MY JOURNEY

MY JOURNEY
DONNA

 BALLANTINE BOOKS   NEW YORK

KARAN

WITH KATHLEEN BOYES

Published in the United States by Ballantine Books, an
imprint of Random House, a division of Penguin Random
House LLC, New York.

BALLANTINE and the HOUSE colophon are registered
trademarks of Penguin Random House LLC.

Library of Congress Cataloging-in-Publication Data
Karan, Donna.
My journey / Donna Karan ; With Kathleen Boyes.—First Edition.
pages   cm
Includes index.
ISBN 978-1-101-88349-5 (hardback)—
ISBN 978-1-101-88350-1 (eBook)
1. Karan, Donna. Fashion designers—United States—Biography.
3. Women fashion designers—United States—Biography.
I. Boyes, Kathleen.   II. Streisand, Barbra, writer
of foreword.   III. Title.
TT505.K37A3 2015
746.9'2092—dc23
[B]
2015025906

Printed in the United States of America on acid-free paper

randomhousebooks.com

9 8 7 6 5 4 3 2 1

First Edition

Book design by Liz Cosgrove

To those no longer with us who made me who I am:
my parents, Anne Klein, and, most of all,
my love, Stephan

And to my family and friends,
who every day create my past, present, and future

FOREWORD

I want you to know how much I love my dear, dear friend Donna Karan . . . and how much I admire and believe in what she is doing as a designer, philanthropist, and visionary.

But first, let me fill you in on the side of Donna you haven't read about that I find so amazing and hard to believe. She is the most scattered, disorganized human being you'll ever meet. Her attention is fleeting, and she's always changing her mind. She can't remember anything . . . including plans you've just made with her. Chaos is her middle name. So I'm constantly astonished by all she accomplishes: the fabulous clothes—Donna Karan, DKNY, Urban Zen—the art exhibits, the fundraisers, the Urban Zen Foundation. I'm always saying to her, "You did this? Really? When?" I'm now convinced that the dichotomy of her nature and all she creates is a sign of her genius. And I don't use that word lightly.

Like everyone else, I met Donna through fashion. It was the late 1970s, and I had just bought a fur, raisin color, and wanted something to wear with it. A friend sent me to Donna, and within minutes Donna was emptying out her personal closet to help me. That is Donna. You like the chic, sexy shirt she's wearing? She'll take it off and give it to you. Literally. And while Donna's styling it on you, giving it just that right twist and tuck, she'll be offering you a nosh, a green juice, asking how you're feeling, solving your problems and your kids' problems, giving you Reiki, applying essential oils, and generally planning your life.

Donna doesn't just dress people; she *add*resses them, mind, body, and spirit. She is a creative visionary. Passionate. Forceful. Nurturing. Extremely hands-on. And generous to a fault. You can't help falling in love with her. As a friend, Donna is thoughtful, funny, and mothering . . . she can't help herself. That day in her studio, I spotted a chenille sweater in one of my favorite colors, burgundy, in a pile on the floor. They were throwing them away because it turned out the fabric was highly flammable. I didn't care. I even offered to sign a legal waiver in case the sweater should ever catch on fire. But Donna said, "Absolutely not—give it back." She wouldn't take the chance. (By the way, I still have that sweater.)

Donna and I bonded immediately. We were two nice Jewish girls from New York, vacationing, dieting, and laughing—sometimes fighting, but always laughing. Throughout our journey, there's always been fashion . . . amazing fashion. To be a friend of Donna's is to dress very, very well.

I was single when I first met Donna and her husband, Stephan, a man I just adored. I became, as she would call me, wife number two . . . told you she was generous! Stephan was an artist who "connected the dots" in his work. He put dots on a page and randomly connected them, allowing a figure to emerge, which he then turned into a painting or a sculpture. Donna continues Stephan's work of "connecting the dots" with everything she does. Especially with her philanthropy.

One of the things Donna and I have most in common is our passion for positive change. How to use our voices and creativity to get something done. How to use our platforms and public profiles to bring attention to urgent matters.

When an earthquake struck Haiti in 2010, Donna became part of the relief effort. In the midst of disaster, she saw potential and made a commitment to help the many talented artisans in that country develop and market their work. Haiti is where all the Urban Zen initiatives come together: A culture that needs to be preserved. A people in dire need of wellness. And a future that depends on education and the ability to sustain culture through commerce. Only Donna would try to take on an entire country! But God love her . . . she never ceases to amaze me.

Barbra Streisand

CONTENTS

INTRODUCTION

I had been up all night, tossing and turning, nervous and depressed. In the predawn light, I could just make out Stephan's two paintings at the foot of my bed—one a big sunny yellow plus sign, the other a thick black minus sign—inviting me to choose my outlook. Easier said than done.

Today was the spring DKNY show, and for the first time since I'd started my company, my husband, Stephan, wouldn't be there. For as long as I could remember, he had always been first row center at my shows, cheering me on. He usually sat next to my daughter, Gabby, my sister, Gail, or maybe our business partners since the mid-1980s, Frank Mori and Tomio Taki. When I walked down the runway for my final bow, his beaming face grounded me. He used to say, "There can't be two of us out there," so I was it. I may have been the face of our brand, but he—the free-spirited artist and ponytailed love of my life—was my rock.

This would have been our eighteenth anniversary (actually our thirtieth, if you start counting when we met and fell in love, but that's another story). I had been doing so well since Stephan died from lung cancer three months earlier. At least I thought I was. But when you've lost someone, all it takes is some small, stupid thought to break you apart. For me, it was that empty seat. I'd come up with a way to feel Stephan's presence at the Donna Karan Collection show two days from now: I would place his life-size red wire sculpture of a man sitting in a chair, a piece he made in the mid-1990s, in the center of the entrance. My spring collection was inspired by Stephan's art, and I wanted him there to see it. But all I felt now was his absence. How did people get through their first anniversary alone, much less on a stage with the whole world watching?

But I had no choice. I had to rally. Not just for me, but for what I refer to as the "we": the enormous company of people whose livelihoods depended on my showing up and putting on that show, from the pattern makers, seamstresses, designers, salespeople, merchandisers, and publicists to the models, hair and makeup teams, backstage crew, and sound technicians to the people who would manufacture the clothes and the retailers who would sell them to the customers who would see them in a magazine.

This time I also had new owners to answer to, as Stephan had arranged to sell our company to the luxury group LVMH Moët Hennessy–Louis Vuitton ten months earlier as a way of taking care of me and our family when he was gone. Sitting out a show, *any* show, isn't an option. Sitting out this particular show was unthinkable.

With these thoughts racing through my head, I drifted into an uneasy sleep, and woke up to someone pushing my arm.

"Donna, Donna. Life will never be the same. It will never be the same!" That's all I remember hearing.

It was Ruthie Pontvianne, a Brazilian healer and massage therapist who had been essential to Stephan during his illness and who now lived with me, taking care of me and running my household. Ruthie was crying.

"You have to wake up, Donna! Now! Look out the window!"

I was living on Wooster Street in SoHo, half a mile away from the World Trade Center. When I looked outside, all I saw were huge puffs of gray and black smoke.

Everyone has their 9/11 story, and this is mine.

Like the rest of the world on that terrible morning, I couldn't immediately absorb what was going on. What was I looking at? An accident? An explosion? Ruthie had the television on. Reporters thought it was an accident, a pilot error of some sort. But that was just wishful thinking.

Then the phone rang, and when I answered, all I could hear was sobbing. It was Gabby, who lived just blocks away. She had been on her morning run when the first tower was hit. I couldn't calm her down, but I insisted that she come right over. "Gabby, it's going to be all right," I told her. "Just get here as soon as you can. We need to be together."

The second I hung up, Patti called. Patti Cohen is my lifelong friend (a sister, really) and was the publicity director of Donna Karan International. She was already in our offices on Seventh Avenue, forty-five blocks north.

"Have you heard?" she asked.

"Heard?" I found myself shouting. "I'm looking at it from my goddamn window!"

"I know, I know. But listen, the show will go on . . ."

Show? *Show?* I shook my head. "You have no idea what's going on here. There's no show—"

Right then, Ruthie screamed. The second plane had hit.

I couldn't stop shaking. If ever I'd needed Stephan, now was the time. He would know what to do; he would handle this, and handle us. The phone in my hand rang again, making me jump. I hit the talk button. Patti again.

"Patti, I can't talk to you—"

"Listen to me. They—the city, the government—want to use the

Armory and our benches for triage," she said, referring to our up-town show venue and the cushioned benches we'd arranged for the audience. "I told them of course, that they can use anything they want. I'm telling everyone here to go home."

That's when I realized that because it was pre-show for Donna Karan New York Collection, we had an office full of people, starting with the seamstresses who had been there all night. I didn't know which way to turn. I had a building full of people I was responsible for, my daughter was breaking down, and my adored city—my hometown, the one I'd named my company after—was under at-tack. It was too much to bear. So I snapped into full mother warrior mode. (Like so many women I know, that's what I do when I feel helpless: I take control and organize.) All I could think was, *I have to get them out of there*. Our offices were near Times Square, and I feared it was the next target, alongside the Empire State Building. No place was safe.

Gabby walked in the door, still in her black running clothes, and we hugged. She was desperate to leave the city, and I was desperate to get to the office. But we quickly learned that we couldn't go any-where. The entire city was shut down: every road, bridge, and tun-nel. No one could leave Manhattan, except on foot.

As the day wore on, we sent stranded staff members to our Home Collection showroom a few blocks away, where we had lots of beds displaying Donna Karan sheets and comforters. Sadly, the Armory never became more than a waiting room for families. There were no sick or injured to speak of. All we could do was sit glued to the TV for news. The air in the apartment was filthy, but opening the windows would only make it worse.

Then, of course, the grief hit me—the overwhelming, suffocat-ing kind of grief I'd been working so hard to fight for weeks. It wasn't just for Stephan; it was for everyone. We were all in this together. On September 11, 2001, my private mourning blended into the world's mourning. I didn't think the city or I would survive.

———————

But if I've learned anything over the years, it's this: somehow, you do carry on. You're never the same, but the truly remarkable thing is that life continues. Bit by bit, you adjust, and one day you even manage to smile and have fun again.

As the days after 9/11 unfolded, I was looking everywhere for a sign, a glimmer of hope that tomorrow would be better. Then it dawned on me. Fashion Week had been all but canceled, but we were still planning spring shows—very small ones, of course. Spring is a symbol of growth, of nature waking up after the darkness and doom of winter. We had two showroom presentations, one for DKNY and the other for Donna Karan Collection, and it was comforting to reclaim our way of life.

After 9/11, our city, our country, and our world came together in unprecedented ways. Support poured in from all over the globe. Our extraordinary mayor, Rudolph Giuliani, told us not to let the terrorists win, to go on with our lives as normally as possible. The fashion industry came together, too. I remember standing next to the mayor, me on one side and Ralph Lauren on the other, surrounded by designers and models wearing the same T-shirt with a heart on it, united in our efforts to raise money for victims' families. To me, it showed that something beautiful happens when a community cares, connects, collaborates, and creates (all my c-words) for a cause that's bigger than any one of us.

I'll never get used to death, but I've learned to live with it, to learn from it, and to build from it. I've lost far too many loved ones in my life—my father, my mother, my stepfather, my longtime psychiatrist Dr. Rath, my uncle Burt, my dear friends Rita Walsh, Lynn

Kohlman, and Gabrielle Roth—and so many acquaintances, associates, and people I've worked with, including most recently my young assistant Clarissa Block, who was also a good friend of Gabby's. (Even Felix, my beloved Great Dane, died before his time.) When I look back, I see that death and birth are a constant theme in my life. Something comes to an end, and something new is born. Your world falls apart, and you're forced to create a new one.

And that new world can be more beautiful than anything you could ever imagine. Without question, the most devastating death in my life has been Stephan's. It changed everything for me. For two decades I had relied on him to fix, smooth over, and soothe any troubles that came up. But his death also led me to create my organization Urban Zen, a marriage of philanthropy and commerce, which allows me to dress people—and *address* people about the things I care about most. Urban Zen helps me find calm in the chaos of my life. Giving, I've discovered, has this whole selfish side, because you get so much in return.

I'm a very young soul, childlike in many ways. Just ask Gabby. She calls me a butterfly, constantly flitting from one thing to the next, never settling down. It's true that I can't stand still—never could. I'm a nomad at heart, forever traveling, searching for answers, and looking for solutions to everyone's problems. Once a Jewish mother, always a Jewish mother.

Life is a journey, an adventure in which every twist and turn has something to teach you. You just have to stay open, be creative, and see where the road leads you. Because, like it or not, your plans will change. Just be sure to pack seven easy pieces and accent it all with a sense of humor. God knows you'll need it.

MY JOURNEY

1 | BORN INTO FASHION

"How did you get into fashion?" People ask me that question almost every day. The answer: I was born into it. Not only did my father, Gabby Faske, make custom suits, but my mother, Helen Faske—known as "Richie" at work—was a model who later turned to showroom sales. Even the man she went on to marry after my father died, Harold Flaxman, my stepfather, was in the business, though he was on the cheap side of the street, selling knock-offs and schmattas.

Fashion was all around me, obnoxiously so. When I was old enough to take the train into the city, I hung out in the back offices of Richie's showrooms. I put on my first fashion show when I was in high school. My first job was selling clothes in a boutique, and I was great at it. I had tons of insecurities, but never about clothes. When it came to clothes, I knew what I was doing.

Designing is second nature to me. It is who I am. I can't help it. I see a problem—a desire to look longer, leaner, and leggier—and I have to solve it. A void? Have to fill it. And fabric, well, it talks to me. I drape it on the body, and it tells me what to do. It's a dialogue without words. I become a sculptor, shaping and coaxing it where it wants to go, accentuating the positive and deleting the negative. You can't teach that kind of design to someone. Like any artistic expression, you have to feel it. It's in your blood, and it was definitely in mine.

————————

I don't have many memories of my father, but I have this one: I had just turned three years old, and we were at his menswear showroom on 40th and Broadway, on the second floor, watching the Macy's Thanksgiving Day Parade. Because I was so small, they propped me up on the radiator box by the window so I could see better. I was enjoying the parade when all of a sudden a group appeared in the lineup dressed like stereotypical American Indians: huge feather headdresses, war-painted faces, jumping around, whooping, the works. To a toddler, they looked like a parade of boogeymen, all coming to get me. I was spooked, really scared. I jumped down and ran into a rack of men's suits for safety. My father's suits.

Little did that three-year-old know she was going to design menswear herself one day, and even dress a president of the United States. I became a tailor, just like my father. He was an amazing one. I like to think he passed that baton, that talent, that gene on to me, because that's where I feel the most connected to him. The photos of my parents and the clothes he made for the two of them— well, the sophistication just kills me. How to capture that, how to create that, how to become that? On some level, those challenges fuel my creative passions.

Photos of my parents tell their story better than words ever could. They're dancing, laughing, and smiling, with hints of the city behind them. My mother looks like a young Ava Gardner; my father is utterly debonair. They lived the high life. My father's tailoring business attracted all sorts of famous people, including celebrities and gangsters—he even dressed New York City mayor Vincent Impellitteri. Everyone told me how charming my father was.

In fact, his whole family was. The Faskes had social status and were always entertaining or out on the town. My father, Gabby, had six siblings: two sisters, Miriam and Leah, and four brothers, Sol, Heshy, Abe, and Frank. Frank was the brother to whom he was closest. Uncle Frank led a glamorous life back then; he owned a Pontiac dealership, and Pontiacs were very chic cars at the time. Montrose Motors was in Brooklyn, where he lived. Once Uncle Frank called my father, all excited. The comedian Red Buttons had just traded in his old car for a new one, and Uncle Frank knew Gabby would love the old one: a 1951 yellow Pontiac convertible. My father went over right away, and that became our family car.

Gabby and Uncle Frank loved going to clubs, whether in New York, in the Catskills, or on Long Island. They were friendly with the owners of the Concord Hotel in the Catskills and made all kinds of show biz connections through them. In addition to owning Montrose Motors, Uncle Frank managed a handful of celebrities, including the comedian Buddy Hackett. He and my aunt Dotty, who had four kids, threw parties at their home in Manhattan Beach with lots of singing and dancing. Stars like Tony Curtis and Janet Leigh would occasionally show up. In the summers, our families would drive to Atlantic Beach on Long Island—an area we eventually moved to—and go to the Capri resort, where we shared a cabana. I was a just a baby, but I remember the festivity, the buzz.

Then on May 1, 1952, the party ended. My father was on his way home from work; his friend Morris was giving him a lift in his green Cadillac convertible. They were on the Brooklyn-Queens Expressway, and the car must have swerved. The passenger side was hit. Morris survived, but my father died in the hospital the next day of brain injuries. He was fifty-two years old.

When death happens suddenly, like it did with my father, everything changes dramatically: How your mother behaves. How you are cared for. How your family functions. How you define your family. *How you define yourself.* And, in those days especially, you were changed financially, because the main breadwinner was gone. You go from being a normal child to one who knows about death, loss, and uncertainty. The impact of losing a parent at such a young age is impossible to grasp unless you've experienced it yourself.

Years later, when I was in my late teens, my then boyfriend, Mark Karan, was opening a men's clothing store in Cedarhurst, Long Island. It was called Picadilly, named after the street it was on. Mark's father was helping us out. He'd just returned from picking up an order of clothes in Brooklyn that hadn't been delivered on time. As he was unpacking, he suddenly stopped.

"Donna, what was your father's name again?"

"Gabby Faske."

I turned, and he was holding a suit on an old wooden hanger embossed with the words *Gabby Faske Clothier*. Stunned, I reached for it, wanting to make sure it was real. What are the odds that after so many years, so many suits, so many stores, so many miles, a Gabby Faske hanger would end up in Mark's store on Long Island?

I look at this hanger framed on my wall, and know my father has been by my side, holding me up, throughout my journey.

———

Fashion was my destiny. Which isn't the same thing as my life's dream. Fashion was actually the last thing I wanted to do. It was too obvious, too predictable, too easy. Like most kids, I wanted to be different from my parents. My fantasy was to dance like Martha Graham or Isadora Duncan and later as a teenager, I wanted to sing like Barbra Streisand. Growing up, I would dance in my room till all hours. Not in front of the mirror—I danced for how it felt, not how it looked. I loved every kind of musical and all the jukebox hits of the 1950s. I signed up for every show in camp and at school. My mother adored my voice and was always asking me to sing. Not that I had a huge talent or anything, but I projected as though I did.

But my main dream was to be a stay-at-home mother—the opposite of mine. She had to work, because we needed the money, but it was also where she came alive. She lived and breathed Seventh Avenue; it was in her soul. When I was a kid, most mothers didn't have outside jobs. My friends' moms got them ready for school in the morning, made hot chocolate when they came home, and cooked dinner every night. My childhood home was nothing like that. I grew up in Kew Gardens, Queens. We lived in a red-brick apartment building—a nice building for Queens. Our apartment wasn't small; it had seven rooms: the living and dining rooms, the kitchen, a small den, my mother's room, which had an attached dressing room, and a bedroom that I shared with my older sister, Gail, and the nanny of the moment. We even had a small terrace. (Young as I was, I remember sitting on that terrace as my father's funeral procession went by.)

I could fill a book with stories of my mother. There are so many ways and words to describe her: *beautiful, grand, polished, stylish*. But also *crazy, dramatic, temperamental, difficult*, and—knowing what I know now—*bipolar*. As I said, they called her "Richie" at work, but her lifelong personal nickname was "Queenie," which kind of says it all. It's hard to know where to begin with her, so I'll start when I was very young. She was distant, depressed, and not there in the ways that mattered—she wasn't there to welcome me home from school and took little interest in my education. My favorite thing to do is climb into my bed with my grandchildren and read to them, but she never did anything like that. My mother worked long days, made even longer by her train commute. When she came home, she was exhausted.

Shortly after Gabby died, she packed me and Gail off to Camp Alpine in Parksville, New York, in the Catskills. That's where New

York Jewish kids went. I was only three and a half, even younger than the minimum age of four years. I stayed in Bunk Zero, where a woman we called Mother Sue watched over us like a hawk. (At one point, there were ten of us cousins there at the same time.) I remember feeling terrified, looking for any sign of my mother all day long, hoping she would appear and take me home. She didn't.

Looking back, I understand that she had major issues, including constant migraine headaches and all sorts of ailments, real or imagined. There were bottles of pills everywhere. As much as she loved her job, she had the pressure of supporting her young family while working in a tough, competitive industry that was based on looking good. She didn't have many friends to speak of, just her sisters, all of whom she argued with. She needed to be mothered herself, yet her parents weren't around—like me, Gail has no memories of them, other than the fact that they lived on the Lower East Side and my grandfather had a pushcart. No wonder my mother could barely cope.

She remarried quickly—to Harold Flaxman, who owned a dress business in Brooklyn. Harold was matinee-idol handsome, a real man's man, with a fabulous head of white hair. It seemed like he just appeared one day. They met at the Concord Hotel in the Catskills (I swear, everything in my early years leads back to that hotel). They married on May 17, 1953, a year and a week after my father died, in a hall at the Hampshire House, a fancy Manhattan apartment building on Central Park South. My sister said the wedding was lovely; I was too young to go. After they married, Gail made the mistake of telling her teacher that our last name would change. Queenie was incensed.

"Your last name is Faske and always will be," she said. My mother loved that name and all it represented: status, glamour, a big social life. Being a Flaxman offered none of that.

Queenie was far nicer to me than to Gail because I appealed to her sense of aesthetics. I was a singing, dancing artist and performer. I was tall, slim, and had a flair for dressing, even as a kid, and as a former model, my mother liked that I had "the look," as she called it. She was outright emotionally abusive to my sister, who didn't take after her. Queenie would call her "piano legs" and tell her she needed makeup or to smoke a cigarette—anything to make her look more sophisticated. I couldn't separate that mean mother from the one who was kinder to me. I still can't.

Queenie was very private. Like I said, she didn't have many friends that I can remember. She had family, as did my father, but they never visited. At work, she was a totally different woman: the elegant, stylish Richie who went into the city with sleek black hair, a perfectly made-up face, red lips, heels, and the impeccably tailored suits my father had made for her, worn over a foundation girdle. (Years later, I got rid of her suits—talk about regrets!) She worked for many Seventh Avenue houses, including for the designer Chuck Howard, who designed sportswear under his own label in the 1960s and later introduced me to Anne Klein. As much as she loved it, turning it on at work must have been exhausting. She'd come home and become, well, nobody. She changed into a robe, tied a babushka around her head, and washed off her makeup. If she had a migraine, which was often, she'd lie on her bed in the pitch dark, and we knew to be quiet.

It sounds dreary because it was. In a way, my mother died when my father died. Gabby Faske was the love of her life. She tried to keep his business open, but couldn't. So not only was he gone, but so was their financial security and all the perks that went with it. I was always aware that our life would have been different if my father had lived. Poor Harold. He was forty-nine when he married Queenie, who was then thirty-three, and it was his first marriage. The youngest of ten children, he had taken care of his parents in their old age—that's how loving he was. Gail and I quickly grew to love Harold, and his family was great to us. But it didn't matter because he wasn't our father. Even worse, Harold never made much money. He worked in the fashion world, but, as I said, he was in the schmatta business. Queenie was the sophisticated one.

Gail was eight years older than I, so she went to school and had friends outside the home. I was alone much of the time, and I didn't feel safe. Yes, there was always a nanny of some sort, but each came with her own problems. One girl asked if she could have her brother over for dinner, and when my parents got home, she and her "brother" were in their bed—naked—with me asleep next to them. Then there was the one who watched me while Gail was at school. When my sister came home, the door was locked. She rang the neighbor's bell, and they called the police. The cops knocked down the door, and there was the nanny, drunk and passed out, and me screaming from my crib. She actually came back to collect her week's pay.

Queenie was constantly telling me to put furniture in front of the door to keep out strangers. I was raised to be scared and worried, just waiting for someone bad to come and get me. To this day, being alone is my greatest fear. I only sleep well when other people are in the house with me. Otherwise, I'm on edge, listening—for what, I don't know.

I was always trying to attach myself to another family. An Eastern European girl, Georgette Beicher, a few years older than I, lived in a one-bedroom apartment down the hall. Her mother, a seamstress who worked at home, used to make clothes for my mother. Georgette's mother was the quintessential nurturer, always offering us food and making a fuss over things we did at school that day. I spent a lot of time at that apartment. Years later, I ran into Georgette at the Clinton Global Initiative and learned that she had become an active philanthropist, as had I.

When I was six, our family moved to Woodmere, one of Long Island's ritzy "Five Towns." It was a big move from our terraced apartment in Kew Gardens. We moved into a three-bedroom split-level house in a new middle-class development called Saddle Ridge Estates. The house was small for the neighborhood, but to me it was a castle. It sat on a canal, and we had a beautiful weeping willow right outside our kitchen window.

Right before moving in, I fell while roller-skating and hurt my arm. I complained to my mother, who didn't believe me. Maybe three days passed. She finally took me to a doctor, and sure enough, it was broken. So there I was, starting my new first-grade class at Ogden Elementary School, midyear, and worse than just being the new girl, I was the new girl with a cast on my arm. I was also tall for my age. I stood out in every way.

When I got sick and couldn't go to school, my mother would pawn me off on neighbors or relatives. Once Gail stayed home with me. She was in high school and I was in grade school. Gail went to cook us some lunch, and her pajamas caught fire (this was the 1950s, before nonflammable fabrics were the norm). She screamed, and I came running. I poured bowls of water over the flames, then wrapped her in a blanket and rolled her on the floor. We called Queenie at work to tell her what happened, but she didn't come home. Despite Gail's severe burns, our mother never took her to a doctor. To this day, Gail has scars on her chest from the accident, and I never use front burners when I cook.

We spent Saturdays at the beauty parlor—I'd get so bored waiting for my mother to get her hair done—and then I'd wait with her some more on Sundays at the laundromat. Beauty parlors and laundromats, those were my childhood weekends. When I was old enough, if I was off from school, I'd take the Long Island Rail Road to meet my mother in the city and wait in a back room while she worked. More waiting—hours and hours of waiting.

My mother was mean to Harold, which really tore at me. She would belittle him the way she did my sister, and he would try, futilely, to defend himself. They fought like crazy because my mother *was* crazy. If she wasn't literally putting her head in the oven, something she did regularly for attention, she was kicking him out of the house, taking him back, and kicking him out again. She was morose one minute, a screaming, hysterical drama queen the next. So even having a loving man around didn't make me feel safe, because I feared I could lose him just as suddenly as I'd lost my father.

Queenie was a perfectionist, and, like so many mothers of her generation, she enforced strict rules to keep our home in order. The fact that she worked full-time made her even stricter. She gave Gail and me cleaning assignments every day. We had white sofas and white rugs, and there was probably a plastic cover over the sofa. Before she got home from work, I had to make sure the carpet was raked in the right direction and put the baked potatoes in the oven at just the right time, depending on whether she was making the 5:35 train or the 6:04. Once my mother discovered wire hangers in my closet, threw all my clothes on the floor, and made me rehang every piece on a wooden hanger. Then she grounded me. This was years before *Mommie Dearest*.

The most difficult thing to live with, more than her mood swings and rages, were my mother's secrets. Façades came naturally to her. There was her artful nine-to-five persona, Richie, the perfectly coiffed, stunning woman who still looked and dressed like the model she once was. Then there were other sides, entire lives she didn't share with us. When I was around eleven, I went up to the attic and started rummaging through old clothes and trunks filled with photographs. I was mesmerized, especially by the photos. There were stacks of paper folders holding single pictures, the kind photographers take of you at a dinner club or studio. One was of my mother in an antique-looking lace dress. In one after another, she was smiling, dancing, glowing. Posing in front of a nightclub with my father, he in a suit, she in a satin dress. By a pool in a two-piece swimsuit, one long leg draped over the other. Wearing a fur coat on a city street. My parents standing in front of a stone lodge, as if they had been skiing. The contrast between this angel and the mother I lived with was startling. Who was this beautiful, laughing woman? Why couldn't she come back to us? Why had she become so sad and withdrawn?

There was also a picture of Queenie with another man. Their clothes looked antique to me. I was riveted by every photo I opened, every dusty item I unfolded. I couldn't comprehend what I was seeing.

"Donna Faske, what are you doing up there?" It was my mother, screaming as she frantically climbed the attic stairs. When she reached me, she pulled the photos out of my hands, threw them in the open trunk, and slammed it shut. "Get out of here!" she shouted. "This is none of your business, young lady. How dare you!" I'd never heard or seen her this angry. She grabbed me by the hair, practically throwing me down the stairs, and grounded me every weekend for a month. I had no idea what I had done wrong, but I knew not to go in the attic again. I also grew to hate secret-keeping of any kind. I'm convinced that I'm completely uncensored and open because my mother was so closed.

I think my mother learned her secretive ways from her family, the Rabinowitzes. My mother had four siblings: three sisters, Sally, Fay, and June, and one brother, Eddie, whom I didn't even know about until recently. No one ever mentioned him because he married a German girl during World War II—unforgivable to a Jewish family. Of my mother's sisters, I especially loved Aunt Sally. When I was very young and living in Queens, she lived near us, in Jamaica Estates. Later she and her husband, Lou, moved to York Avenue in Manhattan. Lou was a noted collector of rare books and manuscripts; he had a bookshop on 61st Street and was one of the world's foremost authorities on Sherlock Holmes. I spent a lot of time in their Jamaica Estates home, sitting in their basement with Uncle Lou while he read his books. Aunt Sally was funky and quirky and she traveled the world, but she was also down-to-earth, with a natural, effortless style. Uncle Lou wore fur-lined coats and had long gray hair and a walking stick. Queenie was terribly jealous of Sally— not on account of her sister's looks or style, because they were opposites that way, but because my mother thought Aunt Sally had it all: the comfortable lifestyle, the adoring, successful husband. I'm sure it didn't help to hear me constantly say I wanted to be just like Aunt Sally when I grew up. No mother wants to hear that about another woman.

———

At home, the fighting raged on. I don't know how my stepfather put up with it, but it was his first and only marriage, so maybe he thought he had to. Or maybe he hung in there for me. The two of us had a close, private relationship, apart from Queenie. Harold gave me the priceless gift of making me feel special and talented. We'd go to his favorite Chinese restaurant, and he'd let me talk about my future. By now I knew I didn't have the talent to dance or sing professionally; fashion seemed the obvious path, given my love of art. He told me I should have my own company, and suggested that I switch my first and middle names and call it Ivy Doná (pronounced "Do-nay") because it sounded fancy. I loved his sweetness and how seriously he took my chatter.

All these years, I was still going to Camp Alpine every summer, and I grew to love it. Camp was my independence; I was away from my mother (and her scolding) and free to find myself. We were all equals there, creating our own community. We slept in the same bunk and wore the same camp clothes. I became a major jock, playing basketball, volleyball, baseball, you name it. Camp Alpine was where I got the nickname "Spaghetti Legs and a Meatball Head." I never felt pretty as a kid; I thought I was odd-looking—tall, skinny, and flat-chested—and the nickname only reinforced that feeling. So I stuffed toilet paper into my bikini top. One time we were in the pool, all lined up, when my top got wet, and shreds of toilet paper started leaking out and got stuck in the pool filter. The camp had to drain the whole pool because "some girl clogged it up with toilet paper." Everyone knew it was me. I was mortified. And then came the song the other kids made up about me:

Spaghetti legs and a meatball head,
Spaghetti legs and a meatball head,
Spider legs, tortoise head,
You'd like peanut butter better instead.

Camp Alpine is where I met my friend Beverly Adwar. Her father, a Sephardic Jew from Israel, was in the jewelry business. Beverly was the shortest girl in the camp, and I was the tallest. We were both jocks and bonded right away. We played a mean game of chicken in the pool. I'd put little Beverly on my shoulders, and we'd knock down every competing team.

Much as I loved sports at camp, Beverly says she always knew I was going to be an artist of some sort. While other kids wrote letters home during our rest periods, I would draw in my sketchbook. I was in all the plays, singing and dancing.

I was into boys, too. I had no issues there, maybe because I was a jock, or maybe because most of my friends were boys and I knew how to joke with them, how to laugh and flirt. My first kiss was in the first or second grade in the school cafeteria. His name was Michael Sprinzen, and he took my bandana, held it up next to our faces, and kissed me behind it. I had a boyfriend named Bruce at camp who was older than I and super-skinny. We held hands and danced in the canteen to the tunes on the jukebox.

Beverly also lived in Saddle Ridge Estates, and during the school year we went horseback riding every Sunday morning at Hempstead Riding Academy. My mom would yell the whole way in the car, her usual stuff, and Beverly thought nothing of it. She admired Queenie because she had a career, while most moms, like hers, stayed home. I loved Beverly's family, and fortunately, they loved me back. In the summer, I joined her and her parents, two sisters, and brother in their cabana at El Patio at Atlantic Beach. I spent the Jewish holidays with them, too. My family wasn't especially observant, and when you don't have religious touchstones in your life, you crave them. At least I did. I hungered for anything that would make me feel the same as everyone else and less of an outsider.

My father's death and my mother's distance shaped me in so many ways. I still hate being alone. I look to create a sense of family everywhere I go. And most important, I've learned that I can live with loss. Losing someone may be devastating, but that doesn't mean there isn't joy ahead.

2 | THE OTHER SIDE OF THE TRACKS

We moved yet again in 1960, when I was twelve. Gail was getting married, and to help pay for the wedding, my mother sold the house. Crazy, I know, but those were her priorities. We moved to the other side of town, closer to the railroad tracks. It was a two-family house, and the people downstairs owned it. They were nice, but living in a shared house by the train tracks was a world away from Saddle Ridge Estates. There was no community to take care of you, no playing safely on the streets like I used to. West Broadway, a major thoroughfare, was just a block away. Queenie was happy because she could walk to the train, but I felt disoriented.

Gail was twenty now, and she was marrying a great guy named Hank Hoffman. Hank had his own recording studio and wrote the 1962 hit "Bobby's Girl." He eventually went to RCA, where he worked for twenty-six years. Gail and Hank's wedding took place at the Hampshire House on Central Park South, the same place my mother married Harold. Gail had no say in the planning and didn't even get to see the space before Queenie made a deposit for Christmas Day, because that was the only day it was available. The room accommodated only ninety people, so many relatives weren't invited, and Gail and Hank could invite only one friend each. Hank's sister Elaine and I were the bridal party.

The wedding was Queenie's show. She wouldn't let Harold walk Gail down the aisle because she said she needed him to walk *her* down the aisle, so my uncle Lou escorted Gail. But first, poor Harold burned his hand while ironing his trousers—his hand literally stuck to the iron! And then there was my itching fit, the worst I've ever experienced. My mother had a dress made for me in silk organza, and during the fitting, we discovered that I was highly allergic to its chemical finish. "Don't worry, Donna, you won't be allergic to it once the dress is made," she said, explaining that the unfinished seams were the problem, as if that made any sense.

Well, I remained allergic—horribly so. I broke out in big, angry hives. In the middle of the wedding reception, I went up to the hotel room we'd rented for the night and put on my white and red sweats, the only other clothes I had with me. I rejoined the party and danced like crazy with my big swollen face. After all her careful preparations, my mother was probably upset to have me looking like that in public, but I'm also sure she was happy to see me dancing. Otherwise, she would have yanked me off the floor.

Gail's leaving home was difficult for me. She was so loving and very maternal, and she let me hang out with her and her friends. I could tell her anything, and she never criticized me. She also knew what it was like to live at home and comforted me in private when our mother was unreasonable. No one knew better than Gail how scary my mother could be. Once Queenie gave me a watch for my birthday. When I lost it the next day while swimming in the ocean, I called Gail immediately. "Oh my God," I cried into the phone. "What am I going to do? She'll kill me!"

"Calm down," Gail said. "I'll replace it somehow. If she notices it's gone, tell her you took it to the repair shop to fix the band." Gail didn't have a lot of money, but she replaced the watch. That's how she took care of me. When she moved out, I lost both my ally and a loving mother figure. When Queenie and Harold weren't arguing, I don't remember hearing any voices in our home.

———

A few years later, Gail, who was now living half an hour away in Hollis, Queens, had a baby. In the hospital, my mother insisted that Gail and Hank name the baby Gabriel after my father, as she had already called every family member, including Hank's, to tell them about "baby Gabby." When Hank stood his ground and refused, Queenie caused a scene so dramatic that the baby ended up going home with no name on his birth certificate. A week later, they named him Glen, the G in honor of Gabby. This did not satisfy my mother. She was so hurt (and probably embarrassed for having told everyone about "baby Gabby") she refused to meet the baby for six months. When she finally did, she wouldn't acknowledge his name. She called him "Mr. G" instead.

Harold visited Glen every Sunday, with or without my mother. He loved being a grandfather, and I loved being an aunt. Queenie loved her grandson, but she wasn't the cuddly type, whereas I could play with him all day long and sleep next to him at night when I babysat. To me, he was pure joy.

———

Maybe because we lived by the railroad tracks, my mother was more paranoid about my safety than ever and was constantly warning me to be on guard. One day I had just gotten a haircut in Cedarhurst and was feeling great. I decided to walk home to Woodmere along the tracks, maybe an hour's walk away. A creepy-looking guy on a bike started following me, saying over and over, "Me alova yua." I got scared. I lied and told him my father was a policeman, but he didn't back off. So I pointed to a house, said, "I live here," and walked toward it. The guy turned toward the house, too. *Damn*. So I knocked on the door. A middle-aged man opened it.

"I'm so sorry," I said in a panicked rush before he could speak. "There's a guy following me. Can you make like I live here and that you're my father?" The man shooed the guy away and wound up walking me home, being very decent about the whole thing. But that story could have turned out very differently.

Another traumatic thing happened when I was a teenager: My dentist sexually harassed me. In those days, dentists put a gas mask on you and completely knocked you out. I remember hearing him say, "Open your mouth wider," which is normal for a dentist, but there was something creepy about the way he said it. The first couple of times he touched me, I didn't know anything was happening, but my body seemed to know. I'd try to fight the anesthesia and cross my legs tightly. One time I felt him touching my breast. I punched him and never went back. These incidents reinforced everything my mother had told me about being alone and watching out for danger, and they left me with a deep feeling of helplessness and vulnerability. To this day, I never drink too much or do recreational drugs because I am terrified to feel even slightly out of control. Once you have a fear, any kind of fear, it's always inside, a part of you.

Of course, if you'd met me back then, you wouldn't have known I was so afraid. I wasn't a rebel, but I had an edge. I've always been a funny mix of insecure and outgoing. I was an oddball, but I grew to own my oddballness. And I've never had a filter. On my first day at Hewlett High School, I went up to Ilene Wetson, soon to be one of my best friends, and said, "You're the girl who just got a nose job, aren't you? How could that be a nose job? It looks just like mine!"

High school was incredibly hard. First, I was a terrible student, awful at reading, writing, and math—all the basics. Years later, I learned that I had attention deficit disorder and dyslexia, but those things weren't diagnosed in those days. You were just a bad student. I'm a visual person, an organic thinker. But traditional education didn't give you credit for that—not really. I was never taught to use my imagination or see the world in my own unique way. I was taught to reproduce what existed—something I didn't have the skills to do effectively. My intelligence was wrapped in creativity, self-expression, and street smarts. It never occurred to me to value and embrace those qualities. I just wanted to fit in.

But I stood out in every way, even physically. I was always among the tallest girls in my class, and by high school I was already a towering 5'7". I must have slumped, because my mother was always telling me to stand up straight. Then there was the money thing. All the families I knew were extremely wealthy and lived in massive houses, not modest ones like mine. That only added to my sense of being different, an outsider.

I skipped classes. I even failed typing—who fails typing? But I excelled in art. I hung out with the creative kids, like Ross Bleckner, the artist, who is still a dear friend today. Ross and I connected quickly, teasing each other in class. We saw in each other a like-minded soul who didn't fit into the conventional Five Towns world. Neither of us was on the road to becoming a doctor, lawyer, or captain of industry.

So art was my salvation. The Hewlett High School art department was a world unto itself—it even had a separate side entrance—and I felt empowered there and part of a community. I had two exceptionally inspirational teachers: Don Dunne, a handsome, cool guy who taught us to draw the body and was more fine-arts-oriented, and Geraldine Peterson, who had us do still lifes. She would line up pottery for us to draw and shade. I loved sketching and could keep at it for hours on end. Mrs. Peterson loved how I drew and would encourage me to stay in the workroom as long as I wanted. My friends and I still talk about the influence those teachers had on us. They urged us to express ourselves. To a kid who felt lost and outside the community, it was validating. The good grades they gave us were the only reason some of us graduated from high school.

As I found my way in high school, I grew more interested in fashion as a means of self-expression. It was the era of the Danskin bodysuit, and I had every style—V-neck, scoop-back, bateau, long-sleeve, short-sleeve—in every color. They looked great with everything. Stylewise, I was a hippie. I liked extremes—hot pants, short skirts, and long skirts to the floor. I was a cut-on-the-bias girl, as opposed to straight-grade shifts, which I considered dresses for temple. I preferred liquid, body-conscious styles because they were less restrictive, and I was all about dance and movement. My mother was now working at the sportswear company Mr. Pants, and I was able to buy hip-huggers and bell-bottoms at wholesale—a real coup for a teenager. For shoes, I loved gladiator sandals that laced up the leg, but I appreciated that every other girl loved Pappagallo shoes, the hot shoe of the moment. My friend Francine LeFrak, whom I saw on the bus every day, had a pair in every color. When she'd get on the bus, my eyes would immediately drop to her feet to see which pair she was wearing.

I should be clear, though: I was only a hippie in terms of my style. I wasn't having sex, doing drugs, or even listening to rock and roll. I wasn't fearless and rebellious; I was wholesome. I liked Disney movies, and I loved Annette Funicello. I listened to the Temptations and the Supremes. I was obsessed with variety shows and adored medical dramas like *Dr. Kildare* and, later, *Marcus Welby, M.D.* (whose young star, James Brolin, would go on to marry my friend Barbra Streisand). For me, the hippie thing was an artistic expression. There were no political or cultural undertones to it.

When I was fourteen, I lied about my age and got a job at Shurries, a trendy fashion boutique on Central Avenue in Cedarhurst. It sold all the hip, young clothes of the time: jeans, T-shirts, maxis, minis, all the must-have pieces. The young girls who came in connected with me because I was one of them. Parents loved me, too, and asked me to create mini wardrobes for their kids, pick outfits for social events, and pack them up for camp. I was great at styling, and I learned the importance of merchandising, not that I knew to call it that then. Instead of hanging up all the tops in one place and all the bottoms in another, I mixed it up. I'd style a great top and display it between pants and a skirt, visually explaining the possibilities to the customers, showing them what could go with what. I rearranged the sales floor and styled the mannequins, adding a tuck here for attitude, a slung belt, a cool scarf. I *still* style the floor whenever I'm in a store that sells my clothes. For me, it's a compulsion. I don't even realize I'm doing it half the time.

The owners of Shurries adored me. They even let me paint a mural on the dressing room wall of a girl walking her little dog—my first real fashion illustration.

Fashion was my comfort zone. I accepted that it was in my DNA, that I was naturally good at it. I put on my first fashion show in high school. It was for a project for Kenneth Goode, another favorite teacher in the art department, where we turned illustrations into clothes. I designed the clothes, and a girl I knew helped sew them: a geometric-print black-and-white halter jumpsuit, a tank top and bias-cut palazzo pants, a short dress. My friends and I modeled. Ilene's mother bought the jumpsuit, and Ilene still owns it. I loved every minute of it. My mother was overjoyed and couldn't stop bragging about me. Once I accepted fashion as my destiny, she became more of a mom to me than she'd ever been.

I discovered another lifelong passion at that time. One day, while still in my teens, I was walking down Broadway in Woodmere when I passed a storefront with a sign for a yoga class. I didn't know anything about yoga but thought I'd give it a try. From the first class, I loved it. It felt like a form of dance, a great excuse to stretch and move my long legs. There was no real spiritual element to it, which was a shame. I could have started my inward path so much earlier! Nonetheless, I was hooked.

Around this time, I started dating my first steady boyfriend and future first husband, Mark Karan. We met while I was on vacation with my mother in Miami during my junior year of high school. She occasionally went to Miami Beach alone, to take a break from her exhausting schedule, always staying at the Eden Roc hotel, where our uncle Lou's sister was head of reservations. As a gift for my six-teenth birthday, she took me along.

Mark was two years older than I, a freshman at the University of Tampa, and he'd driven down to Miami with friends for vacation. We met on the 48th Street beach. He had a hip way about him—he was very comfortable and outgoing and could talk to anyone (he still can). I loved that he was tall and slim; I clearly had a thing for skinny guys. And I remember that he was very, very suntanned. I first thought it was because we were in the Florida sun, but came to learn that he always had a suntan, and still does even now.

Mark took me to a show at one of the clubs—a very grown-up thing to do. We saw Alan King and Bobby Vinton perform. I told Mark I lived in Saddle Ridge Estates, and he thought I lived on an actual estate, which I ran with. "Oh, yeah," I said casually, "we have all these horses and animals on the estate." I toyed with him be-cause I never thought we'd see each other again. It turned out that Mark lived near me in Belle Harbor, Queens. I had never been to Belle Harbor but knew it was on the water, in the fancy part of Rockaway Beach. He called when he came back to New York, and we went to a disco with a few of my friends and a few of his. When he picked me up at our two-family home by the railroad tracks, I told him it was a friend's house. He pulled up in a white GTO con-vertible, and I was impressed. My uncle Frank owned a Pontiac dealership, after all, so cars mattered—especially convertibles, which symbolized freedom and beaches. On Long Island in the 1960s, it didn't get much better than having a boyfriend with a convertible.

From the word *go*, Mark and I had a ball together. I was crazy about him. We both worked long hours in local boutiques—Mark was ambitious, and he wanted to open his own store—and when we weren't working, we were together. Mark's family loved me, as I kept him close to home. Belle Harbor was a gorgeous beach, and I was all too happy to go to his house and hang out. His mother and father were a bit on the rigid side, and I would do things like swoop in and suggest we make French toast, and everyone would get into it. I helped loosen them up, and Mark loved me for that.

Mark and I spent our summers going to the beach clubs, where we would rent cabanas and spend our days swimming and then go back at night for dancing or shows. We would match up Ilene or my other friend Sally Brown with one of his friends and go out as a foursome. Sometimes Mark and I would hole up at a hotel called The Plantation in Long Beach and watch movies and make out all night. Or we'd make out in the entryway of my house, as our upstairs apartment was too small to have any privacy. This was the midsixties (before the free-love generation) and I was saving myself for marriage, so I remember lots of making out with Mark. I wasn't interested in other boys; I liked the security of being with him and him alone.

Mark was incredibly thoughtful. We didn't have air-conditioning at my house, so Queenie always had a cold towel around her neck or on her forehead. One day Mark showed up with a fan. He was lovely and respectful to my mother, always asking about her day, her headaches, whether there was something he could get her. Mark admired her work ethic and felt bad that she was always so tired. The fighting in my house didn't faze him at all. He thought it was normal, no big deal. That was the essence of Mark: he looked for the good in everything. My mother loved Mark because he came from "money"—maybe not Five Towns money, but comfortable money. He had his own car, a job, and a real sense of security about him. Mark could do no wrong so far as Queenie was concerned, which made my life much easier.

Mark took me to my senior prom. Even then I hated getting dressed up, but my mother made sure I was dressed better than anyone else. She bought me an Anthony Muto mint-green crepe satin floor-length slip dress with bugle beads across the neckline. (I'm sure she got it wholesale.) My hair was done up with a fabulous braid extension wrapped around my head. This was not your typical prom look at the time, but that was Queenie. Fashion ruled. We didn't know it then, but she was grooming me for my future.

3 | SCHOOL OF DESIGN

If fashion was my destiny, and I believed it was, I needed a proper education in it. While in 1966 other high school seniors were applying to traditional colleges, I was torn between Parsons School of Design and the Fashion Institute of Technology, both in Manhattan. Since I loved art so much, I wanted to be a fashion illustrator. Illustration was very prestigious in those days, because no one used photos. *Women's Wear Daily*, the magazines, the fashion ads in the *New York Times*—all illustrations. I thought I was good enough to make it.

First I got a job illustrating for Liz Claiborne, probably through one of my mother's connections. Liz loved my sketches, and I admired her tremendously. She was a professional and powerful woman. But this was definitely the other side of Seventh Avenue: more corporate, less creative, not me. Then I got a paying gig, again through my mom, as a still-life model for the famous illustrator Antonio Lopez, who was at the very tippy-top of that world. I'd wear the latest fashions, and he'd draw me for the newspapers. With my long limbs and dancer's understanding of movement, I knew how to make the clothes look good. But I felt very uncomfortable and intimidated in his studio. It was downtown and had a dark, late-sixties psychedelic vibe, and I was a wholesome, naive kid. Finally, I had an interview with *Women's Wear Daily* for an illustration internship or summer job—I forget which—and after reviewing my book, the interviewer told me I should rethink my career direction. It's not that I was a bad sketcher, she said, it was that I wasn't exacting. I was emotional and used bigger strokes.

When the universe speaks, I listen. If *WWD* didn't think illustration was for me, then it wasn't.

I was accepted at Parsons with a little networking help from my mother, which I needed because of my poor grades. I was "on trial," meaning I had to pass everything the first year or I was out. Whatever the conditions, I was thrilled I got in, and so was Queenie. Everything changed for me at Parsons. I gained a sense of direction and purpose. It was also where I met my lifelong friend Louis Dell'Olio.

Louis and I connected immediately. Our mutual friend Leslie Mesh introduced us just before school started. A handsome Italian stallion type, Louis lived in Elmont, a Catholic Italian part of Long Island, just twenty minutes away from me. The two of them drove up to my house in Leslie's Cadillac convertible, and Louis took one look at my gladiator sandals and knew we'd be friends. From that moment on, we were the stars of the Louis and Donna show, always joking and gossiping. We took the Long Island Rail Road to school, the only ones out of the more than two hundred kids in our class who did.

We met Ann Keagy on the first day. An imposing woman in style and stature, she ran the fashion design department at Parsons for three decades and really shaped designer education as we know it. She founded the school's designer critic program, where Seventh Avenue designers work one-on-one with students. I've been on both sides of the program, and it's brilliant, not only for the students but also for the designers, who get to hire rising stars. Mrs. Keagy was a true executive, very polished, very uptown, and there I was in my leotard and flowing skirts. She didn't seem too crazy about female designers, maybe because most of the successful American designers at the time were men: Norman Norell, Geoffrey Beene, Galanos, Bill Blass, Oscar de la Renta, and Halston. At our orientation, she had a special message for girls: "If you think this is home economics and you're here to make some dresses, you can leave right now." Nope, Parsons wasn't going to be easy.

I had no idea, however, just how tough it would be. I don't respond well to discipline and structure, and Parsons had both in spades. We worked around the clock—it was pure torture, like a never-ending *Project Runway* episode. The teachers would often say, "This is nothing compared to what designing is like." And all I could think was, *Who would want to be a designer?*

Fortunately, I formed a lasting friendship with a fabulous illustration teacher named Marie Essex. She was a tiny little thing, motherly and encouraging. Rather than criticize my illustrations, she worked with me and believed in me, and her confidence meant the world. She went on to chair the school's fashion department, and years later, as a designer, I made sure I was always available if she needed anything. I adored her.

Thank God for Louis. He kept school fun. We commuted home together, often very late at night, and then worked more once we got there. We were like brother and sister. We'd sleep over at each other's house. When we stayed at Louis's, his mother made a big Italian dinner; at mine, Queenie served chicken soup and her baked potatoes. We just clicked in every way. Unlike the other Parsons kids, who lived in the city, followed every trend, and hit all the hot clubs, we *liked* living on Long Island.

Another good friend of ours was Linda Fox. She was the daughter of Seymour Fox, a famous coat and suit designer at the time.

Linda wore all her father's clothes, like flared officer coats and A-line dresses with chunky-heeled Pilgrim shoes. She was cool, and it was great having a friend who was a real fashion insider. Linda lived in one of those new white-brick Rudin-owned apartment buildings in Manhattan—ultraposh.

But Louis and I were true partners in crime. He was an amazing sketcher and helped me express my ideas. I helped him sew, something I didn't mind, as I had a used sewing machine I'd bought for $25 with my Shurries money. I was also good at throwing fabric on the form and draping it. It was instinctual for me; my gut knew what to do.

And yet I failed draping at Parsons. Yes, for a designer known for her wraps and ties, it's a great punch line. But school draping was different. It was mechanical and focused on pattern making, and I am no technician. But Parsons believed in educating from the ground up, so you were trained to make garments from scratch.

I survived my first year and was holding my own in my second. I had tried living in the city briefly at the beginning of the year, but it didn't last. I moved in with another Parsons student, but she and her friends were snooty, and I found the city overwhelming. I missed trees and grass, the smells and texture of nature. So after two days, I called my mother and begged her to come get me. Years later, I embraced the city, but at the time, I wanted to leave it at the end of the workday, just as my mother had. I was still a Long Islander. I loved my time with Mark at the ocean and at the beach clubs. He had just opened his shop, Picadilly, so he wasn't spending time in the city, either.

Two assignments stand out from that year. First, the designer Rudi Gernreich, one of my mentoring critics, assigned me to make a swimsuit. I designed two: one very Gernreich in spirit, with huge cutouts on the torso, the other a funnel-neck suit. I wanted to sew the sexy one, but he insisted I make the funnel neck, which looked like a piece of clothing, not a swimsuit. Looking back, that suit was a blueprint for my iconic bodysuit. The other mentoring critic—whose name escapes me—had me design and sew a dress. I settled on a bias jersey style with a contrasting border. For this same critic, Louis's project was a halter jumpsuit with a hood shaped like a flower; I still crack up thinking about that one.

The day of our presentations, we woke up early, showered, got to school, and found out that the critic was on his way over sooner than expected. I grabbed an iron and in my rush melted a hole right through the fabric. I burst into tears. We quickly shortened it to a micro-mini, a fix that eliminated the border, which had been the focal point of the dress. Another student, the future designer Kay Unger, modeled it. She looked great, but nothing could save my burned dress. It landed me in summer school.

In addition to taking classes that summer, I earned class credit through an internship. Queenie got me an interview for an intern position at Anne Klein & Co., where her designer friend Chuck Howard was now working. This was 1968, and though the company was brand-new, Anne Klein was already a big deal. She and her first husband, Ben Klein, had launched Junior Sophisticates in 1948, which gave the petite and junior market a more grown-up, fashion-forward look. Anne's designs had revolutionized that market, which previously had been distinguished by size, not style. Now Anne had a designer company under her own name, in a firm she owned with her second husband, Matthew "Chip" Rubenstein. Their partners were Sandy Smith and Gunther Oppenheim, both industry giants who owned Modelia, a coat company.

Gunther was legendary. Everyone knew, respected, even feared him. He was a huge man who spoke with a deep German accent, chomped big cigars, and rode around town in a custom Rolls-Royce. When I interviewed with Gunther, he asked me what I needed to be paid. I told him, "I don't need money. I'm here for the experience." He didn't believe in free labor and insisted they pay me the going intern rate. I'm sure it wasn't much, but I was happy to get anything. It turned out that Anne needed an assistant—or, more accurately, a coffee getter and pencil sharpener. The day I met her, I wore a blue pinstripe skirted suit and a big white fedora. While walking up Seventh Avenue, my hat blew off into the dirty street, so I put face powder on it to make it look clean.

Anne met me by the vestibule near the elevators. A petite woman with frosted blond hair, she was wearing a short pleated skirt that revealed skinny legs—all very sixties in feeling. What a forceful presence. She took one look at me and said, "Take a walk," pointing to the long aisle in front of us.

"Why?"

"Well, I think you're a little big in the bottom, dear."

"To be a *designer*?"

She thought I was there to audition as a model! To this day, I credit Anne Klein for giving me my first insecurities about my weight. Once we cleared up the confusion, she hired me, but I always felt uncomfortably big around such a small, elegant woman.

I loved working with Anne and her team. Her studio was a whole new world steeped in glamour, sophistication, and clothes. I was a pin picker-upper, a food deliverer, a list maker. I did whatever was asked of me, the most junior stuff, but I got to inhale the design room in action. When my summer was over, Anne told me not to go back to school. "This is what you want to do, right?" she asked. I nodded. "Well, then stay. You'll learn more here than you ever would at school."

I hated the structure of school, so I was happy to drop out. Mrs. Keagy was furious. Her students didn't quit unless she wanted them to. It wasn't that she believed in me, but she would rather expel me than have me quit and work for a Seventh Avenue designer in a job she hadn't arranged. Louis says that out of the 225 students in our class, only twenty-one actually completed the program. Who would have thought a lifetime later I'd be so involved with Parsons educational programs that they'd give me an honorary doctorate or that I'd be partnering with them to establish a vocational education center in Haiti?

That was the moment I began to understand that there isn't just one way to learn, and that experiencing life, not sitting in a classroom, was mine. I knew I had to find my own way, however unconventional my path might be.

For me, everything fell into place after that summer. Mark and I, who already felt and acted like a married couple—it never occurred to us that we *wouldn't* get married—decided to make it official. We didn't have a formal engagement, but it was enough for Queenie to put a down payment on a reception room in the Essex House overlooking Central Park. I was nineteen and loved the sense of security Mark gave me. We were best friends and laughed all the time. We shared the same values, the same love of Long Island and living near the water. Having felt so isolated and alone for much of my childhood, I loved being his constant focus. I knew Mark would provide for us.

He was also rescuing me from Queenie. He was my ticket out of that household and a means to create my own. More than anything else, I wanted a warm, loving home full of family. I didn't want my mother's commuting-to-the-city life. My plan was to work in fashion for a bit and then become a full-time mother. But what's that famous expression? Man plans, God laughs.

4 | THUNDER-STRUCK

There I was, engaged to Mark, and my friend Ilene Wetson wanted to throw me a party. She invited me to discuss it over dinner at her Manhattan apartment. Ilene was my best friend from high school and someone I could be completely myself with. Everyone thought we were sisters because we looked so alike. She had just finished a two-year program in interior design at the Fashion Institute of Technology, and her family had rented a two-bedroom place on 57th Street between Sutton Place and First Avenue, on the far East Side of Manhattan. It was mostly Ilene's, but her family would stay there, too, which is why she had the extra bedroom. By dinnertime, a snowstorm was whitening the windows, and I knew I'd have to spend the night in the city.

Ilene had invited her friend Stephan Weiss to join us for dinner. Their parents were good friends, and he knew her brothers and cousins as well. Stephan, she told me, was separated from his wife and living in a small apartment over a burger joint nearby. Since I was engaged to someone Ilene knew and liked, this wasn't a setup. She buzzed him in, and after he finished shaking the snow off his coat, he looked at me and smiled.

"Hey, you must be Donna. I'm Stephan." Eyes twinkling, he offered his hand.

I can only describe that moment as an out-of-body experience. Stephan was tall, dark-haired, handsome, sexy, charming, and very grown-up in my young eyes. A real man's man. I'm sure my mouth hung open. He kept smiling. I must have smiled back.

I don't remember much about the dinner. But afterward he and I sat together on Ilene's sofa. I didn't have to speak, because Stephan did all the talking in his incredibly soft and sexy voice. He talked about astronomy, quantum physics, all sorts of esoteric things. I had no idea what he was saying, but it didn't matter. I was hypnotized. I didn't think about Mark for even a second. I felt suspended from my actual life. Before the night was over, we wound up in Ilene's mother's bedroom—me, the girl who had been saving herself for marriage.

Because of the snowstorm, there was no getting out to Long Island the next morning. I went home with Stephan, whose apartment was within walking distance on 54th Street. We stayed there into the next night. It's hard to describe how well we clicked and the kind of passion we experienced. I was convinced it was fated, written in the stars—all those things you read about but don't really think will happen, at least not to you. There was no reasoning, no logic. I felt as if I had crossed over into another dimension, one with no connection to reality.

Poor Ilene. This was before cellphones, so Queenie kept calling her to see where I was. My mother was very possessive that way— she needed to know what I was doing at all times and with whom. Ilene must have broken down and given her Stephan's number, because I could hear Queenie yelling when he answered the phone at around 3:00 a.m.: *"Get my daughter home. Right now!"* I couldn't leave the city even if I wanted to because of the snow—and I didn't want to. A couple of days later, when the streets were clear, I finally headed back to Long Island. I told my mother the truth: that I had met a guy I was crazy about and had stayed at his apartment.

"I think I'm in love," I said, as if that explained it all.

"In love?" She was angry. "Don't be ridiculous. He's an older man you've known for five minutes. What about Mark?"

It was a good question. I was committed to Mark. I loved and respected him, and he made me feel secure and nurtured. And to be honest, Stephan's situation was a bit of a mess. He was ten years older than I and separated from his wife, Dale, who lived on Long Island with their two children, Lisa and Corey. He was an artist who held all sorts of day jobs to pay the rent: he worked as an insurance salesman and also for his father's business, I. Weiss and Sons, which made stage curtains and scenery. Stephan was a bohemian, a child of Woodstock, which made him sexy as hell to me. He was also a pothead—he smoked joints the way other people smoked cigarettes, but it never outwardly affected him or interfered with his work. (I smoked my share, too. One time when my nephew Glen was five, he ratted me out to Gail and Hank after Mark and I offered him a toke on our pipe while babysitting him with our friends.) Stephan wasn't exactly looking to marry me and raise babies, which is what I wanted more than anything. He was already devoted to his own two children and had an unhappy and temperamental wife who was not ready to let go. Stephan did his best to get along with Dale in order to see their kids. She often threatened to withhold visitation.

He was also a known ladies' man, something my sister was quick to tell my mother. She knew Stephan from school, and also knew Dale—yes, this is how small my world was. Like my mother, Gail loved Mark. Nothing about being with Stephan made sense. But in my eyes, he was a father figure I could look up to—a man who was fully developed physically, emotionally, and spiritually. He was an addiction.

I told my dad the whole story; I always felt I could tell Harold anything. "What do I do?" I cried.

"You know what you have to do," he said. "You have to break up with Mark." I said I couldn't. I was so embarrassed and upset that my dad agreed to speak to Mark for me. He told Mark that I needed to take a break, that I wasn't ready for marriage, and that I had dated someone else. Mark was crushed—so crushed that *his* father came over that night to talk some sense into me.

"You have to marry my son," he said. "You love each other." Nervous as I was, I held firm.

My mother lost her deposit on the Essex House. She made it clear she wanted no part of this married-with-kids Stephan guy. Even Harold, my wonderful, easygoing dad, told Mark's father he'd punch Stephan if he ever met him.

But I couldn't help myself. I started to spend all my free time with him. I was with him when he adopted Blu, his Great Dane. Blu was all black and the runt of the litter, and he was like a baby to us. I loved seeing Stephan, this tall, handsome guy, with his horse-size dog. His devotion to Blu was yet another thing that drew me in.

———

Meanwhile, my career had its own complications. Still a junior assistant, I was so eager to please at Anne Klein that I was working insane hours and taking on responsibilities far beyond my menial assignments. I thought I was doing okay, but after nine months I showed up at work one day and felt the energy had shifted. Something was going on. Either I was getting a raise or getting fired.

It wasn't a raise.

Anne didn't fire me directly. Hazel Haire, her assistant, did. The official reason was that I wasn't pulling my weight, maybe because I was too distracted by my personal life, which I talked about at work. But deep down, I knew the real reason I'd been fired: Anne thought I was too neurotic, and she was right. Her office was highly professional and structured, and I felt totally intimidated and self-conscious there. I was an unpolished kid from Long Island, and everyone else seemed so adult and sure of themselves. No one offered me any guidance or advice, so I worked day and night, walking around with my head and shoulders hunched over, trying to be invisible. But at the same time, I tried too hard and talked too much. At one point my desk was moved to the sample room to minimize my presence. My anxiety was making everyone around me uncomfortable, and I had to go.

So there I was, devastated, living at home, my love life a mess, a design school dropout, and fired from my first real job. Now what?

Fortunately, I got an interview with Patti Cappalli, the designer for Addenda, a new and trendy division of the contemporary sportswear company Bobbie Brooks. A friend of hers in the fabric business had mentioned that "a wacky girl had just left Anne Klein," and Patti took a chance and met with me.

I loved Patti the moment I met her. The only downside was that Addenda was on Broadway. There's a big difference between Broadway and Seventh Avenue, where Anne was. My mother taught me that when I was a baby, and Parsons only reaffirmed it. Broadway was commercial fashion; Seventh Avenue was designer. Working on Broadway meant you couldn't cut it on Seventh Avenue. Even today there's still a bit of that stigma. But thank God I wasn't stupid enough to get hung up on it, because when I look back, working with Patti was the best thing that could have happened to me.

It was just the two of us, so I got to do pretty much everything. I learned a tremendous amount about the industry as well as how to work within a budget. Unlike Anne, there was nothing intimidating about Patti. With a chic short haircut and an easy smile, she was like an older sister, warm and personable with a laugh-out-loud sense of humor. I could be myself around her, and it was then, free from the pressure to fit into a professional mold, that I began to come into my own.

The first time I met Patti, she told me, "Get a passport. We're going to Europe." A junior assistant would never get to go on an inspiration and fabric-shopping trip to Europe at Anne Klein & Co., where there was a team of designers, all senior to me. Yet here I was being offered a trip almost immediately after walking in the door. I was nineteen and culturally blank, even on a New York City level, much less when it came to Europe. I had only flown once—to Miami for my sixteenth birthday—so the idea of traveling abroad blew my mind, so much so that the whole left side of my face literally went numb from stress. It didn't last long, maybe a day, but it scared the daylights out of me. It added a whole new layer of fear to my already anxious psyche.

Queenie sent me to a psychiatrist, Dr. Frederick Rath, or "Dr. Raaaaath," as he answered the phone. He had long gray hair, smoked a pipe, and looked like Sigmund Freud. I instantly loved Dr. Rath, *loved* him—and I saw him for the next twenty or more years of my life, until he died in 1992. With him, I could explore my insecurities and feelings about everything going on in my life, safe from judgment. I was totally unsettled, and he helped me sort through my feelings. I missed Louis, who was busy with school. I'd lost the security of Mark. And I was struggling with my Stephan obsession. I didn't feel like I belonged anywhere.

On top of all that, there was Stephan's lack of commitment. One night I was staying in the city after work to see the musical *Hair* on Broadway, and I called him and asked if I could stop by his place first. He told me no, it wasn't a good time. So I did what any girl in my position would do: I went anyway. And when I walked in, there was a girl on his sofa. This was exactly what Gail had warned me about.

"Screw you!" I screamed. "We're over!" He called after me, but I ran out of his building and didn't look back.

————

Off I went with Patti to Paris and St. Tropez for ten days. It was a whole new world to me—the architecture, the clothes, the sophistication. At one point in St. Tropez, I threw my black bikini top out of the convertible we were driving, and Patti said, "Donna, women go topless on the *beach*, not in their cars!"

When we got to St. Tropez, I noticed I was called "Marisa, Marisa!" a few times as we searched for a place to stay. Everything was booked, so we wound up at a small, nondescript hotel. We even had to share a bed for a night, which could have been awkward but wasn't, thanks to Patti's easy, breezy personality. One night we went to Byblos, the happening club of the moment, and in the bathroom I saw the actress and model Marisa Berenson standing at the mirror. We looked so much alike—same height, same color eyes, same nose, same tan, same shiny brown hair in a ponytail—that I suddenly realized why people might mistake me for her. I was incredibly flattered.

But I was also overwhelmed by this ultrasophisticated world. I had never traveled anywhere besides Florida before, never heard another language spoken! Patti was single and the consummate career girl: confident and smart, a self-starter who commanded attention. I wasn't anything like her. *Is this the lifestyle I'm going to have if I become a designer? Traveling on my own and feeling awkward all the time? Is this what it takes?* I had no desire to be part of that scene, any more than I wanted to live in Manhattan.

In Paris, Patti and I stayed in adjoining rooms at the Hotel Bristol. Even though I was an ocean away from home, my problems had come with me. Mark called constantly, and I was still conflicted. I wasn't even sure I wanted a career in fashion anymore because I was so intimidated by the scene. I felt so lost that I opened up to Patti and told her Stephan was a playboy and an artist who did not want to settle down. Should I marry the guy who loved me or wait for the one I thought I loved?

Patti didn't mince words. "Marry the man who loves you, Donna."

I knew she was right. Mark would take care of me and rescue me from a world that brought out my worst insecurities. I called him from the hotel and asked him to meet me at the airport back home. Then I called my mother. She phoned Mark and told him he'd better be there waiting for me. The minute I got into his car, I pointed to my naked ring finger. "Yes," I said. He kissed me, and in that moment I was overcome—not with joy, but with relief. I had just made the hardest decision in my life so far. Now there was no more uncertainty.

I wanted to get married before I had a chance to change my mind. Queenie wanted to plan a proper wedding, but I didn't have that kind of time. Three days after I returned from Europe, on a Friday in April 1968, Mark and I married in Rabbi Ronald Sobel's study at Temple Emanu-El off Fifth Avenue uptown. I became Donna Karan in a short jersey knit dress, ten yards of pearls, and an Adolfo fedora. I was nineteen, and Mark was twenty-one.

Mark and I had a small wedding dinner at Trader Vic's in the Savoy-Plaza Hotel—just me, Mark, Queenie and Harold, my two aunts, Gail and Hank, Mark's parents and his sister Ellen, Louis, Patti and her date Maurice, and my nephew Glen, our ring bearer.

After the ceremony, we headed to change at my aunt Jessie's apartment, which was across the street from Stephan's art studio. (What are the odds?) Harold was staying with her because he was separated from my mother at that moment. As we were driving toward the apartment, we saw Stephan walking his big, beautiful Great Dane, Blu.

I pointed at him and said to Mark, "See that man? That's

Stephan, and it's over. I will never see him again." I can't deny it was a weird thing to do, but by saying the words out loud, I thought I could make them true. Good-natured Mark took it in stride.

We honeymooned at the Concord Hotel in the Catskills. When we arrived, they were holding a beauty pageant at the pool. If you won, you got a free room. Mark entered me in the competition, even though I was lanky, hippy, and hardly an American beauty queen. I didn't win, and we had to pay for our room, where we stayed for three days.

The morning after we got home, Stephan called. He'd been trying to reach me. "There you are! I miss you. Can I drive you home tomorrow?"

"Stephan, I'm married—I married Mark on Friday."

He took a minute to digest the news. "That's okay," he said. "We still need to talk. Let me drive you home tomorrow night."

Like I said, Stephan was an addiction. I let him drive me home. The girl at his apartment was a misunderstanding, he said. He missed me; wanted to be with me. But he wasn't exactly asking me to leave Mark. That was clear.

Fortunately, I had a big distraction. Mark's father was so happy we were married that he gave us a blank check and told us to decorate our new apartment in Cedarhurst any way we wanted. I called my friend Ilene, who was working for the famed (and very dramatic) decorator David Barrett. We created a superchic apartment with big leather sofas and animal skin rugs, dark gray walls with a light gray ceiling in one room, and magenta walls with a black ceiling in another. In this ultrastylish setting Mark and I began our married life.

———

I never seem to begin anything without something else ending. Every birth is followed by a death. This time it was my beloved dad's. Mark and I hadn't yet settled into our new apartment, so we were still living in Woodmere, near my parents. My mother was in California for work, and she called and told me to go to her apartment. Harold was sick, she said. Very sick.

"Dad, you must go to the hospital," I said when I saw him.

"No, it'll cost too much money," he said with great effort. "But stay here with me."

I was scared for him, and for me. I lay next to him in the bed, but I couldn't sleep. In the middle of the night I heard him gasp, and against his wishes I called for an ambulance, which took us to a Catholic hospital with crucifixes all over the walls. He died the next day, right after Queenie had seen him one final time. I was distraught—my dad, the warmth of my childhood, was gone. I've often wondered if Harold stayed with my mother to watch over Gail and me and give us refuge from her strictness and sadness.

Harold's death led to a huge family revelation. Mark and I had just come home from the funeral at Riverside Memorial Chapel on the Upper West Side.

"Your mother has now buried three husbands, according to Hank," Mark said, referring to Gail's husband.

"What are you talking about?" I asked. "There was only Harold and my father."

But apparently there was another one. Before Gabby, Queenie was married to a man named Mack Richman. Mack had died, too, which was why Harold called my mother the "Black Widow." Her garment-center nickname, "Richie," came from Richman. Another mystery solved.

So *this* was why I'd been punished when I was a kid rummaging through the attic. My mother didn't want me to stumble on anything—pictures, documents, cards, whatever—that would reveal her secret.

I've thought about it a lot, in and out of therapy. Why not come clean about an early marriage? What harm would it do? Queenie must have been tormented by this secret. I can't imagine the psychological burden it placed on her, and for what?

But I knew not to go there. If she didn't want me to know something, there was no reason to tell her I knew.

DESIGN AWARD
BY
RETAIL FASHION
AUTHORITIES OF AMERICA
TO
ANNE KLEIN & CO.
FOR CREATIVE ACHIEVEMENT
IN THE
WOMEN'S KNITWEAR INDUSTRY
1973

5 | BACK TO SEVENTH AVENUE

The entire year I was with Patti at Addenda, I missed Seventh Avenue. It wasn't Patti's fault. She encouraged me to design what I wanted, and I did a whole collection based on the movie *Midnight Cowboy* with embroidered shirts and velveteen jeans that Bloomingdale's loved. But I missed the pure creativity of the designer world, and I especially missed the fabrics. Patti remembers finding me in the design room one day sewing pants out of the shiny side of interfacing (the stiff fabric used to give some softer fabrics shape). It was an experiment, not something you could sell to stores. Patti designed for a mass audience and had to make her numbers.

I knew now that Anne Klein had been the right job for me, and I had blown it. I loved and respected the modernity of Anne's designs and related to it on a personal and creative level. So, when I heard that Hazel Haire had left, I called immediately and asked for Anne, praying she would take my call. She did.

"Anne, I'd love to come up and meet with you," I began. "You'll see. I'm a different person now. I've been through a lot and have learned so much."

It was the truth. By this point I'd grown up, I knew my stuff, and I had gained a lot of confidence through Patti. I also mentioned to Anne that I was a married woman, which I thought made me sound more settled and mature.

Anne had her doubts; remember, this was a woman who couldn't stand to be in the same room with me. But I was forceful. I invited her to call Patti as a reference. I insisted I would prove myself. She could give me a probation period; I didn't care. I wanted back in.

Anne rehired me, and I made an internal vow: I would not, *could not*, screw this up. I was even bold enough to ask to be her chief assistant, a level up from where I had been. Amazingly, Anne agreed, and Patti, a true friend, was delighted for me.

Anne Klein was an entirely different experience this time around. Even if I was still intimidated by Anne, and I was, I played confident. She saw that I was more focused, and she loved my creative spirit. I was involved in everything she did, from choosing fabrics to creating boards to working with the sample room. Whatever was needed, I did it, even if I had to figure it out on my own. I didn't want to bother her with silly questions.

The first thing I learned was that Anne was the boss. Yes, she had her investors, Sandy and Gunther, and her husband and business manager, Chip. But Anne was as much an entrepreneur as she was a designer. She controlled every aspect of her company—which clothes were sold and where, how they were presented—and everyone reported to her. I admired her strength and appreciated how much she sweated the details. Nothing was too small for her to have an opinion on, from the positioning of darts and buttons on a blouse to the coffee mugs we used in the showroom. She didn't miss a trick.

Anne liked to design at night. Often it would be just her, me, and a model. She'd go into a zone and fit for hours and hours, a practice I picked up from watching her. I'd pass her pins, and she would work painstakingly on the model. Because of Anne, I, too, became a stickler for fit. To me, fitting is sculpture, a three-dimensional creation on a body.

Design-wise, we complemented each other perfectly. Where Anne was all about silhouette and fit, I was passionate for fabric, and she let me shop in Europe. I was among the first American designers to source fabrics abroad—and honestly, I didn't know what I was doing. A classic story: I was twenty-one or so and went off to Frankfurt Interstoff, my first German fabric show. Julie (short for Julius) Stern, Anne's fabric buyer, had arrived a couple of days earlier, so we agreed to meet at the hotel. I don't speak German, but I had the address, which I handed to the cabdriver. He dropped me off at a small building next to an elevated train track and a donut factory. (What hotel is next to a donut factory?) The lobby was barely a lobby—just a desk with a guy behind it. Maybe hotel standards were different in Germany, I thought, and gave the man my name. He had no record of it, but he had a room.

"You'll bring my luggage up, right?" I asked.

"No. You carry yourself," the man barked in broken English. *I guess the standards* are *different here,* I thought. The room was ridiculously small; I couldn't open the bathroom door without putting my luggage on the bed. It was grimy and didn't smell great, either. I opened the window, and the burning sweetness of donuts wafted in. A train rumbled by. I was up all night, thanks to the sounds of pounding and squeaky springs heard through the paper-thin walls. The next morning I called the number Julie had given me.

"Donna, where are you?" he shouted. "I'm at the hotel, looking everywhere for you!"

I connected the dots: the tiny room, the pounding, the stench . . . I was in a brothel. I had checked myself into a Frankfurt brothel! God knows how—a misspelling? a cabdriver's prank?—but I did.

———

As terrible as I was at judging hotels, I was great at sourcing fabric, and Anne gave me carte blanche. I loved her simple, classic palette of black, gray, navy, camel, and gold. When it came to inspiration, she'd say, "God gave you two eyes. Use them!" I think of her words all the time, especially when I'm traveling. Inspiration is all around us; we only need to look up and breathe it in.

To Anne, the customer's needs, lifestyle, and mind-set came first. This modern customer, she'd tell me, was too busy to worry about clothes. In addressing this woman, Anne helped give birth to sportswear and the idea of mixing and matching. Every piece went with every other piece, so you could create multiple outfits with a few key staples. More than anything, Anne wanted to make fashion easy and understandable. When the popular skirt length dropped from mini to midi (midthigh to midcalf), Anne used the same fabric as the season before, so customers could simply switch the skirt, not their entire wardrobe. It was a brilliant way to help women get comfortable with a new proportion.

In many ways, Anne Klein was like her predecessor Claire McCardell, another great American fashion icon. Neither one could separate being a woman from the clothes they designed. I'm often asked if women make better designers than men, and my answer is always the same: "A good designer is a good designer." But women do have the advantage of wearing and living in their designs. We know what feels good and which styles give confidence. We've got the same hang-ups about our bodies as everyone else. Which leads me to the most important thing I learned from Anne: how to balance creativity and reality. Clothes can and should be beautiful, but they work only if you want to wear them in your everyday life. If Anne couldn't imagine wearing something herself, it didn't make it into the collection. In 1967, the year before I joined her, Anne had patented a girdle designed specifically to be worn under miniskirts—not exactly something a man would come up with. (It's no surprise

Spanx was invented by a woman, too.) Anne created it for herself, because she had great legs and loved minis. She understood the relationship between a woman's body and her clothes, and worked to make it a positive one.

Anne and I had very different figures. She was 5'2", built in the front, flat in the back. I was 5'8" and built in the back. In other words, she was belly and no ass, and I was ass and no belly. People called us Mutt and Jeff, like the famous mismatched cartoon characters, because we were always together, this chic little blond woman and her tall, gangly brunette sidekick. She was like a mother to me, which made my real mother more than a little jealous. Mark would pick me up from work and we'd go out to dinner with Anne and Chip. We spent summers with them at their house on Dune Road in Westhampton. She made me feel like family.

Anne and I also got each other because we were both New Yorkers (Brooklyn, in her case) and we both smoked constantly. I think she saw herself in me. Anne had worked her whole life, too. At fifteen she'd gotten an after-school job sketching on Seventh Avenue. At nineteen she'd gotten her first full-time job as a juniors designer at Varden Petites. She saw how unsophisticated I was and joked that she couldn't take me anywhere, but she took me everywhere. And when I screwed up, she took it in stride. One time I forgot to remove an outfit from a mannequin that was supposed to be in a show. We got to the venue, and Anne started reading from the run of show—the order in which the looks would be presented. When she got to a particular number, I covered my mouth with my hand. "Oh my God, Anne! I left it in the studio, on the mannequin!" She peered over her reading glasses and, in a tone that was half angry and half amused, said, "You'll never make that mistake again." Forty years later, I haven't.

We didn't travel together much, but the times we did were remarkable. Our first trip was to Germany to meet with Margaretha

Ley, a stunning woman who ran a knitwear company with her husband, Wolfgang. (They would go on to open Escada in 1976.) Anne and I landed in Zurich with the plan to drive the three hours to St. Moritz, where we would see Anne's partner Gunther, who spent his winters there. Anne Klein & Co. had a fur licensee, so we'd each bought a floor-length silver fox coat for the trip. (In a licensing arrangement, a designer provides her name and designs the product, and the licensee, a manufacturer that is usually an expert in that category, produces it.) Anne's fur had a hood, and mine had a big notch collar, similar to a man's lapel. I paid $1,800 for mine— a fortune on my $30,000 annual salary—but I loved, loved, *loved* it. I wore it over hot pants with over-the-knee boots or a maxi skirt (my two looks at the time) and my bullet belt. *To die.*

We landed in Zurich with a ton of luggage and a Wolf-brand mannequin that Anne planned to use for her knitwear fittings. We expected a big car to pick us up, but instead a compact European car pulled up to the curb. Anne was sick from the flight and could hardly speak. I felt fine but didn't speak German, so I had to refer to my German-English phrase book for everything. Somehow they found us a bigger car, but even so, Anne and I had to squeeze together in the backseat, and the dummy got strapped to the top.

The drive was snowy, twisty, and steep. The whole time, I was looking through the book for how to say something like "Please pull over, my friend is sick." We finally arrived at the Badrutt's Palace Hotel in St. Moritz, the fanciest place on earth, where Gunther lived in a luxe suite. He came out to greet us, saw the dummy strapped to the car, took in our matching silver fox coats, and said in his German accent, "Vat is this, theez matching coats?" To him, we couldn't have looked tackier.

Anne and I went out and bought two new coats. Anne went for a little black fur, and I picked up a chrome-yellow long-haired fake fur jacket. At that moment European fashion was all about vivid color, and you could see this yellow from miles away. I wore it every day of our trip and thought I looked incredibly chic. Once Anne felt better, she took me skiing for my very first time, and we ended up having a highly productive meeting with Margaretha Ley.

Back in New York, I put on my Euro-chic yellow coat one morning and went to Chateau Pharmacy in Woodmere for my usual morning coffee and to meet Johnny Schrader, my friend and fellow commuter, who worked in the fabric business. I noticed people staring at me and was sure it was because I looked so stylish. Then on the train a young boy pointed at me and said, "Daddy, Daddy, look, it's Big Bird from *Sesame Street*." As Johnny and I exited the train at Penn Station, I noticed everyone craning their necks to get a better look at me. *Everyone*. New Yorkers wear mostly black in the winter as they rush around in the slush, and there I was, teetering in my high heels, wearing this gigantic yellow coat. (Johnny wouldn't even let me hold his arm, he was so embarrassed by the attention I was getting.) I ran to the office, left it there, and never wore it again. Fashion lesson learned: one country's chic is another country's cartoon.

————————

We worked crazy hours in those days. Sometimes Anne's husband, Chip, would hang out with us. Anne would have proper dinners delivered and served on china; she was very motherly that way. My trip home to Long Island was a trek, so staying late meant I had no personal life. While she was designing in the evenings, Anne liked her vodka and club soda, which I mixed for her. (Funny, now that's my drink too.) So when I wanted to get home earlier than usual, I would add more vodka than soda, and it worked every time.

Truth be told, the nights I wanted to leave early were Tuesdays. I was still seeing Stephan (we had fallen right back into our routine after I got married), and that was the night he drove out to Long

Island to see his shrink and his kids. It was our weekly ritual. We both knew it was wrong, but it was too intoxicating to stop. In my mind, I compartmentalized our Tuesday night flings. I told myself they had nothing to do with my life with Mark, that I wasn't hurting anyone.

To be clear, Mark and I shared a real physical connection as well. We were sexually and sensually close, always snuggling and touching. He was easy to be with, encouraged my career, and loved making spontaneous social plans with friends. He adored spending time at Anne and Chip's beach house and dining with them in the city. We were house shopping. We traveled a lot, to places like Acapulco and St. Maarten, and we spent our summers on Fire Island, off Long Island's South Shore. We drove great cars, including a chocolate-brown Jaguar convertible, and we had adopted a black-and-white harlequin Great Dane named Felix (I was inspired by Stephan's dog). Life was good, and Mark had no reason to think there was anything wrong.

And then I got pregnant. I was pretty certain the baby was Stephan's—a deep fear in my gut told me so. I called Stephan in a panic, and his reaction was shocking: he was happy for me.

"That's great, Donna," he said. "You've always wanted to have a baby."

"Does that mean . . . ?" I asked, secretly hoping he'd ask me to leave Mark, move in with him, and finally start a life together.

"It means I'm happy for you . . . and Mark."

"But the baby is *yours*."

Silence.

"Stephan? Are you there?"

He was not there—that much was abundantly clear over the course of our conversation. Stephan had no interest in joining me on this particular journey.

"Fuck you, Stephan," was all I could think to say. I felt utterly betrayed.

I told Mark about my pregnancy—and about Stephan. I wish I could have lied about it, but it was so momentous and so devastating that I couldn't hide the truth. I didn't tell him how much time I'd spent with Stephan, only that I'd made a mistake and was terribly embarrassed. Mark saw my resolve. He also understood why I had to have an abortion. I couldn't have this child without knowing who its father was. It was the only possible way we could move forward.

I told my mother, too, and to my surprise she wasn't angry at all. In fact, she was very supportive. She loved Mark and wanted our marriage to work out, and I think she also wanted to protect him a little bit.

"I'm coming with you, Donna," she said.

"It's okay. Mark's taking me."

"And so am I." She was worried, understandably. It was 1973, the year *Roe v. Wade* was decided. Abortions weren't quite as available or mainstream back then.

So Mark and my mother took me to have an abortion—a legal one. I wanted nothing more in the world than to have a baby, and I was inconsolable. Yet the possibility of having Stephan's child while married to Mark was out of the question. This was the right decision.

I was done with Stephan. Finished. Over. The end.

––––––––––

Once again, Mark had saved me. I recommitted to our marriage, heart, body, and spirit. To be loved the way he loved me— unconditionally, really—was a gift beyond measure. We would have our own babies, our own life. In the meantime, we had Felix.

But for me, Felix was also an emotional connection to Stephan. Despite my resolve, I always had an eye out for him, especially on Sundays, the weekend day that I knew he visited his kids. I imagined running into him in Cedarhurst, me with Felix, him with Blu, and having a "Dane chat." You know, "What do you feed your dog? How much exercise do you give him?" It never happened, of course.

I saw Stephan only once around that time. Mark and I went to a friend's party on Woodmere Boulevard, and Stephan was there with his wife. It was as awkward as you'd expect. We said a quick hello, then avoided each other for the rest of the night.

6 | A
BIRTH
AND A
DEATH

"Donna, I plan to travel for a while," Anne said one day in the late spring of 1972. "I need you to do holiday on your own." With Anne away, I felt free, and my mind raced with design ideas.

Holiday/resort is the season that comes after fall. It's less about a whole wardrobe and more about special pieces to brighten your closet, wear to parties, give as gifts, or pack for traveling. Holiday 1972 turned out to be one of my best collections ever. It was couture in feeling, with every piece artisan and special. I used my favorite colors—black, white, red, and vicuña—and incorporated lots of embroidery and leather. I designed small tops with big cowhide skirts, an all-over fringed suede skirt, Lurex sweater dresses, and a black shearling coat with ivory stitching down the front. Very hippie, very me. Kal Ruttenstein, who was president of the department store Bonwit Teller, put the collection in the store's windows, surrounded by a sea of massive red balloons. I thought about how proud and excited my dad would have been to see the displays, and to know that I had realized my teenage dreams.

That collection foreshadowed my future. The truth was that Anne hadn't been traveling that summer; she had breast cancer.

————————

Anne returned to work at the end of August. The only indication that something was wrong was that she was squeezing a small rubber ball all the time, something I'd never seen her do before. (I later learned those balls are commonly used to reduce swelling and help lymphatic flow after a mastectomy.) Still, she was happy to be back at work and impressed with the collection I had done. She named me associate designer, and to retailers and the press she gave me credit. I was bowled over. In retrospect, I appreciate that she was preparing for the future of her company, getting ready to pass the torch.

Our next collection, spring 1973, received rave reviews. The *New York Times* referred to me as Anne's assistant—a far cry from associate designer, but at least they spelled my name correctly. *Women's Wear Daily* omitted it altogether, and I was pissed. To this day, I don't know where I got my nerve, but I called June Weir, *WWD*'s senior fashion editor, to ask why my name wasn't in the review. Big mistake.

"*Never* question the press for *any* reason," she snarled, and hung up the phone.

————————

About six months later, Mark and I learned I was pregnant. I couldn't have been happier. I was going to be a mother—the thing I wanted more than anything. I fully intended to be a stay-at-home mom.

Yet I was concerned about Anne, who was becoming more and more dependent on me. The company was growing, and she relied on me to handle design while she tended to business, especially since we had a new majority owner: Tomio Taki, who headed Takihyo of Nagoya, a two-hundred-year-old family-owned textile business in Japan. To help with design, I wanted to bring in my old friend Louis Dell'Olio from Parsons. We'd stayed in touch the best we could, given our horrendous work hours. Louis was now designing for Giorgini, a new sportswear division of the coat company Originala, a job my mother had helped him get, but I wanted to partner with him again, the way we had in school. I floated the idea with Anne.

She shook her head. "Three's a bad number, Donna. It would be two against one when it comes to opinions and decisions. Let's continue as we are."

Despite my advancing pregnancy, I didn't slow down. If anything, I took on more responsibility. There was a level of trust between me and Anne that I valued. I didn't want to disappoint her; I wanted to help. Having Anne Klein believe in me was validating beyond words.

By October, Anne and I were in the design room, preparing for the famous Battle of Versailles of November 1973.

"My first ball ever, and look at me," I cried, pointing to my pregnant middle, which was expanding by the minute. "What am I going to wear?"

"Wear something black," Anne said. "You'll be fine."

Of all the extraordinary things I've done in my career, the ball and dueling fashion shows were the ultimate. It's not an overstatement to say that this event changed the course of fashion. First, it put American fashion on the global map. Second, it introduced racial diversity to the runway.

It all started because the Palace of Versailles, outside Paris, needed to raise money for restorations. Eleanor Lambert, the grand dame publicist of American fashion, came up with the idea of a fashion "battle," where five American designers would compete against five French couturiers. The idea was almost laughable, because American fashion didn't have an international presence of any kind. But Eleanor saw it as our chance to show the world what we were made of. Through sheer force of will, she spearheaded and orchestrated the whole thing. The Americans were Anne, Halston, Oscar de la Renta, Bill Blass, and the youngest of the group, Stephen Burrows. The French: Yves Saint Laurent, Givenchy, Marc Bohan for Christian Dior, Pierre Cardin, and Emanuel Ungaro. I was seven months pregnant at the time—huge!—but nothing could keep me away from this monumental black-tie ball.

The preparations alone were exciting. We bought Mark his first tuxedo (at $350, it was the most expensive thing we owned) and practiced ballroom dancing at home—me with swollen feet. The office felt like Grand Central Station because we also had a business to run. Kay Thompson, our show choreographer, visited constantly. Kay was an incredibly talented actress and dancer who played the fashion editor in the Audrey Hepburn film *Funny Face,* and she was also the author of the famous Eloise books. Kay had worked closely with Judy Garland and was godmother to her daughter Liza Minnelli, the singer and actress who would open for us at Versailles. Liza had just won the Oscar for *Cabaret,* so I was dying to meet her. We had endless model fittings and rehearsals. We had to make sure everything fit and was in impeccable order, because once we packed and shipped the clothes to France, that was it.

Before Versailles, I had to go with Julie Stern (who'd been my travel companion when I wound up in that German brothel) to a Frankfurt Interstoff fabric show to prepare for pre-fall, the smaller, precursor season to fall, as well as fall itself—as I said, our usual work had to get done. We studied bolt after bolt, vendor after vendor; I used my baby bump as a table to hold swatches and write my orders, and my feet were as big and swollen as my stomach by the end of the long days. I swear, when Gabby was in the womb, she must have rolled her eyes: "*More* fabrics, Mommy?" I can see why she rejected a fashion career.

During that stop in Frankfurt, Julie and I went to a sauna. "Julie, don't take your pants off," I said. "I can't see you like that."

"But it's a sauna, Donna," he said. "Everyone's naked—just don't look." In we went. It was a handful of men—and me.

"Just my luck," said a German. "One girl comes in, and she's pregnant and wearing a swimsuit."

I caught up with Anne and Mark in Paris, and that's where our troubles began. We all happened to be Eleanor's clients, and it was clear that she made her selections to show diversity: Stephen Burrows was African American and new to the industry, and Anne was the only woman on either side. But there was little camaraderie within our group, which was a real boys' club if ever there was one. Anne was a strong Jewish woman, and let's face it, people like her and me aren't the most heralded on earth. When we speak up and fight hard to be heard, we're considered pushy and overbearing. And even though we may seem confident, underneath we are vulnerable and insecure—yet another thing Barbra Streisand and I share. In Versailles, Anne worked hard to be a team player, but the other American designers took all the best staging rooms, leaving us alone in the basement.

The French were even worse. They were on their home turf and extremely snobby about everything. The designers were couture, fancy, global, and well known. They had the whole day before the shows to prepare and rehearse their elaborate stagings, leaving the Americans to rehearse for our shows only very late that night. No coffee, no toilet paper, no heat—and it was freezing!

But there was a magical moment during rehearsals. My feet were killing me, so I went into the audience, propping my ankles up on a chair. Kay, who was silver-haired and reed slim, appeared on the stage. One of her pant legs was rolled up, and to the beat of the music, she mapped out Liza's opening number, step by step, twirl by twirl. It was a scene right out of a movie, right out of my childhood fantasies, and I was mesmerized.

More than seven hundred people came to what was now a globally publicized event, a battle of the old school of couture fashion versus the new school of sportswear. I'd never seen so many limousines, so many diamonds and tiaras. Princess Grace of Monaco was there, as well as other kings and queens, heads of state, socialites (as invited by C. Z. Guest, the American hostess, and Marie-Hélène de Rothschild, for the French side). Even Andy Warhol and Elizabeth Taylor attended. Everyone entered through the Hall of Mirrors, where the servers were dressed in eighteenth-century costumes, powdered wigs, brocades, and slippers. Since I was so physically big, I went with a black turtleneck tent dress and a dramatic turban-style wrap around my head. I didn't wear jewelry—I didn't own stuff to compete with this crowd. As usual, the petite Anne was my visual opposite in a long beige dress with a fox fur jacket.

Now the show. The French went first—of course. They pulled every trick possible, and took more than two hours to do it. The amazing Josephine Baker sang with showgirls from the Kit Kat Club as backup, and Rudolf Nureyev danced with his ballet troupe. There were more performers after that, and the show dragged on and on. When the clothes finally came out, they were backdropped by outrageous props and life-size cutouts: a white Cadillac for Saint Laurent, a spaceship for Pierre Cardin, a rhinoceros for Ungaro. It was overwhelming—too much, too long, too everything.

Then came the Americans. We had no props, just pools of light on the stage. We had planned to have drapes, but because of a wrong conversion between centimeters and inches, they came in too short. Famed illustrator Joe Eula improvised at the last moment, using a broom to sketch the Eiffel Tower on white seamless paper, and it looked sensational.

Liza Minnelli opened, belting out "Bonjour Paris" with a chorus of thirty-six models in trench coats and carrying open umbrellas. The world had never seen so many black models on a fashion stage. We had brought Billie Blair, Bethann Hardison, Alva Chinn, Norma Jean Darden, and China Machado. We also had "The Halstonettes," Halston's regular group of models, including Pat Cleveland and Karen Bjornson. Even my look-alike, Marisa Berenson, modeled.

Anne showed first, a position she got by default after the others duked it out to go last (Halston won). Fine with us. We loved making the first impression and went tribal, exaggeratedly so. Where the French models walked out holding little cards with numbers (an antiquated practice), ours came out gyrating to drums. The clothes were so me—black bras, shrunken tops, hip-slung skirts, and full pants with belly buttons showing. Backstage, I was the dresser. Billie Blair exited, dramatically thrusting out one arm to the audience as she left the stage; inside, I had the other arm, dressing her next look. At the end of Anne's segment, the audience screamed with excitement, throwing their programs in the air. We'd hit it.

The entire production was a proud moment, with America showing its many stories: Anne's sportswear, Stephen's hip edge, Bill's tailoring, Oscar's glam, Halston's minimalism. If this was a battle, the Americans delivered a knockout blow. Victory was ours.

Next came the dinner. Even though it was called a ball, there was no dancing; Mark and I could have saved ourselves hours of practice. I had also insisted we learn to eat formally, as we hadn't a clue how, but it hardly mattered, because the portions were so small. Everyone had five or six glasses at their place setting, a dinner plate the size of a coaster, twelve forks, and several knives—all for what felt like a serving of celery. In the middle of dinner they handed us warm bowls of water with lemon. Mark drank his. I was about to drink mine when Anne leaned in. "That's to clean your hands," she whispered.

Afterward we were starving, so Anne, Chip, Mark, and I went out for dinner at the legendary restaurant Caviar Kaspia on the Place de la Madeleine. The next day, Marie-Hélène de Rothschild held a luncheon at her estate. The Americans were being toasted left and right. Many of the guests marveled to us, "You mean you just pull these clothes on, with nobody helping you?" They were used to hooks and eyes and couture fits. Countess Jacqueline de Ribes told the press that "the French were pompous and pretentious; the Americans' show was so filled with life and color." Even Ungaro declared us "genius." What a triumph for American designers. We were now a force to be reckoned with.

———————

Life being a constant give-and-take, something heartbreaking also happened during the show. While standing backstage, Anne discovered a lump on her neck. She didn't know what it was—a lymph node, maybe—but she knew it was something she'd have to deal with when she got home. When we returned to New York, I told Anne we needed to replace me because I planned to stay home once I had my baby. Again I suggested Louis. I don't think Anne wanted to believe I was going to stop working, but this time she was more receptive, which surprised me. But then Chip pulled me aside privately.

"Donna, you can't leave," he blurted out. "Anne has cancer." I covered my mouth in surprise. "She will be fine," he quickly added, "but we need you here as she goes through her treatment."

It really did seem like she'd be fine. Tomio Taki had just bought into the company, and his insurance carrier required Anne to have a complete physical since she was the principal. They were aware of the cancer and that she had had a mastectomy, yet had no qualms about investing. Anne's friend Burt Wayne, the interior designer, had just finished her apartment on East 57th Street. Only Anne knew the severity of her situation—and that, at the very least, she would need to take some time off. Louis accepted the design position, though his Giorgini contract tied him up until June. We were happy to wait for him, as either Anne or I would need a design partner going forward. I just needed to hang on for as long as this baby would let me.

Because Anne wasn't well, I worked even longer hours than usual; heading home at midnight or later was routine. I wanted to prepare as much as possible before my maternity leave. Julie Stern lived near us on Long Island and drove me to and from work every day. He was the consummate Jewish father, and it was a running joke that my baby would be born in his car. Julie's son drove the local firehouse's truck, so Julie kidded that we were covered, no matter what. I was so big by that time that just the sight of my belly made everyone nervous.

I've always been late for everything, and giving birth was no exception. I was ten days past my due date when my water broke at the office. I went home in a Town Car and had erratic contractions through the night. By 5:00 a.m. on March 8, 1974, they were much closer together. Whom did I call? Julie Stern.

The minute he arrived, I started giving him cutting orders and other instructions. "Julie, you have to follow up with . . ." I paused for a contraction.

"Donna, I don't think you should be worrying about this right now," he said, pacing next to my bed.

"Of course I should. I'll be too busy later."

My labor lasted a full day. While I was in the hospital on Long Island, Anne was at Mount Sinai Hospital in Manhattan with pneumonia—and no one was at work. Our pre-fall collection was due that very week. We spoke on the phone hospital to hospital, discussing how many buttons should be on a double-breasted navy cashmere coat.

I had planned on a natural birth, and I nearly made it—until that last push. "Give me gas," I screamed, and minutes later, out came a ten-pound baby girl. We named her Gabrielle Hope: Gabrielle for my father, a name that began with *H* for Harold. The second I saw Gabby, I fell completely, utterly, madly in love. I was overcome with joy. Finally I was the mother I'd always wanted to be. This little baby girl was all that mattered. I held her in my arms and couldn't stop staring at her, and as if on cue, the radio played Roberta Flack's "The First Time Ever I Saw Your Face." You can't make that up, it was so perfect.

Gabby had no sooner popped out than Gunther called my hospital room and bellowed in that deep German voice of his, "Donna, ve need you to come back to vork."

"Would you like to know if I had a boy or a girl?" I asked. "It's a girl, if you're interested."

"That's nice, but vhen are you returning? Ve have a collection due, and Anne von't be back in time."

I checked with my doctor, who forbade me to go back to work. It was far too soon. "You had a big baby, Donna. You're all stitched up."

"Don't worry," I replied. "I have a roomful of seamstresses who can sew me up if that's an issue." The joke was lost on him. He ordered me to stay home and sit on a rubber donut for ten days.

When I told Gunther, he said, "Okay, ve come to you. Vhen vill you be home?"

Almost a week later, the whole staff arrived at the new white house Mark and I had just moved into on a cul-de-sac in Lawrence, Long Island. I had the bagels and lox all spread out. I assumed they were coming to coo over Gabby and maybe bring flowers and a casserole. Then I saw the trucks arrive, the racks of clothes being wheeled up my driveway. This was business.

We cleared out my new dining room so we could use it as a design studio. Betty Hanson, our head of sales, had no sooner arrived than she answered the phone in the kitchen.

"Um, okay. Yes," I heard her say. Her face fell. She saw me looking at her and turned away.

"What, Betty, what?" I called over from my perch on the donut. She hung up and looked all around, clearly unsure of what to say. "Damn it, Betty what happened?" I shouted.

She came closer. "Anne died."

The shock hit me, and I started shaking and couldn't stop. *Anne died?* How could that be? She was only fifty. I'd thought she was going to be fine. Everyone had thought that. I kept thinking of all the reassuring words I'd heard.

"Someone please get me a cigarette," I shouted to the room. I hadn't smoked since learning I was pregnant. A Pall Mall cigarette and lighter appeared in front of me. As I was taking a drag, Betty knelt by my side.

"Donna, listen," she said in a soothing voice. "This is terrible, but you need to finish the collection. The stores are waiting. Anne would have wanted you to."

I took another drag. Then it dawned on me: *everyone had known.* They'd known all along that Anne was dying. And no one had told me. Not Anne. Not Chip. Not Gunther. Not Betty. Not even Burt Wayne, her interior designer and my friend. This was like my mother's secret keeping. Why hadn't they told me? Who got to make these decisions? I'd just had a baby; I wanted to stay home. Things never turned out the way I planned them. Other people and events had stepped in, and I didn't even get a vote. Anne was leaving me, and I was the last to know. In a state of shock and rage, I exhaled and stood up.

"Fuck you, Betty," I said in my sharpest voice. "Fuck these clothes. Fuck everything. I'm going to the city."

I never got to say goodbye to Anne. Our last conversation was about buttons, for God's sake. She was my teacher, my mentor, my everything. We were so close, and getting closer. She was a second mother to me. I was the daughter she never had. I was twenty-five years old, had just given birth, and Anne was dead.

The insanity of it still galls me. Once again, life and death came hand in hand, and I had no choice but to react quickly and march forward. I see now that I would not be who I am today if Anne Klein had not died when she did. I would not be who I am if not for Anne Klein, period. But in that moment, I stood in the chaos of my dining room, my infant in a bassinet, barely absorbing the news. I had two things to do: get to the city to bury my friend and finish this god-damned pre-fall collection.

7 | FLYING SOLO

A whirlwind. A blur. A 24/7 storm of madness. Those are the only ways I can describe the chaotic days and weeks that followed Anne's death. The entire fashion industry was in shock. The memorial service took place three days later at the Frank E. Campbell Funeral Home on Manhattan's Upper East Side. The chapel seated four hundred, but close to a thousand people showed up. Louis couldn't even get in.

Edie Locke, Anne's great friend and the editor in chief at *Mademoiselle* at the time, spoke, as did Stanley Marcus of Neiman Marcus, the designer Rudi Gernreich, and Anne's lawyer and dear friend Charles Ballon. Tomio Taki flew in from Japan. We sat shiva in Anne and Chip's home. Chip gave Louis one of Anne's lions, a raw-edged copper one. Anne was a Leo; the lion was the company's mascot, and she had a huge collection of lion figurines. The only thing I remember from that day was wearing my long silver fox coat, the one just like Anne's.

All my dreams of being a stay-at-home mom had gone out the window—poof. I was on autopilot, heading back to West 39th Street, sometimes with newborn Gabby at my side, my ankles still swollen. As promised, we delivered the pre-fall collection. Now I had to face the big one, fall, set to show on May 15, 1974. I called Kay Thompson, the actress and choreographer who had been so wonderful to me and Anne at Versailles. "Kay, you've got to come and help me with this fall show," I pleaded. "I feel so lost. I have no idea what I'm doing." More than anything, I needed motherly support and advice.

"I'm here for you," she answered. "I'll help any way I can."

I didn't have a moment to breathe, never mind reflect on all the recent upheaval. I didn't channel Anne in any way while designing that collection; I was still too numb for that. But I did call upon every lesson she'd taught me. I designed for flexibility, creating mix-and-match sportswear a woman could wear multiple ways. It sounds old hat now, but in 1974, women wore "outfits." I knew I had to put my own stamp on this collection, so I made it a little hipper, a little cooler. I wanted the collection to feel young and sexy.

Did I mention I was fifty-five pounds overweight? I was obsessed with losing the baby weight and getting skinny again. I pointed to our leather guy's dummy and said, "I want the tightest jacket you can put on this mannequin." I took the leather and molded it to the form. That was my goal: to fit into that jacket. Everything in the line had to look like that: still sportswear, but slim, bias-cut, sculpted, fitted, maybe balanced over slouchy tweed pants or an easy skirt. My crash diet inspired the whole collection—not that I remember actually dieting. When you have a baby at twenty-five, the weight comes off pretty easily. But I didn't know that as I was frantically designing.

I didn't realize it then, but I was fulfilling my destiny. I knew what I was doing. I was decisive. I had a vision! It was exhausting but at the same time effortless. It was such a mad, mad rush that I didn't have time to think about how the collection would be received. Just putting it together drained all my energy. To keep up morale and build loyalty in the design room during those long days, I clowned around and ordered in great meals. My Jewish-mother instincts had kicked in. And Gabby was occasionally around for people to coo over.

Kay had an idea for the show's music that involved a string of esoteric sounds. I went along with it until I realized it was *my* show and that such a soundtrack wasn't right, so we changed it. That was an important moment. Not only did I have to design a collection on my own, but I had to conceptualize and direct how my clothes were shown. *My* vision, not Anne's, was the one that counted. I ran with it. I added fedoras and ties and gave the whole thing a haberdashery feel.

I came to realize much later that I was operating in a bubble. While I was madly prepping for the show, all sorts of discussions were taking place on the corporate level. I'll never know the whole story, but many people outside and inside the company, starting with Gunther Oppenheim, thought a more established designer should take the reins. Names were being tossed around. And I get it. We were talking about a huge business, with a lot of money at stake. I was a young, unknown quantity. Who knew what I was capable of? I had done one resort collection that had been a hit, but resort doesn't represent an overall design vision, nor is it a money-maker. Also, I was a new mother—maybe they thought I'd be distracted. In those days, many women quit their jobs after having a baby.

Tomio Taki, who had a controlling interest in the company, and had been a partner for only four and a half months when Anne died, bet on me. He felt I knew her vision better than anyone. "We're going with Donna. I believe in her," he said, ending the conversation. But the risk was too great for Gunther. He sold his share in the business to Takihyo. It wasn't just me he was worried about; Gunther also questioned the future of the company under Chip Rubenstein. Gunther had been in it for Anne, and now she was gone.

Tomio transferred the respect he had for Anne to me. They had shared the belief that a good fit was everything. Tomio would say, "The color attracts the customer, the fabric makes her want to touch it, and the design can inspire her to bring it into the dressing room. But the right fit is what makes a woman actually *buy* the piece." Tomio knew I had been trained by the best when it came to fit. He also knew I understood the value and versatility of an Anne Klein garment.

Thank God I didn't know how much was riding on me in the days leading up to that show. People fought for invitations. The press wanted to support a house hit with sudden tragedy, of course. But there were plenty of curiosity-seekers, too. *Who is this twenty-five-year-old kid named Donna Karan? Can she pull this off? Will there even be an Anne Klein & Co. after this?* The fashion world was watching to see whether I would rise to the occasion or fall flat on my face.

On the day of the show, all my usual insecurities washed over me. Who was I to take on Anne's legacy? Would everyone laugh at me for even trying? I was lucky I didn't suffer a panic attack and that my face didn't numb up as it had during that first trip abroad with Patti. I was seeing Dr. Rath every week, but even so I suffered from horrific gas pains and hyperventilation, where I'd get so scared I couldn't breathe. None of that happened on the day of the show, but I was still a wreck. During the presentation in our showroom, I frantically fussed over each model before I let her walk out from behind the curtain, and I held my breath until I sent out the last girl. Then I started to cry. The clothes were out there for everyone to see. My work was done. I felt naked, exposed, and horribly vulnerable.

Then, out of the darkness, over the music, I could hear the sound of clapping, and the applause grew louder and louder. The reaction was immediate and overwhelming. Someone handed me a bouquet of white roses. The knitwear designer Margaretha Ley, who had flown in from Germany, gave me a white stuffed rabbit for Gabby. That set off more tears. When I stepped out onto the runway for my bow, people stood. Blinded by the lights and the emotion, I trembled and tried not to fall over. The collection was a hit. *I* was a hit! Buyers and journalists wanted to talk to me, interview me. *Me!*

The *New York Times* headline the next morning was "At Anne Klein, Young Designer Is Triumphant." *Women's Wear Daily* called it "first rate," adding, "If Anne Klein was a great sportswear designer, she was just as great a teacher. . . . Donna has learned her lesson well." They raved about the "young, fresh touches" throughout. The retailers were just as effusive. Bill McElree of I. Magnin told *WWD*, "We don't need one other collection. It's the greatest group of clothes I have seen in my 20 years of retailing." In the same article, Saks Fifth Avenue's Rae Crespin said, "It was fantastic. Absolute perfection in sportswear." The whole day, I was flying, and I also couldn't stop crying. All the bottled-up tension, heightened by my hormones, came gushing out of me. The show had put to rest any lingering doubts: I was the official heir apparent to Anne Klein. Takihyo signed me to a twelve-year contract.

Given my youth and inexperience, I was hardly prepared for what followed. *Women's Wear Daily* sought to interview me right away. Our company hired a limousine to pick up me and the reporter, Keitha McLean, from the Anne Klein offices at 205 West 39th Street. When we went down to the street, I saw the limo coming and raised my arm, the way you would hail a taxi. Wrong limo.

When my car did appear, I got in before the driver had a chance to walk around and open my door. All in front of Keitha. We rode to Le Cirque for lunch, and the minute we walked in, I asked her if she knew where the "famous, important people" sat, and whether she saw any celebrities. I couldn't stop talking, and I said whatever came to my mind. The gem of the interview was this line about designing clothes: "What can really be glamorous about a rag you put between your legs?"

That quote was the lead of the *WWD* article introducing me to the fashion industry as the woman behind Anne Klein & Co.'s fall collection. The two pull-out quotes in the same article were: "I'm from Lawrence, Long Island, so what do I know?" and "I want to get très chic." Yep, I was a little rough around the edges.

I was also invited onto the *Today* show with Barbara Walters, along with Bill Blass and Oscar de la Renta. Barbara's office asked me to do the honor of dressing her. I told them I'd rather she pick out the outfit, but apparently there wasn't time for that, so I sent up one of our signature looks: a jacket, a shirt, a vest, and a skirt—very layered, very booty. On the show, I asked, "Barbara, so how do you feel in our clothes?"

"Honestly, I've never felt so uncomfortable in my life," she answered, before cutting to a commercial. My smile froze.

———————

What you learn quickly in fashion is that you're only as good as your last collection. There's no time to stop and enjoy your success, not when everyone's asking, "What's next? What's new?" A tiny part of me wished the first show hadn't gone so well. The bar was set so high—what if I couldn't do it again? The fall 1974 collection may have been a hit, but it had taken everything out of me. I needed to be at home with my baby—or at least strike a balance in my life. At that time, collections were huge, maybe a hundred runway looks with another hundred discards (pieces that don't make the collection), versus the forty or so looks we show today. I was desperate for Louis to join me, and when he did, a month later, I was euphoric. He was the answer to my prayers: enormously talented, a fabulous friend, and *funny*—you have no idea. We plunged right in. My first order of business was to announce that we were co-designers. I wanted no ambiguity. We'd rise as a team or fall as a team.

People often asked how we worked together. In a nutshell, we were completely codependent. We sat facing each other across a large desk in the design room. We were always together, talking, bouncing ideas off each other, and cracking up. Louis was dramatic and artistic, and I'd provide the real-woman reality check, reminding him that we just want to look and feel good in our clothes. He did the classic tailoring; I sculpted to the body. He took care of the color and embellishments; I was the fabric and texture person. It was a perfect balance of skills. Louis's MO was create, create, create, and mine was edit, edit, edit. Louis did all the sketching and could design thirty-six dresses in no time. I'd say, "I like this, this, and that." *Basta!*

On a practical level, Louis handled the day-to-day details, and I was big-picture about the brand, the licensees, and our image. He was the more organized one (no surprise) and made sure the *i*'s were dotted and the *t*'s crossed. Because of him, I could catch an earlier train home and see my baby. While I was the workingwoman in the city, Mark was Gabby's primary caregiver. His job was flexible; he could come and go as needed. We also had a full-time nanny named Linda, whom we called "Inda." She was from Barbados, and Gabby adored her. In fact, I constantly worried that Gabby loved Inda more than me. Then came what was truly the worst moment of my life. I was at home in Lawrence, coming down the stairs, holding Gabby. I was wearing bell-bottom pants and platform shoes, and suddenly Felix raced passed us and tripped me. Gabby fell out of my arms and landed on the floor. I must have screamed, because Mark, who was on the toilet, ran out without pants and picked her up. For a terrifying and very long moment, Gabby was perfectly still. Everything about this awful accident spoke to my worst fears and inadequacies. I suffered from the guilt of being a terrible mother and of not being home more with my baby—a guilt born the day Anne Klein died.

My biggest challenge at work those days was dealing with Betty Hanson, our head of sales. Her relationship with Anne went all the way back to 1938, when Betty was a model and Anne was an assistant designer to the dress and suit designer Mollie Parnis. She believed she knew the Anne Klein brand better than anyone, and in her mind she was now in charge. Chip, who was president, was loyal to Louis and me but deferred to Betty given her proven success as sales manager. Tomio, in Japan, wasn't there to referee. We were all feeling our way forward, but Betty made it clear that she wanted everything to stay just as it had been when Anne was alive.

Louis and I had other ideas. We wanted to modernize the fit of the clothes and eliminate vanity sizing, where size numbers are reduced to make a woman feel smaller. We wanted to use softer, more sensuous fabrics. And we wanted sexy proportions. I was young. I wanted clothes cut to the body with more leg happening. I also loved the idea of a man's jacket tailored for a woman—just like my father had done for my mother.

Louis and I would arrange the showroom the way we wanted the collection to sell, pairing our favorite separates and putting them in a particular order of preference. and later we'd find colored notes all over the racks. One of the salespeople told us that Betty had instructed them to sell only pieces with her colored notes. She undermined us any way she could. Admittedly, one of our first collections together ventured too far from the Anne Klein look. A resort collection, it was all raw silk and crepe de chine, everything relaxed and softly constructed. The press and retailers were polite, but you could tell they didn't get it. We were crushed, but we knew we had to believe in ourselves and keep moving forward.

In September 1975, Tomio brought in Frank Mori as our new president. Frank was young and handsome, maybe thirty-five, with a Harvard MBA but no Seventh Avenue experience. He came from Hanes, where he had been executive vice president at Bali, the bra and intimates division. The introduction wasn't smooth. Tomio just showed up with Frank one day, and jaws dropped, since Chip wasn't planning to leave. Takihyo wanted Chip to remain as founder, but with no actual power.

There were too many cooks in the kitchen now, and Louis and I were miserable. Betty continued bossing us around, and then she went a step too far and insisted we design a pre-fall collection. This had been an ongoing disagreement, as I felt pre-fall collections were unnecessary and only served to shorten the time we could work on fall. She overruled me, saying we needed to fill a hole between store deliveries with a capsule (mini) line. I was exhausted, and doing an additional collection—even a small one—was out of the question.

We called a meeting. Tomio, Frank, Betty, Chip, and Julie sat on one side of the table; Louis and I sat on the other. It got heated, and Betty didn't back down.

"That's it. I quit," I finally said.

Louis threw a chair against the wall. "I quit, too," he said. He grabbed my hand, and we got our coats and left the building.

I felt so empowered! We headed to Bill's, the fashion insider bar and lunch spot across the street. As strong as we felt, we were shaking like leaves. The phone at the bar rang, and Carolyn, the owner, picked it up.

"Are you two here?" she asked, her hand covering the mouth-piece.

"No," we said in unison, smiling like two naughty schoolkids.

Soon after, Julie came in looking for us. "Mr. Taki wants to make this right. What can he do to make you come back?"

"Easy. It's us or Betty."

Tomio and Frank made it right. Betty left to open her own firm, which Gunther financed. Anne Klein & Co.'s design direction now belonged solely to Louis and me.

———

It was time to prepare our second fall show. By now, we were feeling seasoned and confident and loved what we were working on. We wanted to create a show that would signal to the world that there was a new team and a new look behind the Anne Klein name. At this time, designers were starting to show outside their showrooms, and we heard that Oscar de la Renta was planning to show at the Circle in the Square Theatre.

"How about we do a Broadway theater?" I asked.

We had a connection to the Shubert Organization, which led us to the Winter Garden Theatre. Stephen Sondheim's musical *Pacific Overtures* was playing there, so we could only book a Monday, when the theater was dark. It would cost a fortune, as we'd have to hire all the theater's union employees and choreographers. Remarkably, Frank and Tomio were on board for the money. But there was another price: we'd have to give up creative control. The theater people would stage the show, select the music, everything. Other than provide the models and clothes, all Louis and I could do was watch and worry.

Our first chance to rehearse at the theater was the morning of the show. "Sit down and have some faith," the choreographer told us. A dancer dressed like a lion ran out and pulled the curtain open, and that was the only successful part of the rehearsal. The models couldn't make their changes in time, so many came out half dressed. The choreography confused some of the girls, and a few went in the wrong direction, causing collisions.

"Women's Wear Daily is going to cream us," Louis whispered, his thick brows knitted in concern. He was right to be worried; the paper was already criticizing designers for using these venues, and ours was the splashiest of all. But there was nothing we could do about it now. The theater was packed, all fourteen hundred seats filled. Louis, Frank, and I sat on the third balcony. We had decided that if the show was a disaster, we'd slip out quickly and go have a drink. We'd even chosen the bar.

But it went perfectly, just like in Versailles. The props were sensational: floor-to-ceiling Mylar screens, blossoming cherry trees, fake horses galloping across the stage. The finale was set to the music of *Boléro*. One by one, models marched out, slowly filling the entire stage. It could have been the height of pretension, but instead the effects enhanced the clothes, rather than distracting from them. The music ended, and there was a second of dead silence. We thought the audience was getting up to leave, and then they started applauding and screaming "Bravo!" I looked at Frank and Louis, tears streaming down my face. It was my Sally Field moment: "Oh my God! They like us! They really like us!"

We received rave review after rave review, starting with *WWD*'s. "Anne Klein Goes Broadway: Fall Line Joins Chorus Line," said the *New York Times*, which also noted that the buyers had put down their pens to enjoy the show. Between my solo show and this one, we had stepped out from behind the shadow of Anne Klein.

A year or so after Frank joined the company, Chip sold his share to Takihyo. Now Takihyo owned the business, with Frank given a minority percentage as CEO and president. I was sad to see Chip go, because he was my connection to Anne. But it wasn't his company anymore. It's hard to stay in a place you once ran—or, as he said to *People* magazine, to "live in the dead past."

———————

Chip. Sandy. Gunther. Anne Klein. Both my fathers. Even Stephan. You'd think that with all the sudden goodbyes I'd faced in recent years, I'd get used to it. But you never do.

In the summer of 1976, I was home in Lawrence with Gabby when Felix, our gorgeous dog, came bounding into the house. He jumped up, grabbed me with his paws, then fell down and died right in front of me. We think he may have been poisoned—Felix was always escaping over our fence and terrorizing the neighborhood. Whatever caused him to die so suddenly, I was traumatized and unprepared. My big goofy dog, my first baby, my living, breathing connection to Stephan, was gone.

8 | FRIENDS FOR LIFE

After the Winter Garden collection, our press office was swamped with requests for fashion editorials and interviews. Louis and I were featured in *Vogue,* while Mark, Gabby (now three), and I were in the New York *Daily News.* Months later, in 1977, Louis and I were nominated for the Winnie, the top Coty Award. The Cotys were the Oscars of fashion, the precursors of today's CFDA (Council of Fashion Designers of America) Fashion Awards. There was even buzz that we could actually win.

Queenie was over the moon. My successes in the fashion industry were a source of tremendous pride; she viewed them as part of her own legacy. I was happy she was happy, but I didn't want her in the limousine with us; I was tense enough. She was hurt and even threatened not to come, but I didn't believe her.

The night of the ceremony, held at the Fashion Institute of Technology, I did my hair up in a bun and wore a pale beige crinkle crepe wrap top with matching harem-style pants that narrowed at the ankle. The organizers seated us in the front row with Tomio and Frank. Mark, my sister, Gail, and her husband, Hank, were behind us, with an empty seat next to Mark for Queenie. I kept looking for her and couldn't understand how she could be late. Then Frank came over. "Donna, you have to come see this," he said. I followed him to the window, looked down, and spotted my mother blowing kisses to the crowd from a horse and buggy—the kind tourists ride around Central Park. She wore a long black dress with a slit up the side and a feathered boa draped over her shoulder. The queen had arrived.

Louis and I won a Winnie, as did Stephen Burrows, my friend from Versailles. After hugging everyone around me, I ran to the pay phone—no cells in those days—and called Dr. Rath. I knew he would understand what this meant to me.

As collaborators, Louis and I had a deal: we would never say no to each other. If one of us truly believed in something, we would go for it. If it made sense, it would stay in the collection; if it didn't, we'd throw it out. But we had to agree in the end. It was the only way we could work together. Outside of the design studio, Louis was patient and nurturing, and got me out of more than a few scrapes. Once, when we were in our late twenties and finding our way in the world, we went to Paris to shop for ideas. We checked into the Hotel de Crillon, an eighteenth-century palace at the foot of the Champs-Elysées, and selected a Marie Antoinette–style salon with two bedrooms, me in one room, Louis and our designer friends Maurice Antaya and Richard Assatly (who would go on to design Anne Klein II with us) in the other. We shopped until we dropped, buying all sorts of pieces— some designer, some not—that could spark an idea. Along the way, one of us (okay, me) got the bright idea to deliver and charge all our purchases to the hotel. That way, we wouldn't have to worry about money or schlepping bags while we bounced around the city.

When Louis went to check out on the morning of our departure, he was asked for approximately $20,000—in cash. Apparently, the hotel had paid in francs for our purchases, and because of the value-added tax and conversion rates, it wanted hard currency in return. Louis came rushing into the suite and found me, Maurice, and Richard lounging in the hotel's plush terry robes and eating a decadent breakfast.

"We've got a real problem," he said. "We have to come up with $20K or we'll be cleaning rooms here for the rest of our lives."

"Don't worry," I said calmly, placing my cup back into its saucer. "I'll call Frank and ask him to wire us the money."

"What did you buy?" Frank screamed so loudly I had to hold the phone away from my ear. Before I could answer, he hung up on me.

Right at that moment, our Parsons friend Linda Fox came into the room with her French boyfriend, Jacques. We explained our predicament, and he assured us we could work something out with the front desk. I don't know what Jacques said, but sure enough, we were able to put our purchases on a credit card after all.

I called Frank to tell him all was fine.

"Fine?" he screamed. "You spent $20,000!"

As we packed, I told everyone to cut the labels out of our purchases to avoid declaring them—yet another bright idea. We had shipped a lot of it, but I wanted some pieces right when I got home.

We landed at JFK, and there were Mark and Gabby, waving from the other side of the glass dividers. Louis sailed through, no problem. Me they detained and led into a small room.

"Why are you stopping me?" My voice was loud, my heart pumping. "Do I look like a drug dealer?" I showed them my clean arms.

Then they dragged Louis into the room with me. I was still shouting and talking, shouting and talking, mostly because I was scared. Louis just rolled his eyes, exasperated.

"You've been traveling with this woman for two weeks?" the customs agent asked Louis.

"Yes," he sighed. "And you can imagine how anxious I am to get home without her."

They released us. I went home to Lawrence and hid our purchases under the sofas and mattresses, in the attic, and in the china closet, convinced that federal marshals would come knocking at the door.

———————

Louis and I were now considered to be in the top rank of American sportswear designers, up there with Ralph Lauren, Perry Ellis, and Calvin Klein. Calvin's offices were in our building on West 39th Street, and because of his last name and boyish looks, many people thought he was Anne Klein's son. Calvin and I weren't especially close back then (now we're the best of friends), but I'd run into him often in the elevators and at various fashion events. Calvin was notoriously focused, with absolute control over everything he did. He was also the essence of cool, with his edgy ad campaigns and Studio 54 nights. I was definitely not cool. I was still the awkward, uncensored Long Island girl I always was.

"Calvin," I said to him one day, "listen, I've got this great idea. Since we're both Kleins, how about if we combine the two collections, call it Klein, and you do fall and we do spring? We'd each get half the year off!"

He smiled politely. "Are you crazy? I love working. I'm not looking for time off."

I don't think he got my goofy humor, and that was okay. I didn't mind not being one of the cool kids. My personal life always mattered more.

I met Patti Cohen, my great friend and publicist of almost thirty-five years, on a tennis court. It was the summer of 1976, and Mark had rented a house in Sea View, Fire Island. We'd spend one month there and another month renting Perry Ellis's home in the Pines, where Louis also had a house. Fire Island was my escape, a place for happy family time under the sun.

I decided to take up tennis because everyone out there seemed to play. I went to the local club, where they were assigning partners, and no one picked me. No one picked a sweet, cute, down-to-earth redhead in tennis whites, either.

"Hi, I'm Donna." I held out my hand to Patti. "I guess it's just us."

We hit it off immediately, on the court and off. Patti said I was exhausting to play with because my arms and legs were so long I could reach the ball in one or two steps. But, as a lefty, she had a killer backhand. We agreed to play together every Saturday morning at eleven. Unfortunately, I had no idea how to get in touch with her, so I stood her up the very next weekend. When I saw her the following Saturday, I told her why.

"I had a work thing. I had to go meet the queen of England at Bloomingdale's." I shrugged. Patti thought I was insane, as she knew me only as Donna, her new tennis partner.

(I *had* met the queen of England at Bloomingdale's, along with Louis, Calvin, and Ralph Lauren. It was July 9, a couple of months after our Winter Garden show; she was in the country as part of the United States' 1976 bicentennial celebration and wanted to have a New York experience. We were invited to meet her and present our designs. Louis and I took the subway from our office on West 39th Street so we could stand and avoid wrinkling our clothes. I wore a pale blue linen little jacket, a skirt, and heels. Because of the linen jacket, I held on to the pole as to not crease my sleeve. I also wore a fedora and gloves. Some guy on the subway saw us and said, "Where you going? You look like you're going to meet the queen of England." "We are!" we replied.)

Patti and her husband, Harvey, became great friends to Mark and me. We summered together, traveled together, and went out all the time. Harvey was in his family's paper business, but Patti didn't work.

"What do you do all day?" I asked, fascinated.

"I shop," she laughed. She was my kind of gal. I love working with friends, and I wanted to bring her into the fold. I just hadn't figured out how.

———————

After our Winter Garden show, the company grew by leaps and bounds, and Frank managed it all well. Everyone was knocking on our door, offering us licensees. There was already an Anne Klein Studio, a department spread across a floor where we designed all the Anne Klein licensee products. But Louis and I wanted to control it better. In 1977, we called the interior designer Burt Wayne, my style mentor since Anne's death.

"Uncle Burt, darling, I need you—full-time," I said. "You have to head up the Design Studio. You won't believe how much we have going on here."

"I do homes, Donna, not handbags and shoes," Burt sniffed. He wore huge diamonds and long fur coats and had his copper hair colored and blown. His Connecticut home was a mini Versailles.

"Okay, and now you'll also do those furs and jewelry you love so much, and a few other things, too. Think of all the fun we'll have."

I had him at "furs." Burt was named president of the Studio, and his life and business partner, John Doktor, was named creative director. Together, they oversaw a world of Anne Klein–licensed knitwear, coats, scarves, eyewear, watches, umbrellas, intimates, menswear, handbags, and shoes. Louis and I touched it all, following Anne's mantra: "Good design is good design. It's as important in a toothbrush and a hospital gown as it is in an evening dress."

With its tremendous output, Anne Klein Studio was a perfect place to engage and launch all the new designers we were now mentoring and critiquing at Parsons, including Narciso Rodriguez and Edward Wilkerson, the chief designer for the sportswear company 148 Lafayette and Xiomara Grossett, who went on to become an integral part of Donna Karan New York. Other young designers, such as Cynthia Steffe, Rozann "Ro" Marsi, and Jane Chung, came straight from Parsons to work with us. (Rozann and Jane worked with me for more than thirty years. Jane is to me what I was to Anne Klein: a protégé, a colleague, a daughter, and a great friend, though she's the short one and I'm the tall one. We fit into the same jackets, but not the same bottoms.)

Even though I was in my early thirties, I thought of these designers as my children. Because Anne was so good to me, I tried—and still do try—to give back. I've hosted countless birthday parties and baby showers and attended just about every wedding, including Xio's, an almost-two-hour Catholic ceremony in the South Bronx on a snowy night. I go to brises, baptisms, and anything else that celebrates a personal milestone. (Edward, my former assistant, still jokes that I may forget your name, but I'll remember to throw you a birthday party, even if I'm out of the country.) Like Anne did with me, I'd invite our designers to my beach house and hold meetings in my apartment, where I'd serve nutritious food. If someone's sick, I make sure they get chicken soup and send them to my doctor. I don't just mother, I *smother*.

I lack boundaries in other areas, too. For instance, just about everyone I've worked with has seen my breasts. It may seem an odd thing to mention, but everyone else mentions it, so I feel I should explain. I'm a very hands-on designer—I love to try on everything—and I happen not to wear a bra. Never have. First it was because I was a free spirit, but then I started to wear a bodysuit for yoga every day and a bra was redundant (besides, I hated the strap across my back). I need to feel the clothes on my body. How does something drape? Can I move in it? Does the fabric give? Yes, I could use a model, but it's so much better when I use myself. Edward says I was the first naked woman he'd ever seen. Ro's teenage brother was stunned when he walked into the design room and met me topless. I offered my hand, forgetting my bare boobs and nude hose. This happened more than thirty years ago, and he *still* talks about it. Narciso once thought he walked in on a private moment between Louis and me. He froze, unable to take another step. "Don't just stand there," I said impatiently. "Come on in. What do you need?"

One time, Frank asked me where models could change. He was dating one named Peggy and wanted her to have some privacy. I was probably topless when I said, "Seriously, Frank? This is a design room!" Louis swears there wasn't an editor from that period who didn't see my boobs. We'd be showing the line, and I'd tear off one top to pull on another. Ro became my cover-upper, handing me a cashmere robe when executives or other non-designers came into the room. I should add that male designers try on women's clothes, too, including the heels. Trust me. I've seen it firsthand many times, not that I'm going to mention names or instances. And I don't blame them. It's all part of the creative process.

As a designer, I am always creating. Everything talks to me. First and foremost, fabric. But the sun talks to me, too. The flashing lights on the street talk to me. The rocks on the beach talk to me. It's actually hard to have so much visual stimuli talking to me. I look at the beach, and I see the wet part and the dry part. The wet is more yellow, the dry is more blue. Warm versus cold. I've brought rocks with me to Europe and wet them so the mills know what I'm talking about. I once traveled with a potato because I loved the color variation of its skin. And then there was the time in Italy when I discovered the most perfect color gray ever in the toilet paper at an Autogrill, one of the rest areas on the *autostrada*.

When you're in that zone, you forget yourself. I cut off Louis's tie once—it was the most vibrant shade of red and perfect for resort, so I helped myself to a fabric swatch. Another time, my great friend and shoe designer Andrea Pfister's partner, Jean-Pierre Dupre, came to lunch in the most beautiful fuchsia cashmere sweater and linen pants; I needed samples of both. Patti's husband, Harvey, has lost a couple of Japanese jackets because I needed to dissect the construction. Edward came to work one day in to-die-for plaid pants. I tried snapping them with a Polaroid camera and even had him sit on a Xerox machine. When nothing else worked, I reached for the scissors. I recently persuaded a young woman at my favorite juice store to snip off a piece of her teal-colored hair. It's going to make an amazing sweater.

Then there are the *people* who inspire me. Let's start at the top: Barbra Streisand. I know, I know. Every man, woman, and child on the planet loves Barbra Streisand. Since I was a young teenager, I have related to her on a visceral level. I cut my hair into a bob like hers and dressed like her. I listened to her music all the time, deeply connecting to the soul and emotion behind her mesmerizing voice. I aspired to *be* her. She was a strong, glamorous, creative, Jewish, unconventional-looking woman from New York who made it big. She was my idol. I couldn't imagine ever meeting her, but I desperately wanted to. Thanks to my friend Ilene Wetson, I finally did.

It was late 1977, and Ilene called me at work. "I'm with Barbra Streisand, and if dreams can come true, I'm going to deliver yours."

Ilene was dating a guy named Joachim Springer (whom she went on to marry), whose brother Karl Springer was a famous luxury furniture designer. Barbra was in Karl's showroom, and Ilene went up to her and said she had a designer friend who would love to meet her. Barbra happened to have just bought a raisin-colored fur coat that Louis and I designed for our licensee, Michael Forrest, a furrier. She had also fallen in love with a chenille sweater I designed that was featured on the cover of *Harper's Bazaar*. Yes, she told Ilene, she'd love to meet me.

I froze with fear. "But Ilene, who is going to pay for what she picks out?" The fact that my mind jumped to something so trivial shows you how flustered I was.

"Do you want to meet her or not?" Ilene asked. "I can send her over tomorrow."

This was far bigger than meeting Queen Elizabeth. Barbra was my royalty. We cleaned the showroom and canceled all appointments. I had my hair and makeup done. Since we were showing our spring collection at work, I brought all my fall clothes from my personal closet and set them up in the design room. When she arrived, an assistant walked her into Frank's office so I could greet her there.

When I entered, Barbra's back was to me. I took a deep breath. "Hi, I'm Donna."

Like a scene out of a movie, Barbra turned around slowly and smiled. "Hello," she said in the most recognizable voice on earth. I was taken aback by how short she appeared (she's 5'5"). I was expecting a six-foot goddess.

"I'm overcome," I said. "I need to sit down and have a Valium or something."

Barbra smiled. "I have your raisin fur coat," she said, "and I'd love something to match it. Like one of those chenille sweaters I recently saw in a magazine."

This would not be possible. A month earlier, I'd worn one of those sweaters to Dr. Rath's office. The cigarette I was smoking had set it on fire, and that was how we'd realized they were highly flammable. My mind flashed to Gail's pajamas catching on fire when we were kids.

"I have some great pieces laid out in my design room to show you," I said, hoping to distract her.

But on the way, we had to pass the shipping room, and wouldn't you know it, maybe twenty-five or so of those chenille sweaters, just recalled from stores, were spread out on the floor.

"Yes, yes, this is the sweater I want," said Barbra, entering the room and dropping to her knees to pick one up.

"Unfortunately, we just found out it's quite flammable," I said, imagining Barbra Streisand bursting into flames at Studio 54. "I'm so sorry."

"You're kidding."

"I wish, but no. You really can't have one."

"I want the sweater." The Voice turned steely.

I don't know how we got through that meeting, but we did. Despite giving her many of my own personal fall pieces, I could tell she was distracted and fixated on the sweater that got away.

The next day, she called me and said, "I really would like the chenille sweater."

"No. I told you, I can't take that chance."

"This is ridiculous. May I have the name of the yarn supplier? I'll call them myself and have it knitted up."

"I can't."

There was an uncomfortable silence.

"All right," she said. "I have an idea. I will draft a legal waiver indemnifying you and the company should the sweater catch fire. How's that?"

I never saw the document, nor did I send the sweater. But my dear friend says she still has that sweater. (Who knows how she got it?) Months later, she was on the cover of a magazine wearing one of our nonflammable off-the-shoulder sequined sweaters with those gorgeous legs of hers. And a chenille hat on her head.

When Barbra gets something in her head, she will move heaven and earth to make it happen. I knew I had met my match—and my soul sister.

Barbra, Louis, Patti, Jane—they were all soul matches. When you first make friends with someone, you never know if it's for life, but these people came along for a reason and quickly became family to me—the kind of family I never had.

9 | REUNITED

As much as my life had changed with my recent successes, I was still a suburban working mom taking the Long Island Rail Road to and from the city. I was on the train one morning when I heard a familiar voice say my name. I looked up to see Eric Weiss, Stephan's younger brother.

I hadn't seen him in years, and we quickly caught up. He told me that Stephan was still single and that he was living downtown and using a studio in Long Island City. "If you speak to him, tell him to give me a call," I said, trying to sound casual.

Stephan called that very morning, and we arranged to meet up that night. It was February, ten years to the month after we first met, and there was a major snowstorm brewing. History repeated itself. I couldn't get out of Manhattan. I called Mark and told him I had worked late and was staying with Burt.

Stephan and I met and walked down Central Park West in the snow. In the four or so years since I had last seen him, he hadn't changed at all. Neither had our connection. It was instant and passionate, as if no time had passed.

Stephan was still married. His wife refused to grant him a divorce, and he'd chosen not to fight her. He was working in his father's business more and more. Money was a constant issue, so he wasn't able to devote much time to his art, which tore at him. But he was still traveling to Long Island every Tuesday night to see his shrink and visit his kids.

I couldn't believe we'd found each other again, and this time I wasn't letting go. You wouldn't think I would have time for an affair: I was a successful designer with endless deadlines. I was mother to a four-year-old daughter whom I didn't see enough of. And I had this ridiculous train commute. But I made the time.

My life quickly turned into a comedy of errors. Louis and my assistants were already on Queenie patrol, because she was constantly calling or popping in. My assistant, Ro, would answer, and my mother would say, "Don't let Donna know I'm on the phone," at which point I would signal to Ro to say I wasn't there. Queenie would then hammer poor Ro with questions about what we were doing. With Stephan back in the picture, the studio phone became the Peyton Place hotline. He would call, and I would slip out to meet him somewhere. Mark would call asking what train I was making that night. And my mother, now suspicious something was going on, would call and grill Ro about where I was, where I'd been, and whether she knew my plans for the night.

Louis and Ro were my beards, and Uncle Burt was my confidant. We'd talk through the night on the phone, not that we reached any conclusions. I honestly didn't know what to do. This was no longer just a love triangle. I also had Gabby to consider.

It wasn't like Mark and I were unhappy. We were truly best friends. He was the most easygoing, supportive man on earth. We had a great life together and rarely argued, which only made things harder. I didn't often see Gabby in daylight anymore, and my commute was getting to me, so we decided to move into the city. Mark was apartment hunting for us, scouting out dozens of places. I should have stopped him, but I didn't. He called me at work one day, very excited. "I found it—the perfect apartment. It's huge! You've got to get here ASAP."

"Do we really want to rush into this now, Mark? I have so much going on with the fall collection . . . ," I said, trying to stall.

"What are you talking about, Donna?" Mark said. "We've been planning this forever."

I met him at the apartment at 211 East 70th Street, and he was right: it was perfect. Palatial by Manhattan standards, it was a three-bedroom that had been attached to a studio apartment. An actress had lived there. I couldn't come up with a reason not to go for it and immediately called Uncle Burt for ideas on how to pull it together. He knew about Stephan, but he also knew it was useless to talk me out of the apartment. Mark and I put the Lawrence house on the market.

Confusion, passion, sadness, love, guilt—I cycled through those feelings all the time. Yet I couldn't and wouldn't give up Stephan, the center of my emotional turmoil. I even asked him to design a set for our fall show. Given the nature of his family business, it would give him a legitimate reason to be around, and I knew it would be fabulous. Louis was on board. He didn't judge me because he knew how much I loved Stephan, how much I had *always* loved Stephan.

Besides, our affair was my greatest inspiration for the collection. The clothes dripped raw sensuality: Fur coats. Skin on skin. Big, seductive cashmere cardigans. Satin wrap shirts. Suede jodhpurs and palazzo pants. Skirts with thigh-high slits. All in earthy shades of vicuña, camel, wine, and gold. Each piece was so modern, so timeless, so chic, I'd wear any one of them today.

Finding a way to be alone with Stephan was another story. His downtown apartment was disgusting, so Uncle Burt let us use his opulent Connecticut home. I would tell Mark I was with my sister in Queens, and then Gail was stuck covering for me, which was especially tricky because she worked with Mark two days a week as a bookkeeper and assistant manager. Gail liked Stephan; you couldn't *not* like Stephan. But she was less than thrilled to lie to Mark, who was family.

My old friend Ilene Wetson was an unknowing godsend. She had just moved in with her boyfriend Joachim, and her apartment on 64th and First was empty. I asked if I could stay there while we renovated the East 70th Street apartment. Her only condition was that I not lose the key, a real possibility with me. Every time we spoke after that, she'd ask me about the key, and I'd say, "All good."

When she came to the fall 1978 Anne Klein show and saw the big, organic stretch fabric backdrops on stage, she knew. She looked up at the projection box, and there was Stephan, smiling down at us.

"Of course you didn't lose the key, Donna," she said, hitting my arm. "Stephan's been living there the whole time!"

One night Stephan whispered to me in bed, "I think I'm falling in love with you." It was the first time he had ever said it, and I felt like I was floating. This whirlwind affair was turning serious for him. It certainly was for me.

––––––––––

The Friday before Mother's Day that year, 1978, I saw Dr. Rath and couldn't stop crying. I loved Mark, and we had created a beautiful, perfect child. How could I destroy our family? But I knew that I was making everything worse by deceiving him. If I could have pulled back from Stephan, I would have. But he was my north star. I was drawn to him with every cell in my being.

Just as I had poured out my heart to Harold all those years ago, I told Dr. Rath I knew what I had to do, but that I didn't have the strength or the courage.

"You can do this, Donna," he said. "I'm going to call Mark and have him come in right now. You will speak with him today, in front of me."

Incredibly, Dr. Rath was Mark's psychiatrist, too. He was also my mother's, something I found out years later. (Gabby and I have gone to the same psychiatrist, too. It must be a family thing.) At the time, Mark was working at Gabby's, his new Cedarhurst shop that sold only Anne Klein clothes. My sister, Gail, was there as assistant manager when Dr. Rath called, and it was she who answered the phone.

There's no easy way to end a marriage. The details of that meeting have long escaped me—they were far too painful to keep. All I remember is that I was crying, and Dr. Rath was comforting Mark, who was in shock. I felt awful, and, as stupid as it sounds, I wanted to protect Mark. He was completely blindsided. He had had no idea I was seeing Stephan, not a clue. I wanted to do anything to fix it, to soothe it, to make it better. But I couldn't, of course. I had to sit there and own my betrayal. Mark left first. He later told me that he was so angry and devastated he wanted to run me over with his car. My sister was waiting for him at the store. She said he returned a different person—white as a ghost. Then he broke down.

Mark stayed at Gail and Hank's for the weekend. He cried the whole time.

———

Out of guilt, I gave Mark everything. The Lawrence house. My interest in the store. The cars. I only wanted one thing: a pair of beautiful, worn-in cowboy boots we'd shared (we were roughly the same size). I called Mark from a pay phone to ask him to give them to Gail for me.

"Nothing doing, Donna," he said. "They're mine."

"I've given you everything I own, and you won't give me a pair of boots?"

"That's right."

"You shit." I slammed down the phone. We weren't exactly even, but it felt good to be angry about something.

After several back-and-forths, Mark came home, and I moved in with Gail and Hank for a while, sleeping on their sofa, until my lawyer told me I could lose Gabby if I stayed away too long. So Mark and I alternated staying at Gail's until the city apartment was ready. Gail let me know that Mark was having a tough time, but boots aside, he was very cooperative—especially when it came to Gabby, who would be starting school in September. He even let me and Stephan have the East 70th Street apartment.

That summer Gabby stayed with Mark in Lawrence and went to camp during the week, and I gradually introduced her to Stephan. We'd pick her up with Stephan's kids and go riding at a nearby dude ranch, or take her to an amusement park. In September, Gabby, now four, moved with me and Stephan into the new city apartment and started school. It was going to be all right.

Only Queenie was unforgiving. She loved Mark, really loved him, and refused to meet Stephan. "Mark is your husband, Donna," she told me. "Stephan is a married man with two children. I want nothing to do with him."

Uncle Burt helped us design a beautiful apartment, my first city home. Vicuña suede sofas, Coromandel screens, a huge mirror with two plush chairs in front—it was chic, simple, and warm. (Years later, I realized how much it looked like Coco Chanel's apartment. It must have been a coincidence, because Burt, who had since died, would have been the first to tell me if that was his inspiration.) We had Gabby's room, the nanny's room, and a den-like room we could use when Stephan's kids visited. The studio became our large master bedroom; I removed its kitchen and replaced it with a big walk-in closet.

Gabby adored Stephan from the beginning. Corey and Lisa, Stephan's kids, lived with their mother but visited all the time. Their home life was difficult and unstable because their mother acted bipolar (called manic-depressive at the time) and could be irrational on occasion—kind of like my mother. The kids viewed their stays with us as an escape. Stephan and I wanted them to feel like part of our primary family, never as visiting stepchildren. I'd always say, "This is an apartment. There are no 'steps' here."

For a single man, Stephan was a very hands-on dad. Corey was a young teenager, around thirteen, and going through the typical acting-out stage. He later admitted that he was probably angry at Stephan for creating a whole new life and being a full-time father to Gabby. Lisa was eleven and madly in love with Gabby, whom she treated like a doll come to life. They were inseparable. (I'm not proud to admit this, but I was jealous of just how much Gabby loved Lisa. I was jealous of anyone Gabby loved.) To Lisa and Corey, I was the cool stepmom. I had the fun car, great clothes, and uncensored personality. We clicked in a very organic way.

———————

Even Stephan's wife, Dale, came around to accept his new life. She looked forward to seeing Gabby when we visited the kids. She still wouldn't grant him a divorce, but I didn't care; I was as married to Stephan as a woman could be. Then, on Valentine's Day, 1979, he went all the way. I was on a fabric-shopping trip in Paris when I got the Western Union telegram.

DON'T BE ALARMED. BUT WITH THIS TELEGRAM I AM
ARMED TO ANNOUNCE MY LOVE FOR YOU. THIS CHANCE

I WILL TAKE THAT YOUR LOVES NO FAKE AND THAT MY
WIFE YOU WILL CHOOSE TO BE. THE PRECEDING HAS
BEEN A FORMAL REQUEST OF MARRIAGE. HAPPY
VALENTINES DAY. LOVE YOU. STEVE

I screamed; I cried; I melted; and then I immediately called him to say yes. We both knew it was up to Dale when and if we'd marry. But it was still nice to call him my fiancé.

————————

Six months later, Queenie became ill. She had always been a hypochondriac, so it was hard to know when to believe her. But this was real. First the doctors thought it was her appendix; then they thought it was her ovaries. Weeks later, when they discovered it was cancer, it had spread throughout her stomach.

Gail took her to every doctor's appointment. A month after her diagnosis, the cancer worsened, and we checked her into Valley Stream Hospital. Gail, saint that she was, visited every day. Since I was living and working in the city now, the most I could get there was once or twice a week. Louis and I were gearing up for a resort collection and were working round the clock.

My mother still wouldn't meet Stephan. So Stephan took matters into his own hands and did something I'll never forget. He made an audiotape message:

Queenie, I'm Stephan. I love your daughter. I'm sorry we've never met and that things have been like this. If I ever hurt you in any way, I apologize. Don't worry. I'm going to take good care of Donna and Gabby. They mean the world to me. I love them.

Even in her illness, my mother didn't soften; she refused to listen to the tape.

My parents, Helen aka "Queenie" and Gabby Faske

Me at three months

With my sister Gail, who has always taken care of me

Mom and me

Gabby and his girls

Queenie and our yellow
Pontiac convertible

My sixth-grade
school picture

Mom and me at Camp Alpine—
I was eleven

Queenie and my stepdad, Harold Flaxman

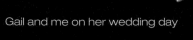

Gail and me on her wedding day

Prom night in my Anthony Muto dress

Senior year of high school

Modeling the jumpsuit from
my first fashion show

The hanger from my father's business

An Anne Klein look I could easily wear today

new york

Designing in my first Manhattan apartment

With Louis Dell'Olio in the Anne Klein design room

A publicity still of Louis and me

In my silver fox coat (the same one Anne Klein owned)

Me with a year-old Gabby

With Gabby and Mark on Fire Island

Practicing yoga with a young Gabby
in our East 70th St. apartment

With Gabby
in the Anne Klein
design studio

With Stephen, our good friend Saul Zabar, and our kids

FIRE ISLAND

Smoking my Pall Malls

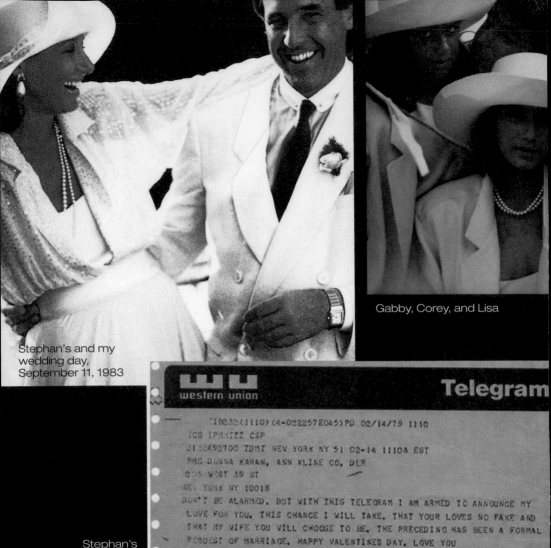

Stephan's and my
wedding day,
September 11, 1983

Gabby, Corey, and Lisa

Stephan's
proposal
telegram

With Uncle Burt Wayne

My old friend Ilene Wetson with Stephan and me

The New York Times Magazine

DESIGNER DONNA KARAN

How a Fashion Star Is Born

BY CARRIE DONOVAN

The Donna Karan presidential campaign, 1992

Bodysuits in the Spring 1985 show

Draping on house model Gina DiBernardo

THE NEW YORK TIMES, SUNDAY, FEBRUARY 2, 1992

THING

Hal Rubenstein

The Cold Shoulder

What do you see at every turn?
A look that makes women feel
like Hillary, Liza or Candice.

WHAT: They peek out of gowns, cat suits, unitards, sweaters: women are flashing more deltoids than there are blondes in beer ads — all because of a design inspiration so eerily simple, anyone could do it with a black turtle-

Karan was not the first, that it was "just something in the air." But much as she is touched by her husband's loyalty, Ms. Drugn, president of Ta-pomeasure, confessed: "I saw Liza on the Academy Awards. I think Mi-

The Donna Karan versa On Hillary ham Clinto Candice Ber Liza Minnelli and a Donna Karan mod

The first Seven Easy Pieces, featured in *Elle* magazine

My Donna Karan and DKNY design teams in East Hampton in the early '90s

DKNY on the move in NYC

In my favorite anorak and
jeans from my first DKNY line

The DKNY family (as inspired by my own)

With Jane Chung, my DKNY other half

Taxicab yellow—
an essential inspiration

Our iconic neoprene
scuba dress

DKNY's Fall 1994 campaign

A DKNY Men's suit

Our first DKNY fragrance ad

Announcing DKNY Jeans

Me and Stephan,
photographed by Lynn Kohlman

The two of us at work

In his Greenwich Village studio

Hiking at
Canyon Ranch
in Arizona

Celebrating my fiftieth
with Barbra and Jim in Greece

Susie Lish,
our family chef and caretaker

Stephan with wife number two

Like mother, like daughter

Stephan racing his Ducati

My long-haired love

Boating buddies

Stephan's last Christmas in Parrot Cay with our family

The CFDA uniting after 9/11

With Anna Wintour and Carolyne Roehm at the first Seventh on Sale fundraiser

With Stefania and Gabby at Super Saturday

My spa and travel buddy, Linda Horn

Kids for Kids: With Liz Tilberis, Hillary Clinton, and Elizabeth Glaser

Stephan and me with Liz Tilberis, Kate Moss, and Johnny Depp at Kids for Kids

Kathleen Boyes, Patti Cohen, and Marni Lewis

With Peter Speliopoulos and stylist Nicoletta Santoro

With Denise Seegal, Mary Wang, Linda Beauchamp, and Sonja Caproni

Bonnie Young and Gabby

Tommy Tong, Julie Stern, Kyoko Nagamori, and Nelly Biden

Urban Zen designers Bessie Afnaim and Oliver Corral

From bottom left: Xio Grossett, Shelly Bromfield, Bonnie Young, Beth Wohlgelernter, Istvan Francer, Jane Chung, Robert Lee Morris, Julie Stern, Alida Miller, Patti Cohen, and Edward Wilkerson

Lynn Kohlman, Colleen Saidman Yee, and Rodney Yee

With Marisa Berenson

. . . and Christy Turlington Burns

. . . With Trudie Styler and Sting

Barbra on stage in Donna Karan

. . . and Ralph Lauren

. . . With fellow yogi Russell Simmons

With my idol, Giorgio Armani

With Deepak Chopra and Arianna Huffington

. . . and Bernadette Peters

Watching the Oscars with Oprah and Mary J. Blige

With Natasha Richardson and Gabby

With Susan Sarandon when she presented me with the CFDA Lifetime Achievement Award in 2004

With Angelica Huston

. . . and Demi Moore

. . . and Richard Baskin

. . . With Patti Cohen

. . . and Leonard Lauder

. . . and Sandy Gallin

With Michelle Obama and Gabby

. . . and Calvin Klein

. . . and Robert Lee Morris

With my creative partners
Hans Dorsinville . . .

. . . and Trey Laird

Peter Arnell and Patti Cohen

DONNA KARAN
CORPORATE GODDESS

THE MOST SUCCESSFUL WOMAN ON SEVENTH AVENUE HAS GONE
NEW AGE, AND NOW SHE'S GOING PUBLIC. WILL WALL STREET LOVE
DONNA AS MUCH AS HER CUSTOMERS DO? BY REBECCA MEAD

$2.95 • MAY 6, 1996

Steve Ruzow, me, Stephan, Tomio Taki, and
Frank Mori at our opening on Wall Street

WWDTODAY

Ready-to-Wear/Textiles

Donna Karan

LVMH: A Deal for Don

By Lisa Lockwood

NEW YORK — Donna Karan called it.
That was the the code name for
ations between the designer and
Hennessy Louis Vuitton that too
several weeks in Paris.
"I've always perceived it as a p
said of the negotiations, in an exc
office Monday. "You know when
happen. It was incredible."
LVMH, in the latest in a blist

The Flag Flies High
For Wall St. Donna

By David Mois

Karan: Day 1

Our celebratory sail around
Manhattan after going public

At one point, Gail had to go on a four-day business trip to Puerto Rico with Hank, and we decided to transfer Queenie to Mount Sinai in Manhattan so I could take over the visits. Stephan was with us when the ambulance arrived, and said hi to my mother while she was sedated. He knew this was the only way he would get to meet her.

I visited Queenie every day that Gail wasn't able to. My mother was failing quickly and would slip in and out of consciousness. I talked soothingly to her, told her stories about Gabby, and described the resort collection I was working on—all the things I knew she cared about.

The morning Gail returned from Puerto Rico, she came straight to the hospital, and Queenie got upset because she was tan. How dare she go on vacation while her mother was in the hospital! Gail headed for the door. I begged her to stay, but she wouldn't. I had a powerful feeling that my mother was going to die that day. Our resort shows were that afternoon, so I couldn't stay, either. We were doing two shows, back to back, because we had to split the audience in our small showroom.

"Mommy, don't go anywhere," I begged. "I have a show to put on, and I'll be right back. I mean it—don't go anywhere!"

She listened. When I returned, I sat with her as she drifted in and out. I wanted her to leave with a clear conscience, so I approached the big "secret" as gently as I could.

"Mommy, I know that you were married before my father," I whispered. "Don't worry, I know everything, and it's all okay." She may have nodded; I'm not sure. She died soon after that, with me at her side.

I pulled out all the stops for Queenie's service at Riverside Memorial. Uncle Burt did the flowers, and he filled the room with white Casablanca lilies. I sent someone to our New Jersey warehouse to get a new black suit for my mother. I asked Rabbi Sobel, the man who had married Mark and me, to conduct the ceremony. At least three hundred people attended, including my friends, Gail's friends, and our extended family.

True to my father, Gabby, till the end, my mother was buried beside him, along with the rest of the Faskes. Another death, another beginning. My mother died just as I was starting my life with Stephan.

10 | ACT TWO

Everyone loved Stephan. He was handsome and charming, but more than that, he was sensitive and kind. My teenage nephews Glen and Darin adored Mark, so they didn't want to like Stephan. But the day I took him to Gail's house, he asked them to walk with him to go buy cigarettes, and the boys came home with a look of hero worship on their faces. People couldn't resist him. It wasn't just me.

In 1978, we had thrown Louis a surprise thirtieth-birthday party at Studio 54, and it was the first time many of my friends met Stephan. It was as if I'd walked in with Warren Beatty or Mick Jagger. Everyone was smitten, especially my gay friends, who threw me over the minute they met him. That's the thing about handsome men: without even trying, they get all the attention. Sometimes Stephan's attractiveness caused problems. Women openly flirted with him. Some would tell me that they "knew" Stephan. I'd shrug and smile politely, but the minute we were alone, I'd hiss, "Want to explain that one?" It was hard not to be jealous.

Our relationship was hot—in the sexy, passionate sense, yes, but in the volatile sense, too. Where Mark had been my supportive best friend who never argued, Stephan stood up to me. He loved me and was completely committed, but he didn't tolerate my bullshit. I was a strong woman and wouldn't back down. So we fought. Like crazy.

We had huge conflicts about whose work was more important. We fought about Gabby. He thought I spoiled her rotten (true) and wanted to instill more discipline, much as he did with his own kids. I was such a guilty Jewish mother that I defended my right to overindulge. I still traveled weeks at a time for work, and that was another issue. Stephan would say I was allowed to be gone for three weeks. If I was one day late, my ass was grass. I'd call and say "Hi, honey, it's your wife." And he'd answer, "What wife? If I had a wife, she'd be here."

Our biggest source of tension, however, was money. More specifically, what was *our* money versus what was *my* money. Stephan had two children to support. By this time, I was making a healthy income, but it didn't seem right that I should support his family. I wanted to empower him to provide for them, not emasculate him. Stephan was forced to take all sorts of jobs to make ends meet. He worked at his father's business, but he also sold Jacuzzis and high-end showers and for a time made Lucite furniture. He squeezed in his art on the weekends. If I have one regret in life, it's that I didn't financially support him more back then. He should have had the time and energy to pour into his art. But you get an idea in your head and dig in your heels. It was stupid of me, I see that now.

Stephan and I almost broke up a few times, but we never gave up. We did a lot of work together: therapy work, spiritual work, soul work. He wasn't big on what he called my "woo-woos," but he would do anything to talk things out and improve our relationship. He had been in therapy for as long as I knew him, and was open to new ideas and ways of approaching our differences. As with all couples, sometimes the work involved accepting the very differences that had initially brought us together. He could be stubborn and set in his ways, whereas I was impetuous, scattered, and indecisive. He loved to sit still, and I loved to move. We had to find a way for our temperaments to live together.

Luckily, the kids got along. Over the next few years, we squeezed in as many family vacations as we could. We went to dude ranches and went whitewater rafting and hiking. At Christmas we'd ski in Aspen, Telluride, or Sun Valley. Summers were about the beach. Our first years together, we went to Fire Island, which was perfect for the kids. There were no cars and no worries, just bikes and red wagons. The house was always filled with friends and family, including Patti and Harvey, who had embraced Stephan without missing a beat. We lived next door to Carole and Saul Zabar of the famous Jewish food emporiums. I took up cooking and was known for my pasta dinners. I was quite the domestic at the beach—except for the topless part. I wore only string bikini bottoms, which drove my more conservative husband nuts. I know, it's probably not the best way to bring up children, including Stephan's teenage son, Corey, who had friends coming in and out all day long. But I felt totally myself: a mother, deeply in love, immersed in nature.

I was finding myself, and it was liberating. For instance, at work, I hired a model many people didn't understand: Lynn Kohlman. The new face at Perry Ellis, Lynn was anything but the standard blue-eyed blonde of the day. She had spiky, boyish brown hair and had lived with David Bowie for a year in Europe. I called her in to model for an Anne Klein show and then insisted we put her in an ad. The day of the shoot, I directed Lynn to give me hard and sexy, and she did. Stephan, who had designed the set, took one look at her and said, "Who is that bitch?" Lynn was a rebel and very androgynous. I related. Not that I was androgynous, but I still consider myself an outsider, not part of the fashion crowd. I liked this nonsuburban Donna I was becoming. It was the most *me* I'd ever felt.

"We need an Anne Klein Two." Everyone kept saying it, from Frank and Tomio to all the customers Louis and I met on the road. And for good reason. Anne Klein had reached almost $30 million in sales, more than triple from when Anne was alive. But as a designer company, we had hit our ceiling. In 1982, there were only so many $500 blazers you could sell.

I welcomed a new project, a change. We decided to call the line Anne Klein II, which I could shorten to AKII. I envisioned doing casual weekend clothes, but management had a different idea. They wanted a cheaper Anne Klein: wool instead of cashmere, suits for the young working girl. I wanted to dress that girl, too, but in clothes more in line with her age—sexier, cooler, edgier.

Louis and I brought in our old friend Maurice Antaya. He had been with us on our Hotel de Crillon escapade and had also known Queenie in the sixties; she had helped him get one of his first jobs. Maybe she was still networking in heaven, sending me Maurice right when I needed him. We also needed a new publicity director. Finally I had found a place for Patti Cohen. "But I've never done PR," Patti said.

"You'll figure it out," I said. "You're such a shopper—you get fashion better than anyone." Patti had great taste. It was fun to see her come into work in high-end labels like YSL and Sonia Rykiel and get genuinely excited over our more commercial line. Patti has always been one of my most supportive, tell-it-like-it-is friends. She's a great sounding board, because as enthusiastic as she is, she's also realistic. I can get very caught up in the moment, and she'll be the first to tell me why something doesn't or won't work. You need that in a friend and PR person. She's also loved by every editor in town and is very plugged in. You need that *most* in a friend and PR person. With Patti on board, my work family was falling into place.

Our first AKII collection, which launched in February 1983, featured novelty sportswear: boyish jackets, leather vests, white shirts, pleated or skinny skirts, tweeds and trousers. We added lots of fresh twists, including a group of tailored pieces cut in sweatshirt fabric. It was an instant success. There was nothing out there like it. Editors raved as much as the retailers. And with prices only a third to half those of our Anne Klein designer clothes, sales soared. Without even trying, we'd pioneered a new category in sportswear, called "bridge" because it bridged the gap between designer and contemporary clothes.

My vision for Anne Klein II was always a lifestyle one, not just a work one: the sweats should be as important as the suits. But Marilyn Kawakami, our new president, saw it as a workingwoman's wardrobe, period. She wanted to edit the line and how we sold it. I saw shades of Betty Hanson's "I know better than you do" attitude in her, and it bugged me.

I follow my gut, not a marketing plan, when designing, not that I'm always right. When Maurice first showed me the pink version of Anne Klein II's iconic blazer, my teeth hurt. I'm not a big fan of color, never have been.

"Does it have to be so bubblegum?" I whined.

"Donna, we need a color, and women love pink," Maurice said. "And look how chic it is when we pair it with gray flannel pants." I added a tie for a funky haberdashery look and let it go.

By then, my friend Lynn Kohlman was working both sides of the camera. Arthur Elgort and Irving Penn had mentored her when she modeled for them, and from her time with David Bowie, Lynn was well connected and shot rock stars and personalities for *Interview* magazine. I asked her to photograph Anne Klein II's first ad, featuring that bubblegum jacket. We went on to sell more than three thousand of them. I'm convinced that Lynn's photograph, which had her signature edge, helped.

Still, my creative struggle for Anne Klein II continued. Marilyn kept saying, "More suits, Donna!" It drove me crazy. I appealed to

Frank and Tomio, but it's hard to argue with success—our sales were in the tens of millions right out of the gate.

––––––––

Stephan and I had been living together for a little more than six years, when Dale granted Stephan a divorce. Committed as we were to each other, I was thrilled to make it official and plan the wedding to go with it.

We married on September 11, 1983, the hottest day of the year, at Stephan's mother's house in Hewlett, Long Island. I had designed our upcoming spring collection (the one which would be my last Anne Klein collection), based on the colors of the wedding party, to kill two birds. I wore a sequined shirt, a full chiffon skirt, and a large wide-brimmed hat. The kids wore pastels.

Uncle Burt and I art-directed the whole thing, from the tents and flowers to the seating chart and place settings. But we couldn't control the heat. All my flowers wilted and died, every last one. People were dripping with sweat. Thank God for sequins is all I can say (that's why performers love sequins—you can't see the sweat). We all drank far too much and danced late into the night.

Despite the sweltering heat, the wedding was magical. My past, present, and future came together under those tents. Ten-year-old Gabby danced with her teenage siblings Lisa and Corey. There was Stephan's mother, whom I adored. There were Gail, Hank, and my nephews, and Louis and his beautiful girlfriend Jac, who modeled for us. Patti and Harvey. Lynn and Mark. Jane Chung and so many others from my Anne Klein family—many of whom would go on to join Stephan and me at the Donna Karan Company.

At the center of it all was Stephan. Sixteen and a half years after meeting my sexy, creative soulmate, the love of my life, I was finally marrying him. Stephan wore a white linen double-breasted tux and the biggest smile you ever saw.

11 | FIRED AND HIRED

Birth, death. Death, birth. The same year I married Stephan, my contract with Anne Klein & Co. came to an end.

Anne Klein was doing as well as ever, and with the birth of Anne Klein II, the company was flying high. But success makes me restless. What was next? I saw my contract renewal as an opportunity to redefine my future. The problem was I didn't have a clear picture of what I wanted to do. I needed help.

Dr. Rath was my primary sounding board, of course, but I'd recently heard about est from some friends in the fashion world who had had extraordinary experiences and thought, why not give it a go? Est, or Erhard Seminars Training, was wildly popular in the 1970s and early '80s. Supposedly it helped people achieve clarity so they could reach their potential, and seminars took place over two weekends (sixty hours). I attended a seminar called "The Power of Being" at a midtown hotel in New York City. I asked Louis to go with me, and he said no. A few more designers declined. Finally I told Jane I would fire her if she didn't go. I was kidding, of course, but she saw how much it meant to me and came, as did Edward.

I had a life-changing breakthrough at est. I remember sitting on the stage in front of hundreds of people. I was asked to think of a three-word phrase that I wanted to say to the room, and then repeat it over and over again. Since I was being pulled in a million directions in my life at that time, the phrase that popped into my mind was "Leave me alone." I said it many, many times. Leave me alone. *Leave me alone. LEAVE ME ALONE!* Then the est leader pointed out that being left alone was actually the *last* thing I wanted. I had a fear of being left alone. If anything, I fostered other people's dependence on me, so I had to respond to their needs and demands rather than face myself and ask, "What do *I* want?"

It sounds so simple, right? But women are taught to put others first. We're so attuned to everyone else's needs that we rarely ask what *we* need. That was the question I had to answer.

Creatively, here's what I wanted: to design a small collection of clothes for me and my friends. I was tired of designing for other people. Anne Klein had an established customer who wanted a certain look, but it wasn't my look. I wanted to explore what *I* wanted to wear, which was basically a Danskin leotard with a large scarf wrapped around my hips—the same clothes I'd worn in high school! I also wanted fluid, flexible pieces to take me through my nonstop days, especially when I was on the road. Like every urban workingwoman I knew, I didn't have time to go home and change into evening clothes; I went straight from the office to dinner. Last—and this was huge—I wanted clothes that made me feel sleek and sophisticated. Every morning, I had to face the mirror. I was far from a perfect size 6, or even 8. When you're not bone-thin, dressing is a crapshoot: *Do these pants make me look fat? Is this jacket flattering enough?* And I was a designer! Imagine how a regular woman must feel.

At the same time, I didn't want to give up my professional success and security. Couldn't I have a little collection under the Anne

Klein umbrella, a place to pour my creative juices? My collection would be small, with no major fashion show, and a very limited distribution—maybe just Bergdorf Goodman and Neiman Marcus. Couldn't something of that size coexist with Anne Klein?

I met with Dawn Mello, the president of Bergdorf's, to gauge her interest. Dawn was beautiful, tall, and slim—as elegant as the store itself. I told her my idea for a seven-piece wardrobe.

"Everywhere I look there are clothes—clothes, clothes, clothes," I told her. "Yet women like us—sophisticated, stylish, professional women—have nothing to wear. I want to design the perfect seven pieces that every woman needs, no matter what she does or where she goes. Just seven pieces that will take her from day into night. And every season I'll introduce seven more pieces that build on the last."

"Seven pieces, Donna?" She looked at me disbelievingly.

"Yes, seven pieces," I said. "Look at it this way. There are so many of us who are on the go, constantly traveling to Europe or wherever. What do we pack? We've got the one suitcase, so it's about essentials. What's going to take me to work, take me out at night, and, if I have the time, let me take in a museum? What if it's cold, or if it's hot—what can cover me up if needed or show some skin? You don't want to bring a trunk of clothes, just the *right* clothes. Seven pieces feels perfect. That leaves you room for the accessories, the scarf, and the change of shoes."

Dawn considered my words for a moment, then said, "Donna, we'll support whatever you do. But we'll need more than seven pieces. How about thirty?" Whether the pieces numbered seven or thirty, she thought the small collection was a great idea, and that I should take it to my bosses.

The answer was an unequivocal no. "You couldn't do anything small if you wanted to," was how Frank put it. They wanted my full attention on Anne Klein. They were protecting their brand; I understood, I did. But I hate hearing the word *no*. I met with lawyers left and right trying to come up with a scenario where I could have it all under Anne Klein & Co. But the other side wouldn't budge.

Finally my lawyer Charles Ballon, who had been Anne's personal lawyer as well, said, "Stay or go, Donna. They need you to make a decision."

It was the most difficult career decision I'd ever faced. I was in such agony, I really thought I was losing my mind. I will never forget sitting on the toilet in the office bathroom early one evening, scratching the paint off the walls with my fingers out of sheer frustration.

But then fate intervened. We were in the midst of preparing for our spring 1985 show. The design room was in full bloom, bustling with models, assistants, seamstresses, and shoes being lined up. Louis wasn't there, but I didn't think anything of it. Then the phone rang.

"Donna, Mr. Taki and Mr. Mori would like to see you right away." This wasn't a request; it was an order.

At that instant, Louis walked into the room. His face was ashen, and his eyes avoided mine. The air was thick with tension. I didn't have time to ask what happened, because they were waiting for me.

"Donna, you're fired," Tomio said, staring right at me.

"Excuse me?" I was sure I had misheard.

"This back-and-forth has gone on too long," Frank said. "We've made the decision for you. We're not renewing your contract."

"You're joking."

Frank shook his head. "No. This is difficult for us, but it's clear your soul isn't here anymore."

Before I could fully digest what was happening, Tomio continued. "We believe in you, Donna. Which is why we would be happy to support you in your own company. You can choose us or someone else. Personally, I think the devil you know is better than the one you don't. It's up to you. But Anne Klein is not an option anymore."

My head spun. *I'm fired?* I'd been at Anne Klein longer than Anne Klein had been. I *was* Anne Klein. They couldn't fire me!

But they did. There were no smiles or hugs. They told me to take the weekend to decide about partnering with them, that we could work out the details on Monday, that I could use the Takihyo conference room as my new base of operations. Or not. It was really up to me.

Stunned, I stumbled my way back to the design room. Louis must have just been told, at least about my firing. We didn't speak. I called Stephan to come and pick me up, then gathered my things, picked up my handbag, and headed to the elevator. I'm sure I looked serene and in control, but I was numb with shock.

———

"Donna, I'm just not seeing the bad side. This is great news," Stephan said later that night after dinner as we lingered at the dinner table. "It's everything you've dreamed about—only with partners to support you, to support us!"

I loved Stephan's fearlessness, but I didn't share it. I was terrified. Who was I, Donna Karan, without the solidarity of Anne Klein & Co. behind me? I didn't know the first thing about running a company. All I had was my gut, my own sense of what I wanted to wear. Who knew if anyone would respond to my vision? My design ideas were so personal and specific to my lifestyle. I didn't know from trends or what women outside of my zip code would like.

Stephan didn't share any of my doubts. "Put the business equation out of your mind," he said. "You have me. I'm your partner. I'll handle what needs to be handled. I'll deal with Charlie, with Frank, with Tomio. I'll protect you. You just need to design."

"Stephan, I love you, but you're not exactly a businessman," I said. "You're an artist. You need to spend more time in the studio, not less."

"Business *is* creative, Donna. You analyze it, you sculpt it, you create something from nothing. This will be my art for a while. We'll start it right here," he said, hitting the table. "We can do this, I just know it."

"What if we can't?" I whispered.

"Then we fail," he said, smiling with that ever-present twinkle in his eyes. "Never be afraid to fail. That's the first step to succeeding."

At that moment, at our dining table, the Donna Karan Company was born.

We went into partnership with Takihyo Inc. Tomio and Frank offered us 50 percent of the business with a token investment on our part. Stephan asked for three million dollars to get us going, which they gave us, no problem. Three million sounds like a lot of money, but it's nothing when you add up the start-up costs involved in a business. Keep in mind, Tomio and Frank had no idea what I was planning. I barely had a plan! We were all operating on faith.

As promised, they gave us the Takihyo conference room to get started, which was convenient because I was still finishing up the Anne Klein spring collection with Louis. After this collection, Louis would be chief designer of Anne Klein & Co., an amazing opportunity for him, just as mine was for me. But still. I had such a heavy heart about losing my partner in crime. I valued Louis's talent, opinion, friendship, and steadiness so much. Louis and I had been a team for so long, we were so in sync, that in order to separate, we really had to separate. We couldn't chance overlapping ideas. We were now competitors in the same way we were with Calvin or Ralph. Creatively, I was on my own again.

Stephan handled all our business and legal transactions. We were four partners now, and Frank and Tomio had a lot more experience than my husband and I, but Stephan rose to the challenge, reading all the legalese and agreements, asking questions, and challenging details where we disagreed. We met at Tomio's lawyer's office to finalize the deal. There were seventeen documents to sign. I was named chief designer and chief executive officer. Most important, I retained ownership of my name under an entity called Gabrielle Studio. This meant that no matter what happened with this new company, my name was mine to do what I'd like with, including take it away if it ever came to that. This was key. We saw what selling one's name had done to Halston, who lost control and prestige when his label started appearing on cheaper goods. Bergdorf's even stopped carrying his designer line.

Someone was pouring champagne, but I passed. Great as these terms were for us—and by any measure, they were—I couldn't stop crying. The thought of separating from Anne Klein and starting under my own name was too much. Letting go of anything big in my life terrifies me. Could I really do this?

————————

There are things in life you block out because they're too painful. My last Anne Klein show was one. Even though it was the spring collection inspired by my wedding, I don't remember it. I only remember sobbing as Louis and I walked down the runway. The last time I cried that much was my first solo show for Anne Klein. Once again, something had to end for something else to begin.

12 | SEVEN (NOT SO) EASY PIECES

New husband. New company. New job. All in New York, a place where ten million things happen at once. At thirty-six years old, I was a wife, a mother, and a designer starting over. I was constantly moving, constantly juggling. There was so much to do, touch, remember. I was learning how to keep all the balls in the air, how to hold on to myself, and how to shrink my multifaceted world down into something manageable. Everything I designed was in answer to the urban lifestyle I was living. As I started this venture, I knew one thing for sure: I wouldn't just dress this woman. I would *address* her, too.

The transition from my old job to this new one was an emotional jolt. One day I came into Anne Klein, and the design room, with all my stuff in it, was blocked off to me. On the door was a Do Not Enter sign with a skull and crossbones on it. The conference room they gave me had no windows, no air, and no space to set up even half of the things I needed to lay out. That's when I knew I had to move my new business to my apartment.

For me, the best part about being busy is that I don't have time to think. I just *do*. And there was so much to do. First I had to se-

cure the right people, because you're only as good as the team behind you. Next I had to find a space and set up a design room. Then
I had to create a sample room from scratch, hire fitting models, recruit salespeople, and hire merchandising and production teams.
Budget everything and plan a time line, a marketing strategy, a retail rollout. Gather supplies—design, office, backroom. Develop a
brand strategy—we didn't even have a company name. And after all
that, where and how would we show these clothes? My head spun,
but I forged ahead.

Creatively, I needed fabric to get going. I called my friend Alida
Miller, who was Bottega Veneta's vice president of development and
merchandising at the time and asked her to come work for me, to
be my first employee. Alida was a former YSL model, as talented as
she was gorgeous, and I asked her to come with me to Ideacomo,
the Italian textile fair. "Alida, you have to be in charge of money," I
said. "I lose it around fabrics. They're my drug." I had $100,000 in
total to make the collection—far from the blank check I'd had at
Anne Klein. The trip was frustrating. The last time I was there, I
had worked to develop a specific stretch wool-cashmere blend at
Loro Piana, the luxe fabric house. But the fabric now had Louis's
name on it, not mine. Worse, he had the platform; the mills made it
clear that Anne Klein orders had priority. For a fabric junkie like me,
that stung.

Then a miracle happened. Someone showed me a piece of black
stretch crepe, and I fell in love. It was light and comfortable, with a
natural give, and I knew immediately that this fabric would change
everything. It was very expensive, something like $35 a yard—
unheard of in those days, when the top fabric was maybe $20. But
I knew this crepe would let me make exactly what I wanted: jackets,
skirts, pants, everything.

While I was in Italy, I looked up Jane Chung, my former assistant at Anne Klein. Jane had left the company just a few months

back to live and work in Milan, which proved prophetic, since I wasn't able to poach from Anne Klein. Jane was one of the most creative assistants we had. I was once *this close* to firing her for not pulling her weight, but her talent—and a good talking to—saved her. Our dynamic reminded me of Anne Klein and a younger me: a mentor disciplining and nurturing a promising protégé.

Creativity is everything to me, and Jane was a visionary. I saw it when I first mentored her at Parsons (where she happened to use Gabby as her model), and I saw it time and again at Anne Klein. A true design talent isn't a one-noter. He or she appreciates the breadth of fashion: day, evening, sportswear, dresses, precise tailoring, sensuality. You can be an excellent tailor, but can you see what is in front of you and create something you haven't done before? Do you have the itch to innovate something that goes against the grain of what's expected? That's what I look for in a designer. Once Jane was trying out a new silhouette, one with deeper armholes. Louis said it wouldn't work because you couldn't get a jacket over it, but whether or not it worked, I appreciated that Jane wasn't guided by the past. She looked to the future. You can't teach that.

When Jane and I met up, I begged her to join in my new venture. "But Donna, I just got here," Jane said. "I have a two-year contract with my new job, and I've got a boyfriend. . . ."

"I hear you. But this is a *brand-new company*," I said. "We can design anything we want! You'll never have this opportunity again. What do you need? Two, three weeks?"

"Try two or three months—at least."

"Okay, I'll share you."

"Can I have some time to think about this?"

We smiled at each other because Jane knew I wasn't giving up. I was determined to have her by my side.

Back in New York, my first order of business was hiring an executive assistant—not a phone answerer, but someone who could help source everything necessary. I had the perfect person in mind: Beth Wohlgelernter. Beth was Mary McFadden's assistant, and Mary was the president of the CFDA. Beth had been organizing and running the award dinners for three years—not an easy job, especially with all the clashing egos. I offered Beth the job straightaway, making her my second official hire after Alida.

"Donna, you should know I observe the Sabbath," she said.

"So?" I wasn't sure what she was getting at.

"That means I'm tied up Friday afternoons and all day Saturday."

"Oh, okay. But you should know I don't observe at all," I told her, adding, "I even work on Yom Kippur." I had a flashback to Anne Klein and me, two Jewish girls, pushing racks to Lincoln Center for a show and hearing the shofar (a ram's-horn trumpet) blowing to signify the end of the holy day. At least we'd known to feel guilty about working. Beth told me that was my business, but years later she revealed she purposely didn't schedule any outside appointments for me on that highest of holy days. Maybe my future Kabbalah teacher Ruth Rosenberg had sent her to prepare me for what was to come.

Beth came to my apartment for our first meeting, and we met in my bedroom, where I handed her four manila folders stuffed with preliminary research and listed the many jobs we had to fill. "Most critical," I said, "is that I need a space to design in while we wait for our permanent home. Stephan doesn't like all these fabric bolts in the apartment." Until we had a proper office, Beth could set herself up in Takihyo's conference room, and I could come in for meetings as needed, but I was stuck designing at home.

Designing, of course, was my main focus. Xiomara Grossett, like Jane, was another Anne Klein designer who'd left the company to live in Italy. I heard she was back in New York and called her immediately. Xio is an extraordinary artist—her drawings tell a story of a woman, her clothes, and her attitude, and they perfectly capture the point where art meets design. (That's her work on page 186.) With just a few words and gestures from me, she can create a fully realized illustration of what I have in mind, and take it to the next level. Unlike Jane, Xio could join me right away. We had our third employee.

We worked out of my small den, which had a huge gilt-framed mirror and center chaise. We pinned Xio's sketches all over the gold-colored walls and created a mood board around them. Working at home in those early months, I got to maximize my time with Gabby, who was ten by then. She loved the commotion and the novelty of having me around with my cool young friends.

Gabby also loved seeing Patti all the time. Patti was the only employee I could safely poach from Anne Klein & Co., as Frank knew she wouldn't stay once I left. She was set to start after the New Year, but she still came to my apartment for moral support and brainstorming. We had similar taste in clothes, and Patti was one of the friends I wanted to dress in my new collection. We'd also gossip about the industry and whose clothes we loved and whose we didn't. Patti was the redheaded me. She knew me better than I did myself, and she still does. The fact that our husbands were best friends and motorcycle buddies made it all the more fun. The four of us had planned a ski trip for Christmas together, figuring we'd need that calm before the storm.

Our temporary studio was at 80 West 40th Street, and it had double-story ceilings and huge windows facing Bryant Park and the cityscape beyond. Apparently it was the very studio where Liz Claiborne had started her company—a great omen. We threw the space together so quickly there was no time to customize. Alida, Beth, and Patti used built-in cabinets as desks (they had to turn their legs out to the side when they sat). The space's showpiece was a sleek black kitchen, installed by the previous tenant, an interior designer, which we used as our mini showroom. For our reception desk, Patti brought in a black faux-leather card table and chairs she'd received as a wedding present. And near the center of the room we put two oversized Parsons tables for me and Xio—as well as Jane, who was commuting between New York and her job in Milan. A winding staircase led to a small room where the pattern makers worked. Creatively, I'd never been happier.

"Donna, we need a name already," Patti fretted one day. "We need to brand ourselves, if only to have a logo for stationery. I've been using yellow legal pads—it's crazy! Who are we?"

"That'll be your job. Find us a graphic person to create our identity and get us out there in the books," I said, referring to the fashion magazines. Our business may have been new, but I had been around the fashion block for ten years and knew who and what had to happen. We had already hired a public relations agency, Cristina, Gottfried and Loving, the same one we had used at Anne Klein. The Gottfried was Carolyn Gottfried, a former *WWD* fashion editor and a good friend of mine from Fire Island. Patti interviewed various branding and image agencies, including a newly formed company named Arnell/Bickford. Peter Arnell had recently done a small project for Dawn at Bergdorf's, and she adored him. That was the extent of Peter's fashion experience, but he and I instantly bonded. For me, it's all about the connection when I meet someone, especially on creative matters. Either it's there or it isn't. Peter was physically huge, a barrel of fun. He wore round owl glasses, a white shirt, khakis, and white sneakers. He spoke a million words and spewed a million ideas a minute. We talked for hours, him fueled by a pot of coffee and me by endless refills of my boiled water and lemon. He got me, my message, and the essence of what I wanted to do: dress the day-to-night lifestyle of an urban workingwoman like me with ease and sophistication. Without realizing it, I had written my mission statement.

Now for the name. The obvious thing was to put my name on the label, but it didn't feel right. It didn't seem like enough. When you've been designing under another name for so long, you feel protected. It's not *you* out there; it's your job. My name felt flimsy in comparison to Anne's, and I struggled with it. Then one day I saw one of the shoeboxes stacked in our studio's black kitchen for our upcoming show. Maud Frizon Paris London, it said. Suddenly, it hit me. "Hey, what about Donna Karan New York?" I said it aloud. "Donna Karan New York." *That* sounded bigger than I.

I passed it by Peter. "That's the dumbest idea I've ever heard," he said with a scowl. "What about people who live in LA? What are they supposed to do?"

"Peter, New York is the world," I told him. "It's the most international city of all. New York exudes sophistication, modernity, innovation, power, everything I want this label to stand for." Peter got it then, and he came back with the most inspired portraits of New York I'd ever seen: Black and white. Highly romantic. Blurry views of bridges and passing architecture. There were no clothes and no woman in the images, which was great because we couldn't afford a model. It was nothing but city views, with "Donna Karan New York" stamped in gold on the bottom. Patti and I were speechless, which doesn't happen often, trust me.

"This is the customer's view of her world," Peter explained. "Speed, light, motion, pure energy. If we can sell Manhattan, communicate the fantasy and the emotion, we show her where the clothes come from. If she relates to this, then she relates to what you're doing."

I was struck dumb with joy. If Donna Karan New York was our baby, this portfolio was our birth announcement.

———

It's hard to describe a million things happening at once, but that was my life in that period. Every morning after I had breakfast with Gabby and kissed Stephan goodbye, my new driver, Marvin, picked me up in the new stretch Lincoln Town Car bought by Takihyo and drove me to the studio. (I had never had a car and driver before, and I was delighted by the idea of slipping into a quiet place all my own, black mug with hot water and lemon in my hand, before facing the office. Marvin, who was with me for years and years, was from North Carolina, and I swear, our relationship was like *Driving Ms. Donna*. I just adored him.) Once I arrived, the chaos commenced. Phones rang. People dropped in. Fabrics arrived. My days were filled with appointments (with suppliers, stores, and press), and I spent evenings with my design team, Patti, and Peter. He was with us all the time in the early days. I was flying, fueled by adrenaline. I couldn't believe I was really doing this.

"Donna, I have *Women's Wear* on the line," Patti would call over. "We really need to nail down a date for the photo shoot."

"Oh my God," Jane would exclaim from another corner. "This looks so chic. Donna, come see this jacket. You were right about the pitch."

"I need Donna Karan's signature over here," a man in a UPS uniform would say, holding up a box addressed to Donna Karan New York.

"Andrew, get that," Beth would tell our receptionist. "Donna, pay attention! I need you over here." Beth kept track of everything and screened visitors. She held the keys to the studio, turned on the lights, paid our bills, and barked orders at all of us. If Patti was my work sister, Beth was my work mother.

And Julie Stern was our father. Frank had loosened the "no poaching from Anne Klein" rule for him, too, and he became our president. Julie was always exasperated and rolling his eyes, and he was the first to scream when frustrated with me for any reason.

He'd met me when I was a kid, and he still saw me as one. One time years before, we'd been flying to Europe on a fabric-buying trip. I was late getting on the plane, and I stopped to ask a seated Julie whether he had any money on him. "Why are you asking?" he said, his bushy eyebrows arching.

"I was rushing and forgot my wallet," I said. This was pre-ATM days, when airports barely checked IDs.

"You forgot your wallet?" he yelled. *"We're going away for ten days, and you forgot your wallet?"* The whole plane was looking at us, but Julie didn't care.

He reprimanded me in front of my design team all the time, telling me to *just choose already* between thirty-two shades of black, or insisting that I couldn't have that divine $200-a-yard, hand-painted, embroidered double-faced cashmere, no matter how much I wanted it. Julie reported to Frank, so there was a level of accountability—but not too much. For all his bluster, Julie was a softy and a very endearing man.

We set up the business and designed the first collection simultaneously in early 1985. We were scheduled to move to our new showroom at 550 Seventh Avenue and show the very same week in May, just over four months away. The mere thought of it was enough to make me hyperventilate.

———————

Black. The color that does it all. It's sophisticated, says New York, looks good on everyone, goes seamlessly from day into evening, matches everything, doesn't get dirty, travels well, sets a canvas for jewelry, erases extra pounds, and allows a woman's skin and personality to shine. Do I need to go on? I will anyway. You never regret buying a good black piece. It is timeless, seasonless, and ageless, and it looks right anywhere in the world. To me, it's a uniform you put on and don't have to think about again.

Creatively, black lets a designer—this designer—focus solely on silhouette, shape, and proportion. For my first collection, black was the solution to many a problem. We had the several bolts of black crepe I'd fallen in love with in Italy. Then we ordered a ton of black wool jersey to use as our muslin (the raw fabric designers typically use to create prototypes). I loved using jersey because it had a natural stretch. In fact, I loved it so much that we kept it in the finished line.

Our design mission was perfection, not quantity. I wanted a concise wardrobe. Whatever the piece, it had to be perfect, the only one of that kind you'd need. That was key, because I wanted fewer pieces that could do more things: an entire day-into-evening wardrobe in seven easy pieces. Each item had to be flexible and ready to shift in attitude and purpose, depending on what you teamed it with. It had to have a mix of masculine and feminine, because there's nothing sexier than a woman in a man's jacket, coat, shirt, or sweater. And it had to accentuate the positive and delete the negative, because that gives you confidence. And for the urban woman, confidence was power.

I called them my seven "easy" pieces, but let's be clear: designing them was anything but.

THE FIRST SEVEN EASY PIECES

1. **The bodysuit.** The foundation, the base, the starting point. Put it on, and you were dressed—whether you added a pant or a skirt, a jacket or a sweater. Inspired by my love of yoga and dance, the bodysuit ensured sleekness underneath it all. We came up with a perfectly fitted crewneck and a turtleneck, both in either jersey or cashmere. How did you go to the bathroom, you wonder? Three snaps at the crotch—a huge improvement over my Danskins.

Alternatively, we had a white body blouse—a sensuous, feminine take on a man's big white shirt. Chic and feminine in glossy charmeuse, it had a notch collar and folded cuffs. The white lit up the face and accented all the black. The plunging V elongated the neck, while a bodysuit bottom kept the neckline in place.

Tights finished the foundation. Jane and I found our dream version in Italy, made by a woman who had set up a small factory in her garage. They were the most opaque tights we'd ever seen. When paired with the bodysuit, you were covered—literally. If your skirt accidentally opened or rode up (when getting out of a car, for instance), no problem.

Why so dark? Because I wanted one long line from head to toe, with no distractions. Not only is the effect slimming, it directs all the attention where it should be: on the face, the woman, the personality. Dark legs also deleted the leg issue. So many women are self-conscious about their legs—they're too short, too heavy, too skinny, too whatever. These tights eliminated all of that angst.

2. **The wrap-and-tie skirt.** This was Jane's idea. It had to be tailored in a way that would slim and elongate the body. I've always pegged skirts (narrowed the cut as you get closer to the knee) because it makes you look slimmer. I can't tell you how much time we spent on this skirt to make it look effortless. Xio was the only one who could make the wrap as flat as I could, so she was called in to dress the models for every presentation. We also had a pencil skirt. Wear it with the matching bodysuit, add a wide contoured croc belt at the waist (which covered the waistband) and you had a dress. Minimal. Luxurious. Genius.

3. **The pants.** Women never like how they look in pants, my-self included. They worry about their hips, their stomachs, their butts. I was determined to change that. We offered a choice of two: classic trousers inspired by menswear, and pull-on pencil pants that went straight to the ankle. Cut in my favorite crepe, either was incredibly slimming. With the matching bodysuit and contoured belt, you had a jumpsuit. And for the most fashion-forward look of all, wrap the skirt over the pull-on pants. (This cut down on luggage weight, too.)

4. **The jacket.** I was a tailor's daughter, so I knew precision. Whether in black crepe or camel cashmere, ours were sen-sually tailored to the body. Since women shoulder so much in their lives, I wanted to give them an authoritative shoul-der. I also wanted a strong lapel, a sculpted torso, a for-ward slouch, and pockets perfectly arched on the hip. Our jacket was long enough to skim the hips and stomach, but not so long they'd truncate the legs. Despite the structure, I wanted to infuse a sweater-like sensuality and ease to how it felt on the body. Hours and hours later, after many trials and many errors, we got there. This was a jacket you never needed or wanted to take off—it was that comfort-able.

5. **The suede wrap jacket.** This piece gave the lineup a sporty kick. In vicuña suede, the waist-length jacket had a long notch lapel, a drape front, and raglan sleeves. You could wear it with the pants, over the skirt, or with your own jeans—it didn't matter. To me, skin on skin is as essential as a touch of cashmere. It adds a sexy dimension and tex-ture to an urban wardrobe. I've never done a collection without a suede or leather jacket of some sort, whether a

sleek biker or a cozy shearling. (This vicuña suede went on to be one of the notes in my first fragrance.)

6. **The camel coat.** To me, a coat is a wardrobe essential, not an afterthought. Based on the classic trench, this coat was a mix of masculine and feminine. The shoulders were strong, the sleeves were raglan (so you could throw it over a jacket), and a self-belt nipped the waist with attitude. We went for a goldish camel cashmere. It was timeless, and a warm accent against all the black, white, and gray in our line. Just like gold jewelry.

7. **The gold sequined skirt.** This evening element was key. You needed a piece that could transform any of the above into evening, whether you were headed to a dinner party or a gala. Gold sequins did it for me. It was our wrap skirt, only cut to the floor. Wear it over the bodysuit, add some striking oversized jewelry, and you had a modern take on a sequined ball gown.

There were more pieces: A fabulous swing coat. A draped, wrap-front tunic. A cuffed at the hip full skirt. Sensuous evening dresses. But those seven were the core essentials, the chic and easy uniform you turned into a wardrobe. Structure was kept to a minimum, which was unusual for the day; I wanted everything to wear like a second skin, with nothing pulling at you as you moved. It was a new kind of classicism—like a man's wardrobe, but tailored for a strong woman. Just like those suits my father had made for my mother.

Last, I added a personal touch. Given my love of art, I wanted a true artistic stroke to accent the clothes. It had to be expressive—not just jewelry, but a marriage of fabric and metal, of soft and strong. At Anne Klein, I had worked with the jeweler Robert Lee

Morris and felt deeply connected to his sensual, tribal sculpture. There was nothing fashiony about it. Every element had a touch of warrior goddess, just like my vision of the urban woman.

When I approached Robert about collaborating with me on my new venture, his face lit up. He opened up his jewelry cases for me, and I played for hours. It was like Christmas, me pulling out piece after piece and exclaiming, "More of this!" and "This, only bigger, bolder!" He had huge gold pearls, disc cuffs, ropes of segmented snakes. I envisioned metal slice belts and hand-sculpted buckles. These gold pieces would define the simple clothes, and the combination of black and gold would become the Donna Karan New York signature. Our partnership felt destined.

We had a personal connection as well. Like me, Robert is a young soul with a childlike enthusiasm for creating. I knew this from working with him at Anne Klein. Robert works from the gut; he's a true sculptor who brings the primitive to the modern. Neither of us can stand a structured environment. We collaborate intuitively, loving the process of me wrapping the body with fabric and him molding just the right organic metal piece to light it up.

To those key elements we added a dramatic, organically shaped felt hat by the milliner Maeve Carr, as well as jersey head wraps accented with an RLM pin. We finished with a contour croc belt, simple suede pumps to continue the line set by the matte jersey fabric and matte tights, suede gloves, and the perfect leather workbag—big enough to hold everything you need for your day and sleek enough to become part of your body. We made a cashmere blanket to throw over your shoulder by day and wrap around you at night (or to use as a blanket on a plane or in your hotel room). We thought all of these clothes, jewelry statements, and accessories would be small in wholesale volume, almost like limited edition pieces. We had no idea what was to come.

We were on our way. It was exhilarating to create something so special, modern, and right on every level. Everything I had done in my life had brought me to this moment. It almost didn't matter if anyone else agreed. In my mind, these were the clothes I was born to design, the pure essence of what I wanted to say. I had experienced a huge creative breakthrough, one that would shape the rest of my career.

13 | SHOW TIME

"Hi, darling. I'm only in town for the day, so let's meet up." It was Sonja Caproni, my fashion merchandiser friend from I. Magnin in San Francisco.

Busy as I was, I couldn't pass up the opportunity to spend time with Sonja, who was passing through New York on her way to the shows in Milan. A dead ringer for Sophia Loren, Sonja was sophisticated and worldly. She was also incredibly supportive: At a recent Anne Klein trunk show, I had confided to her that I was thinking about designing my own collection. "Do it, Donna!" she'd said encouragingly. She went so far as to present me an open order form with her signature on it, saying, "We will buy whatever you design."

Sonja and I went to the Whitney Museum, which was showing a Jonathan Borofsky exhibit called "All is One." Borofsky is an American sculptor who specializes in multimedia exhibits. Everything in this show was three-dimensional. Instead of passively looking at the art, we interacted with it, walking around and under it, listening to it, experiencing it. It was incredibly modern. I told Sonja, "I want my show to be exactly like this!"

"Speaking of which, how's the design going?" Sonja asked.

"Come back and see for yourself," I said. "You'll be the first." I trusted Sonja and was eager to get an early opinion.

"This is just so, so chic," she exclaimed later, seated in our little black kitchen. She loved it, I could tell. I asked her to try on the bodysuit, which fit her beautifully.

"Take it, take it," I insisted. "Wear it in Europe."

Sonja wasn't gone for more than half an hour before Julie started yelling at me. "What are you, crazy? You gave her the key piece of the collection, and she's off to Europe? Get it back, *now!*"

Sonja went to Europe without the bodysuit, but she told everyone how much she loved what I'd shown her. Word of mouth is everything in fashion, so the phone immediately started ringing with requests to preview the collection. Despite the buzz, every time someone sat in our little black kitchen with our fit models Gina and Doreen, it felt as if we were handing them an exclusive. We were such a start-up that we had to show the clothes just feet from where we were actually designing them. It was like presenting dinner in your kitchen; there was nowhere to hide. So we did our best to make it look professional, even elegant. Patti schlepped in her good china, silverware, and linen napkins. Beth scrambled to order lunches in advance. Alida picked up flowers from the Korean deli on the corner. And Andrew, our receptionist, would run out and get fresh fruit to cut up and present on one of Patti's platters. To prepare for a visit from Bergdorf Goodman, my retail holy grail, Patti called Ira Neimark's office—he was the store's CEO and chairman—to ask what he'd like for lunch. "He loves chicken pot pie," was the answer. Beth went to two delis to find just the right one. Forget fancy catering; we could barely cover the electric bills.

On April 5, 1985, a month before our show, *Women's Wear Daily* officially previewed the collection in a cover story:

The (Very) First Look at Donna Karan

In a salute to sensuality, Donna Karan is creating a fall collection that embodies the spirit and luxury she's always wanted. For her first collection, Karan hasn't forsaken her taste for the tailored, but she's added a fluid body-consciousness that is consummately feminine.

The cover photo was of Doreen and another model in head-to-toe signature looks, complete with hats and Robert's jewelry, standing in front of our big window with the city behind them. Inside was a double spread of the whole collection. That's all it took. Poor Patti and our public relations agency were inundated with pleas, threats, and ultimatums from people who wanted to attend our show. The match was struck.

———————

Just days before the show, we moved into our new home, which had been designed by architect Nicholas Goldsmith. Nothing said we'd arrived more than moving into 550 Seventh Avenue. All the big names were headquartered there: Oscar, Ralph, Bill Blass, Geoffrey Beene, and Karl Lagerfeld. The only ones missing were the Kleins— Calvin and Anne—who had too many floors at 205 West 39th to ever leave. At 550 Seventh, the fourteenth floor happened to be available, so we grabbed it. (It was really the thirteenth floor, which I considered yet another great omen, as my apartment was also on the thirteenth floor.)

The space was still under construction. Our fourteen employees literally carried their things from 80 West 40th, each of them making several trips. Beth rented dollies for the heavy boxes and enlisted some Anne Klein friends to help with the Parsons tables. Julie and his wife, Nina, arrived with a paper bag of cleaning supplies and wiped the chrome tables and chairs with Windex. This was quintessential Julie. He was the president of our new company, but he was also the most unpretentious man who ever lived.

Imagine us laying out the clothes, fitting the models, trying music, and working on seating plans while workers completed the bleachers and platforms in our three connecting showrooms. We added a graphic, architectural touch of white stretch fabric across the ceilings, a look similar to what Stephan had done at that Anne Klein fall show years ago. The effect was very intimate, like a cocoon. The crew finished at one-thirty in the morning on the day of the show. We were all still there, of course. I went home an hour or two later, long enough to lie down in bed for a bit, hug Stephan, and get Gabby off to school. Marvin came for me at 7:00 a.m.

On Friday, May 3, 1985, my copy of *Women's Wear Daily* was waiting for me in the car, and we had made the cover. "Karan Today," it announced over a shot of a model wearing our cashmere knit bustier evening dress against our white scrim. This was it.

Inspired by Borofsky's exhibit, I had all the models lounging on the different platforms in nothing but bodysuits. When everyone was seated, the girls started getting dressed, adding layer upon layer. The clothes came alive right in front of the audience. The whole thing was a blur for me—I was backstage, just trying to remember not to forget anything. It ended with what would become our signature show song: Billy Joel's "New York State of Mind."

This time, as I walked the runway—really a meandering aisle through the three rooms—I wasn't the only one crying. The audience was, too. Stephan. Frank. Tomio. Uncle Burt. Dawn from Bergdorf's. Grace Mirabella, then *Vogue's* editor in chief. Polly Mellen, the legendary fashion editor and stylist. Carrie Donovan from the *New York Times Magazine*. The audience gave me a teary standing ovation that seemed to last forever. We had three shows that day—the rooms were tiny—and each one ended the same way. In that moment, even my deepest insecurities couldn't eclipse the fact that I'd been universally accepted and validated.

That night Stephan and I hosted a small dinner party in our apartment for our employees, family, and closest friends. At 10:55, Patti and Ilene took a taxi to a newsstand on Second Avenue to pick up the next day's *New York Times*. I noticed Patti's water-filled blue eyes as soon as they returned.

Donna Karan Stars on Her Own

by Bernadine Morris

Pandemonium broke loose after the last three models appeared in their sultry black cashmere evening dresses with strapless tops or midriff cutouts. Everyone in the showroom was trying to touch, kiss and congratulate Donna Karan. Closely linked to the Anne Klein organization for all of her working life, the designer introduced the first collection under her own name yesterday. It was an immediate smash hit.

Women's Wear Daily called my show the "highlight of the Seventh Avenue season . . . New York fashion at its most sophisticated," and described the collection as "sheer perfection." The headline in the *Chicago Tribune* read, "Karan's First Collection: An Instant Hit."

The madness that followed was even more extreme than after my first solo show at Anne Klein. My life was a flurry of interviews, shoots, magazine exclusives, store meetings, and negotiations with my partners. I wanted to keep things exclusive and sell only to Bergdorf's and Neiman Marcus, and maybe Brown's in London. But Frank told me we had to sell to the other big stores because we were tied to Anne Klein. *If we can't buy Donna Karan,* the retailers said, *we won't buy Anne Klein.* (Fashion can be very political.) We weren't set up to produce all those clothes, so we scrambled to source more and devised a rollout strategy to give a little bit to one store one week and a little to another store another week. The system was far from perfect, and retailers were far from satisfied, but we managed to sell that first collection in 120 of the most prestigious stores in the country, including Bloomingdale's, I. Magnin, and Saks Fifth Avenue; Saks put us in eleven of their forty-one stores.

I had a very specific vision for our retail space. I insisted that stores give us head-to-toe boutiques with everything we made—clothes, handbags, shoes, jewelry, hosiery—in one place. I didn't want my customer to have to schlep off to different departments to complete a look. None of the big stores was happy about this; they want to sell shoes in the shoe department and handbags in the handbag department. This led to lots of negotiations and head-aches, but in the end, we were able to stake our claim.

I was feeling my way forward. I had been a designer, not a busi-nesswoman, and this was a whole new world. Once I came in and sat at Alida's desk, which faced Patti's, and started opening the pile of mail in front of me.

"What are you doing?" Patti asked. "That's Alida's!"

"My name is on it," I responded, perfectly serious.

"The whole company has your name on it, Donna," Patti said, laughing. I didn't see how this was funny; I just felt weird. Donna Karan was now a brand, not a person. It was my name, but owned and traded on by everyone else. This marked the beginning of my evolution from a private woman to a public fashion brand, and I won't pretend I was comfortable with it—I'm still not. My name would never be mine and mine alone again.

Our first trunk show, a small gathering where VIP customers preview a collection and place orders in advance, was at Bergdorf's on June 18, 1985. We were going to be in all of Bergdorf's Fifth

Avenue windows—my ultimate dream come true—and Patti was helping set up the displays. Around ten o'clock on the Tuesday night before the show, I looked across my office to Beth and whispered, "Want to peek?" We called Marvin, hopped into the car, and headed uptown to 57th and Fifth. I was still holding my mug of hot water and lemon when we got out of the car, and when I saw that sheets of brown paper were still covering the windows, my heart sank. But one of the guys recognized me. He put his finger to his lips and rolled up the paper, and there it was: black background, black clothes, black hats, highlighted by the white shirt, the gold sequin skirt, the camel coat, and all of Robert's gold jewels. *Donna Karan New York* was etched in gold on the glass.

My mind jumped back to 1972 and the time I'd found myself standing in front of the Bonwit Teller windows displaying the first holiday collection I'd done for Anne Klein. I had missed Harold so much in that moment. *You did it, Donna, you did it,* I imagined him saying now. "You're right. I did it, Dad," I whispered to the night.

The next day was bedlam. Our space was the first thing you saw at the very top of the escalator. Women went wild, and I looked on in wonder.

"What do you think, Donna?" It was Dawn Mello, who had come to stand next to me.

"I honestly never thought it would sell," I said, without a hint of false modesty. "Not like this."

The *New York Times* reported that in our first season, we produced the highest sales per square foot of any designer in Bergdorf Goodman, and Saks said the same about their stores that carried our clothes. Bergdorf's became our brand's home away from home. My memories from that time are endless and treasured. I wanted our in-store boutique to feel exclusive, so the clothes were hung behind sliding doors instead of just on racks (so elegant). Once I insisted on black cubbyholes to hold our sweaters, only to realize you couldn't see our black clothes in them (not so elegant). And I was constantly running into friends.

"Barbara Walters is in the dressing room," Patti said to me one day when we stopped by the store. "You have to help her."

I did more than help. I literally gave Barbara the clothes off my back, which weren't yet in the store. Barbara looked so chic and felt fabulous—a far cry from when she'd worn my Anne Klein clothes on TV all those years ago. Patti got me a terry robe from the intimates department, and I slinked out of the side entrance into my waiting car.

Another time, I solved a woman's medical issue with a fashion remedy. I was doing a personal appearance for our accessories on the first floor when she approached me. "I'd love to wear your jewelry, but I can't," she said, pointing to a neck brace in her handbag. "Follow me," I said, pulling her to the hosiery department. We opened a pair of black tights, made a black sleeve for her brace, and stuck on an RLM pin. Gorgeous. You'd be amazed what black tights can do in a pinch.

They can also save face. My friend Sonja Caproni of I. Magnin once went to a Fashion Group dinner in a bodysuit, hosiery, and gold sequined skirt. She started to dance with Michael Coady, the *Women's Wear Daily* editor, and Michael, a practical joker, purposely untied the skirt, so it fell down to the dance floor. The press covered the moment, of course, but Sonja just laughed it off. "Thanks to the black bodysuit and tights," she said, "it wasn't half as embarrassing as it sounds."

———

Speaking of black hosiery, Stephan and I agreed early on that we wanted to control everything about our business and make everything in-house. We would license our name only if we needed the expertise, and that's how we came to work with Hanes.

Hosiery had become an obsession with me. The black tights from the Italian garage lady weren't cutting it. The material didn't have the kind of memory I needed. This was fine for a show, but real life was another story, and the knees of my tights were getting baggy! Cathy Volker, a brand-new executive at Hanes, came to my office. "I want one thing and one thing only," I told her. "I want a pair of matte tights you can't see skin through. Not even a hint. Not even when your knee is bending. I will personally test it. And they need to suck you in from your toes to your neck, so you don't need a girdle."

There was a reason I was insisting on total opacity. My next fall collection would be all short skirts. I wanted one fluid line, and I didn't want women getting hung up about their legs. I didn't want to chance anyone rejecting a new proportion because she was feeling self-conscious about her thighs or calves.

Cathy got it. She went back to the Hanes factory and made them innovate the technology to achieve the opacity I demanded. She told me they went through thirty iterations to get it right. It wasn't just using a heavier yarn; it was the way the yarn was knitted and the technical manipulations of the needles. Like me, Cathy didn't know from the word *no*. She made it happen, and a new hosiery machine was born in the process.

The black tights were so crucial to my looks that I insisted that every dressing room have a pair in it so women could wear them when trying on clothes. My reasoning was that a woman buys her fall clothes when it's still warm and she's not wearing hosiery, and everything looks too new and heavy against a bare leg. (It's the opposite of buying a swimsuit in the middle of winter—neither situation is ideal.) When stores told me I was out of my mind, I fired back, "Yeah? See how many more garments you sell with the hosiery in the rooms, and then tell me I'm out of my mind." Today, having hosiery on hand is a given in high-end stores.

———————

"Stephan, are you out of your mind?" I asked. "I've already said no." I would do many things, but hawking a deodorant was a step too far.

"We need the money," he said. "They've raised the offer to $100,000, plus another $100,000 if they use it next year. We can't afford to turn it down."

He had a point. We were going through our original $3 million like water. When the ad agency for Gillette's Dry Idea first came to Beth with a $25,000 offer to feature me in a commercial, I said no, absolutely not. But the agency raised the offer, and Beth took it to Stephan, because she knew he would get on board. We signed the deal, and they even invited us to help write the copy. They asked us to come up with three "nevers," which all ended up in the ad:

KARAN: There are three nevers in fashion design. Never confuse fad with fashion. Never forget it's your name on every label. And, when showing your lines to the press, never let them see you sweat.

ANNOUNCER: That's what new Dry Idea solid is all about. Maximum control. It keeps you drier than any other solid.

KARAN: Feeling tense is understandable. Looking tense is unfashionable.

ANNOUNCER: Dry Idea. Never let them see you sweat.

There I was on TV, wearing as many Donna Karan New York pieces as I comfortably could—it was, after all, a national commercial. The spot was a hit, and given all the buzz I was getting, Gillette quickly renewed our contract for another year and another $100,000.

Now I had another line: never turn down a free commercial for your brand.

14 | WOMAN TO WOMAN

I realized I had truly made it when I landed on the cover of the *New York Times Magazine* on May 4, 1986. There I was next to the headline "Designer Donna Karan: How a Fashion Star Is Born" for a feature story written by famed fashion editor Carrie Donovan. I was already feeling pretty fabulous. Right out of the gate, I'd won the 1985 CFDA award for womenswear designer of the year for my first collection, as well as a 1986 special CFDA award for influence in head-to-toe dressing. But that cover story meant more than any award. For a native New Yorker raised on Seventh Avenue, it didn't get any better.

It was also terrifying. Success is tricky that way. You never trust it or think it will last. I had poured my heart, soul, and life into that first collection, and now I had to do it again, and again, and again. What if I didn't have anything new to say?

Meanwhile, Peter Arnell was pouring my life into the ads. "We've shown the view from your car," he said. "Now's the time to turn the camera around on you in your home, in your office, in the car with Marvin."

"Peter, my life is a mess," I told him, my mind flashing to the piles of paper on my desk and the heaps of clothes all over my bedroom. Even any hotel room I stayed in looked like a cyclone had hit it minutes after I arrived. (When Julie and I traveled together, he always threatened to take pictures.)

"But that's the point," he said. "*Everyone's* life is a mess. You've created a brand in answer to the mess."

"Okay, but they can't be about clothes. Nothing bores me more," I said. I meant it. Fashion for fashion's sake had never done it for me. What fascinates me is the woman who wears the clothes. My goal with designing has always been to make the woman be the first thing you see. If you comment on her clothes first, I haven't done my job.

Peter and I decided to tell an intimate story in a series of ads, to document how a woman (me, my customer) lives on the move, juggling the private and the professional. Like me, her only quiet time would be in her car. If it looked like she was self-conscious or posing in any way, we'd throw it out.

We cast the model Rosemary McGrotha as my alter ego. (So many people thought she actually was me—I *wish* I looked like that!) We gave her a husband, the actor Peter Fortier, and a baby, Mackensie—Lisa's baby, who was actually Stephan's and my first granddaughter. The fabulous photographer Denis Piel caught our woman getting ready in her bedroom with her baby sitting on an unmade bed playing with jewelry. He captured her having a pedicure, on the phone at work, walking off a plane with her bags, being hugged by her husband in the kitchen, and in the car with her baby playing with a phone. You'd only see hints of her clothes because *she* was the focus. That was the whole point of the campaign. Of course, this was a rather airbrushed view of things: she still looked amazingly serene no matter how much luggage she carried, and her baby never cried or drooled. There's reality, and there's *reality*.

My reality was filled with messy, unplanned moments. The day before my spring 1987 show, I had Naomi Campbell, Christy Turlington, and Linda Evangelista (the original supermodels) in my design studio for a fitting. These were the years when models were paid exorbitant rates with two-hour minimums ($7,500 for a fitting and show, and they did multiple shows a day). My mouth was full of pins when Beth put a phone up to my ear and told me it was Stephan.

"Gabby's in the hospital," he said. "She had a cigarette, which triggered a bad attack." Gabby was a teen now and had chronic asthma. "Look, I've got this one," he continued. "Come up whenever you can." Pulling the pins out of my mouth, I started crying. Should I stay or should I go? What was the right thing to do? Like any juggler, I did both. I stayed for the fittings, and Patti and I went up to the hospital late that night. I wound up sleeping in Gabby's room and heading straight to the show the next morning.

As women, we all have the same issues, insecurities, and how-do-I-do-it-all moments. It doesn't matter how famous, rich, or accomplished you are. No one looks in the mirror and thinks she has it together. Women have to go to work, take care of their families, travel, and constantly be "on." We don't have a lot of time to spend on ourselves. We just do the best we can. I haven't met the woman who thinks her body is perfect—even the ones with perfect bodies! We're all looking to feel good about ourselves, to feel sensual, to feel comfortable in our skin.

Since my first show, I had met and dressed so many celebrities, women I'd long admired and assumed led charmed, ideal lives. But the minute I got them in a dressing room or into Patti's office, we'd start sharing personal stories. I came to think of them as private people with public lives.

What I loved most was that we were dressing women, not girls—people who had a sense of who they were and what they wanted to project, and who knew their bodies. Anyone can dress a beautiful girl. They look great in anything. But to dress a woman, a true peer, who wants to look fabulous, sexy, confident, and still age-appropriate, was an accomplishment. We dressed Susan Sarandon and Bernadette Peters, both of whom still wear our clothes today. In the 1980s, Candice Bergen, who was starring on *Murphy Brown* at the time, shopped the line without any stylists and wrote up her own order. She looked amazing in our clothes, as did Patti LaBelle (who later sang at our Christmas party), Anjelica Huston, Isabella Rossellini, Sigourney Weaver, and Annette Bening, who visited us with her husband, Warren Beatty. Annette and Warren asked us to dress them for the cover of *W*, and proudly showed us a photo of their first baby. We even met with Raisa Gorbachev, who arrived with four bodyguards. We dressed Uma Thurman, and she and I eventually became friends through our philanthropic work. And we regularly outfitted Marisa Berenson, my old twin from St. Tropez.

I'd known Diane Sawyer since I was at Anne Klein and was honored that she embraced Donna Karan New York, both on and off the air. No one has a stronger, more confident presence in clothes. She came to us looking for an outfit to marry Mike Nichols in, and she fell in love with a cream-colored lace jacket and pencil skirt. She said she'd just wear the sample (she was model size) even though Patti wanted to give her a new one. Talk about easygoing. Natasha Richardson asked me to design her wedding dress for her marriage to Liam Neeson; it was the first time I had done a wedding dress, really a couture piece. I made a simple ivory strapless dress with a sheer organza coat. Everyone in the design room looked forward to her fittings because she was so beautiful, sweet, charming, and so in love. (And who wouldn't want to marry Liam

Neeson?) Theirs was a great love story, which made Natasha's sudden passing in 2009 especially tragic.

––––––––

"We've been asked to be on *Oprah!*" Patti screamed one day in the early 1990s. She was beside herself. Somehow we figured out the logistics of getting the models and clothes to Chicago, and everything went surprisingly smoothly. I did my best to act like talking to Oprah about clothes in front of a zillion people was natural. The actress Linda Gray of *Dallas* (another star we dressed) was her other guest. After taping the show, Oprah came into the green room to thank us.

"I'm flying to New York for dinner," she said to us and Linda. "Would you ladies like a ride?"

Patti and I jumped at the chance, though I'm sure we acted cool about it. The flight back was a wonderful two hours of lively girl chat. Oprah mentioned that she was thinking of starting a book club on television, an inconceivable idea at the time. We talked about fame, and Oprah shared that she'd known she'd be successful the minute she'd stopped worrying whether everyone liked her. Women, we agreed, get too caught up in being liked. But the highlight of the flight was when she pointed to my outfit.

"Donna, I love what you're wearing," she said. "I wish I was wearing something like that for my dinner." Within seconds, I pulled off my clothes and handed them to her. We got off the plane with Oprah in the very clothes I'd worn getting on it.

––––––––

Right around now, my friendship with Barbra Streisand was starting to take off. I had called her when I saw her in a magazine wearing one of my off-shoulder pieces and complimented her on how gorgeous she looked. We got to talking, and she asked if I'd like to go with her to an antiques show. (This time I do remember what I was wearing: the camel jacket from the first collection.) We got along famously, and afterward Barbra invited me back to her apartment on Central Park West—a triplex.

"I'd love to see if you have sweaters that would match some of my stones," she said.

We were in Barbra's bedroom, which was very feminine, very elegant, very Barbra. It was all white, with vintage touches like an antique four-poster bed and crystal chandelier. (During that first visit, klutz that I am, I broke two of her 1920s candlesticks. I was mortified, but she was very gracious about it.) All her "stones" were laid out on her white carpet. Not emeralds or lapis, just necklaces with semiprecious or costume colored stones. She wanted exact matches. And I mean exact.

Barbra matches color like no other human being I've ever met. The only woman who comes close is Demi Moore, another good friend. They are precise and very detailed, catching things that mere mortals don't. (Coincidentally, they also both have antique doll collections.) Performers are used to being magnified on the big screen. They know their bodies from every angle, and a sixteenth of an inch matters. They've taught me more about fashion than anyone. They've also shown me the power of celebrities versus critics as style influencers, which was a new concept back then.

I got my first taste of this in 1992, when I designed a dress called the Cold Shoulder, which had cut-outs on the shoulders. I had two thoughts in mind: First, a woman never gains weight in her shoulders, so everyone is happy to bare them. Second, it would look conservative under a jacket by day and supersexy at night. For our fall show, I put it on Linda Evangelista under a jacket, which she took off as she walked the runway. *Women's Wear Daily* hated it—I mean really hated it! Thinking it was an embarrassing flop, I shoved the Cold Shoulder dress in the back of my discard closet, and that was that.

Until Liza Minnelli, whom I'd been friendly with since Versailles, came to visit. She was heading to Europe and needed some clothes. She went into my closet, pulled out the Cold Shoulder, put it on, and screamed, "Divine! I love!" Her eyes danced as she twirled around in it. She wore it all over Europe, and when she returned, she asked me to make it into a gown, which I did. I must say, when I went to see her perform, she looked sensational in the dress (except that you could see right through it under the bright lights—that's when I learned the importance of the right underpieces). Liza went on to wear it to the Academy Awards, and Candice Bergen wore a version of it to the Emmys.

Not long afterward, our new First Lady, Hillary Clinton, wore my Cold Shoulder to her debut state dinner. I found out when everyone else did: when her photo from the dinner appeared on the front page of the *New York Times*. She looked chic and modern, and ushered in a new generation of First Ladies. Apparently she bought it at a store in Arkansas and paid for it herself. We've gone on to sell tens of thousands of Cold Shoulder bodysuits, sweaters, and dresses, both in Donna Karan Collection and in DKNY. Take *that*, fashion critics!

Long before menswear was even a thought in our company, the entertainer Peter Allen, once married to Liza, asked to borrow our gold sequined shirt to wear onstage. "But Peter," I said, "it buttons up on the girl side."

"It's a gold sequined shirt, for God's sake!" he laughed. "Do you really think the button side bothers me?" Years later, I met Hugh

Jackman while he was performing on Broadway in *The Boy from Oz*, a musical about Peter Allen. I told him about the gold sequined shirt, and he said it wouldn't have bothered him, either.

It certainly didn't bother Edward Wilkerson. My former design assistant had left Anne Klein and had been Calvin's assistant and associate for three years. He had just come back to me at Donna Karan. I was thrilled. No one makes me laugh like Edward, and he's the only guy who wears my clothes better than I do. A six-foot-one African American with dreadlocks, Edward loved to play dress-up with all my most dramatic pieces—the RLM jewels, the gold sequin wrap skirt, everything. It wasn't exactly drag; it was, well, Edward.

I've had so many assistants in my career, but no one got me like he did. When he sensed that I was in a bad mood, he'd quietly put on Barbra Streisand music to calm me down. He thought I didn't notice. Once I was in such a truly horrible mood that I looked at Edward and snarled, "Don't even try with the Barbra!" I got Edward, too: When he'd complain it was late, that he was tired, I'd say, "Act like you're at a club," because he never was too tired to dance. Edward was with me at Donna Karan for fifteen years before he went off to design his own collection under the successful label 148 Lafayette.

So many truly remarkable talents have passed through Donna Karan New York and DKNY. Many of them have also worked for Ralph and Calvin, which isn't ideal, because you're always afraid they'll take your best and worst secrets to the competition. Then there are those you just know will leave to do their own thing because they're so gifted.

A perfect example is Mark Badgley of Badgley Mischka, who was with me in the early years. He was so elegant and handsome. Naturally, he designed eveningwear for us, and his talent was extraordinary. Then there was Christopher Bailey, who thoroughly modernized Burberry and was recently named the company's CEO. I am not at all surprised—Christopher was one of the most organized people I've ever worked with, as well as one of the least pretentious. I'm so proud of him.

Istvan Francer, who has designed Theory for many years, was also with us for a long time. Istvan brought a European sophistication to the clothes that you simply can't find in America. He also brought in a lunchbox from home, like a schoolboy. His wife made him a sandwich and a dessert every day, which I thought was so funny until I tasted how delicious they were. Edward, who was so flamboyant, would tease the more conservative Istvan by slowly putting on lipstick in front of him.

Even our shoe designers have gone on to achieve fame and glory. Edmundo Castillo designed our shoes for years and gave me my all-time favorite pair, which I still wear today: black suede lace-ups, the modern version of my gladiator sandals from high school. Paul Andrew took over for Edmundo in 2003. Paul's shoes are works of art, but every season we argued about heel height. "Paul, we both want them to look good," I'd say, "but I'm the one who has to wear them!"

The early years of Donna Karan were as fast and blurry as Denis Piel's first photographs. We worked late into the night, with friends like Uncle Burt coming over from Anne Klein after work in his fur coat, holding his Diet Coke, or Liza and Barbra stopping by to have dinner in my office and see what I was up to. We were constantly in the news, and the Donna Karan look of black bodysuit, wrap skirt, and gold jewelry was being ripped off left and right, something that bothered others more than it did me. My standard answer was, "They can only copy what I did yesterday, not what I'm doing tomorrow." Of course that fed into my insecurities about what was next, what was new, what hadn't been done before.

The collection was selling off the charts, but I was spending money as quickly as we were earning it. I was still a fabric junkie and spared no expense. By now I had hired Cristina Azario, a chic and proper British girl, to help me develop fabrics in Europe. Cristina had lived in Italy with Jane, which was all the recommendation I needed. She met me at the Milan airport and hopped on the speeding train that was Donna Karan New York. Cristina was born into fine fabrics: her parents owned Nattier, which had supplied all the Parisian couturiers in the 1960s. I hardly knew her, but I handed her a blank personal check and a long fabric wish list. Mostly I wanted her to ask the mills to figure out how to infuse stretch into luxe fabrics like lace and cashmere. Unless it was a natural stretch, like jersey had, stretch in those days was primarily used for swimsuits and ski wear.

I still squeezed in my own fabric sourcing trips whenever possible, scheduling back-to-back meetings without a minute to spare. Edward would complain. "You make my time with Calvin look like a luxury vacation," he'd say, describing the stretch Mercedes that greeted him and Calvin at the airport and their cushy stays at the Plaza Athénée in Paris. On our trips, we'd land, then hop right into a car that would take us to mills on small mountain villages, and we'd stay in tiny, unglamorous hotels. Poor Cristina would carry a bag of Tuscan cookies to keep up her strength because I wouldn't stop until midnight. We'd have eight or nine suitcases with us and fill them with inspiration: a scrap here for its color or texture, a scrap there for its shape or detail. I don't have the best memory, but somehow I possessed a photographic recall for every single swatch we brought home.

"Can you give me that piece of mink?" I'd shout out to them from my room.

"What piece of mink, Donna?" Cristina would shout back.

"You know, that amazing chocolate-colored one with the black tips. I so see it as a sweater, don't you? We definitely packed it."

I could picture Cristina and Edward rolling their eyes as they rummaged through the bags.

Dyeing was my other fixation. I'm the first to make fun of Barbra, but I, too, would insist that every item in an outfit match perfectly: the cashmere jacket, the sweater, the bodysuit, the shoe, the hosiery. And not just match, but match in every kind of light. I drove everyone insane, myself first and foremost.

Other times, when the situation called for it, I was more relaxed. When we first started out, I had an idea for a washed silk collection for resort 1986 using the same inexpensive silk the sportswear company Go Silk was using.

"No, no, *no*," Julie yelled. "You'll destroy the company with that cheap stuff."

I didn't care because I was designing as a woman with personal needs, not as a businessperson. Resort means traveling; you just want to throw something into the suitcase and not worry about it. Washed silks in hot ombre colors like fuchsia, tangerine, cobalt, and teal looked great with a tan and for going out at night, too. The fabric was affordable, which helped customers take a chance on the saturated colors and soft, billowy silhouettes. It was one of our most successful collections.

I was becoming a star in the hosiery world now, too. By insisting on the blackest of the black matte hosiery, I had created a luxurious new fashion essential, because even if you couldn't afford our clothes (and I knew the average woman probably couldn't), you could afford our tights. At $11 a pair, they were twice the cost of the average department store pair, but everyone had to have them.

Hanes predicted it would be a $3 million specialty business, but the first season we took in orders for $6 million, and the number kept doubling. Once again, Peter took an innovative approach to advertising. He and Denis Piel photographed a beautiful, sensual ad of a nude woman. That's right, we used bare legs to sell hosiery, to show what your legs would feel like in ours. I thought it was extraordinary, and it was certainly revolutionary: in 1987, the CFDA honored us and Arnell/Bickford Associates with a joint special award for the campaign.

In 1988, just three years after starting our company, we were invited, along with eight other designers, to participate in the Bicentennial Wool Collection fashion parade in Australia. Held at the Sydney Opera House, it had all the same elements as Versailles: the grandness, the international designers jockeying for position, the royalty (this time in the form of Princess Diana and Prince Charles—Patti and I swear we saw him nodding off during the show). There we were alongside Oscar de la Renta, Kenzo, Missoni, Gianni Versace, Claude Montana, Bruce Oldfield, Sonia Rykiel, and Jean Muir. We had flown over on the same plane with Oscar, and Patti and I marveled at how pressed his suit still was when we landed all those hours later in Sydney. But that was Oscar: the consummate elegant gentleman. We'd first bonded in Versailles, and we both had offices at 550 Seventh Avenue, where we enjoyed what we called our "elevator relationship." Oscar loved women, and it showed in his work.

Every experience in Australia was wonderful, from visiting Rupert Murdoch's farm to the day our group went to Tamarama Beach, otherwise known as "Glamourama." For some crazy reason, we were driven there in a white limousine, which we had drop us off a block away. There we sat, a bunch of fully dressed fashionistas, including *Women's Wear Daily*'s Patrick McCarthy, enjoying the natural beauty of sand, waves, and sky. Being on a beach like that within a huge, vibrant city was nothing short of magical.

———————

The more successful I became, the stronger my conviction grew that women needed to access their power and believe in themselves. I didn't consider myself a traditional feminist. The movement at that time seemed to pit women against men. I saw us as equals, each bringing something unique and valuable to the table. A woman's leadership style is very different from a man's: we're more inclusive, bringing out everyone's best side while encouraging and nurturing.

For spring 1992, I decided to do a collection that embraced a woman's strength in a more overt way. I envisioned navy and gray pinstripe suits with stretch lace tops, and finished with pearls, of course. We had an idea for an ad campaign inspired by the infamous line "Don't f——k with me, fellas!" from the film *Mommie Dearest.* Joan Crawford says it when she confronts the board of directors of the Pepsi-Cola Company, which is trying to dismiss her after the death of her husband, Al Steele, who had been chairman. I wanted to show a commanding woman with strong shoulders, her hands down on a long rectangular table. Peter Arnell and I conceived it together, and Peter Lindbergh was all set to shoot it in Manhattan.

The night before the shoot, I had an epiphany and called Peter and Patti. "Why settle on a businesswoman?" I asked. "Let's make her the president of the United States!" Patti still can't believe how Peter turned the shoot around on a dime. The very next morning, he had Rosemary, Peter Lindbergh, hair, makeup, and extras on a plane to Florida. If our woman was going to be president, she needed to be outdoors for her swearing in—and it was winter in New York.

The campaign was iconic, our most talked-about ever. There

was the serene-faced Rosemary in dark pinstripes and pearls, hand on a Bible, surrounded by American flags and a team of men. The tagline said it all: "In Women We Trust."

———————

Barbra and I saw each other as much as we could. I'd fly to Los Angeles, and she'd come to New York. We just clicked. We had the same passions, obsessions, and taste in clothes and décor. Stephan called her "wife number two." I'd also figured out how to work Stephan: just have Barbra ask him for something. If we wanted to take an extravagant vacation together, Barbra would present the idea to Stephan first.

People often ask why she didn't come to more of my shows, and the answer is simple: she came once, and we were totally unprepared for the insanity of the photographers and reporters mobbing her. The show started more than an hour late, and we really paid for it. Everyone was angry at us. Glamorous as fashion shows may seem, they're work for those in the industry. Also, a late show screws up the designer who follows you. Barbra was happy to watch the video.

So there I was, hanging out with Barbra, flying around with Oprah, and dressing celebrities. My name was quickly becoming synonymous with New York and powerful women. We even went to a White House dinner and were seated at President Reagan's table, where I found myself next to Sly Stallone. The one person who wasn't impressed by my new high-profile life was Stephan. He knew me as Donna Faske and had no tolerance for pretension. He refused to be my plus one; if an invitation said "Donna Karan and Guest," he wouldn't come (and Patti would). If I was late to meet him somewhere, he'd leave.

I felt like I was leading a double life. I ran home for dinner almost every night. If it was near showtime, I'd go to the apartment, make dinner, return to the studio, and work all night. I attended all of Gabby's school functions. And, unless I was traveling, weekends were exclusively family time. I did my best to maintain this balance, but Stephan let me know when I was slipping. I never, ever forgot that I was a wife and mother before I was a designer.

DKNY

PARK
Left On Houston

RENAISSANCE
& DAVID Z SHOES

BIRD
7.61
24 HOURS
12.69

Amoco
REGULAR 119
SUPER 129
ULTIMATE 139

TDI

DR
DRUGS

15 | DKNY: A FAMILY AFFAIR

An elusive pair of jeans. A teenage daughter. A restless young designer. Those were the factors behind the birth of DKNY. And yes, my partners were after me to make money. We had long since gone through our reserves, and Takihyo had put up more funds to keep us going. The logical thing to do was launch Donna Karan II, just like Anne Klein II. But I always choose instinct over logic.

So, jeans. I really needed a pair. Until that moment, women's jeans were made either for moms (that frumpy fit, God forbid) or models (people with no curves). I wanted a pair for people like me. The jeans needed to be either slim and sexy or cool and comfortable. I also needed clothes for my downtime—weekends, vacations, days I was running around the city. My collection was too sophisticated for everyday life.

Second, I wanted to dress my fifteen-year-old daughter, Gabby, who was constantly raiding my closets, with and without her friends. She'd take out a hand-painted velvet evening dress and add a chunky leather belt and cowboy boots, then maybe throw a jean jacket on top. Cool as she looked, I hated seeing my beautiful, luxe pieces tossed about. Gabby needed her own clothes.

Then there was the restless designer Jane Chung, my assistant since the Anne Klein days. After four years of designing with me at Donna Karan New York, she resigned when an outside company offered her the chance to do her own collection. Truth be told, Jane had never been a Donna Karan New York customer. She was a chic rock 'n' roll type. She wore ripped jeans to work, sometimes with a Chanel or Matsuda jacket. She had long black hair and loved her high, high heels.

"I get it, Jane, I really do," I said. "But you can do your own clothes here."

"I need time and space," Jane said. "To travel, explore, and be inspired again."

"Then go travel, see the world," I told her. "Just be sure to come back with ideas."

In April, right after showing our fall collection, Jane went off to Europe and Asia and came back a couple of months later raring to go, armed with sketches, fabric swatches, and sourcing ideas for a new collection.

Here's what Jane and I agreed: these clothes would be the pizza to Donna Karan Collection's caviar, equal but different. I love pizza, and I love caviar. One is not better than the other. You need both. This line would represent my other side, and there'd be no overlap with Donna Karan New York whatsoever. We saw it as a sportswear collection: unisex, accessible, friendly, and fueled by life in New York City. Our pizza just needed a name.

God bless Peter Arnell, who, with his team, came up with DKNY's name, logo, and brand identity. Just weeks after we conceived of the new collection, he presented us with a short film and a huge fake newspaper to illustrate what these clothes were and who they spoke to. For the name, he used the acronym DKNY for Donna Karan

New York (to make sure we got it, he wrote out "Donna Karan New York" with small dots under the *D*, *K*, *N*, and *Y*). Peter spoke rapidly as we flipped through the mocked-up newspaper. "Here's why I love the name," he said. "It has the energy and street cred of FDNY [Fire Department of New York] or NYPD [New York Police Department]. You have to say it quickly. FDNY. NYPD. DKNY."

Our mouths dropped open at his complete and utter genius. Then on to the graphics. Where Donna Karan New York's logo was slim, elegant, and etched in gold, DKNY's was bold and clean in black-and-white Helvetica typeset. Icons—a subway token, a manhole cover, a billboard—were lifted from the city streets. At this point in the presentation, we were all crying. I called in Xio, Istvan, Edward, and our house models Doreen and Gina, and right at that moment, Peter had six pizzas delivered, each with DKNY spelled out on it in black olives.

Trey Laird, a young account executive who worked with Peter and went on to become our creative services director, was the one who had stopped at the pizzeria to assist in the laying out of the DKNY letters while holding on to the bag with the logo materials after the team was up all night producing them. When you're on the receiving end of a fabulous presentation, you don't appreciate all the details and stress that went into pulling it off. It's like a fashion show: the audience sees a calm-looking, pulled-together model, but none of the backstage hysterics, never mind the countless sleepless nights.

To kick off our new brand, Peter handed out T-shirts emblazoned with the DKNY logo. It was couture to me, an exclusive peek into a club before it opened. Boy, did I love that T-shirt; I wore mine every day. It made everything look young and fresh.

From the beginning, I saw DKNY as a *family* collection, for women, men, kids, dogs, everyone. One night, I was telling Stephan over dinner that I planned to do a DKNY men's collection, and he stopped me. "You can't open a DKNY menswear until you do a Donna Karan New York men's collection."

"Why not?"

"Because once you go cheap, you can't come back expensive."

I have no idea how he intuitively knew that, but he was right: you design from your top line down, not the other way around. We had to do Donna Karan New York menswear before DKNY menswear. So I scrapped the coed thing—for the time being, anyway.

For DKNY, Jane and I started with a woman's essential seven easy pieces of street style. It was everything you needed to look modern and classic, sexy, and sporty. Most important, the pieces invited personalization. No two women would wear them the same way.

DKNY: THE SEVEN EASY STREET PIECES

1. **Jeans.** I wanted two kinds: sexy and comfortable. The sexy jeans curved to the waist, hugged the hips and thighs, and elongated the legs. The comfortable pair had a relaxed boyfriend cut. We did two washes, light and dark. We probably went through two dozen pairs before we landed on our first prototypes. It helped that Jane and I had entirely different styles and bodies (she slim and me curvy). Our goal was to make them look and feel great on all shapes and sizes.

2. **The boyfriend blazer.** We all steal clothes from the men in our lives, especially blazers, since anything masculine looks extra sexy on a woman. Cut in navy gabardine, ours was roomy but not gigantic. And—this was key—we refused to make a matching skirt. Instead we did paper-bag pants (with a full waist, purposely cinched in with a belt so they looked like men's pants). The last thing I wanted to

make was a workingwoman's wardrobe. This was a jacket to throw over jeans.

3. **The T-Shirt.** Ours was a white canvas for the logo, something to be worn as an underlayer or on its own. We did skinny-ribbed muscle tanks and racer backs, as well as classic and oversized tees. We even did a tank bodysuit.

4. **The jumpsuit.** I *love* jumpsuits. They combine the one-stop ease of a dress with the sportiness of pants. (When Gabby was a kid in camp, she was so embarrassed when her fashion designer mom showed up in denim overalls.) The first DKNY jumpsuit was inspired by the utilitarian uniform of street workers. Lots of pockets to hold your stuff. Wear it over the T-shirt. Undo the top half and tie the sleeves around your waist (which is how I still wear it today.) I loved its casual, cool vibe.

5. **The jumper dress.** Our short denim dress was as young and sexy as it was casual. This one had a modified overall top, hence the "jumper" name. You could wear it with a T-shirt or bare it with nothing at all. You could funk it up with sneakers by day and dress it up with killer heels by night.

6. **The trench.** Jane and I loved trenches—for attitude, not rain. They're sexy and strong. This was DKNY's answer to Collection's camel cashmere coat.

7. **The anorak.** When you live in a city, you live in an anorak. It's your staple for traveling, walking the dog, running out to the store. You need the hood, the pockets, the all-weather fabric. Ours was utilitarian, with DKNY touches like stamped hardware and rubber zip pulls.

Unlike Donna Karan New York, DKNY had dozens of other pieces. It wasn't a concise, seven-pieces-only type of thing; it was more like, "Here are the tools—choose what feels good." We didn't have shoes, so we showed everything with a white Keds sneaker. DKNY later became known for its sneakers of every variety: neoprene, mesh, reflective, open, wedged, heeled, you name it. In the early 1990s, we were among the first to make a high-heeled platform sneaker.

I loved DKNY from the get-go. It spoke to my inner hippie and made me feel liberated and natural. I also adored designing with Jane and her team. We brought in Lynn Kohlman (my model and photographer friend) as fashion director, and she gave it that androgynous edge. We scored with DKNY's business team, too. We interviewed more than a dozen executives and were just about to sign with someone when I acted on a hunch. I heard Ralph Lauren had a great women's sales leader named Denise Seegal, and I called her directly.

"Hi, this is Donna Karan. I'd love to meet with you to discuss a new collection we're introducing."

"Great," she said. "Is there a day you have in mind?"

"Yes, today. In five minutes."

Denise was totally Ralph: blond, petite, classic, and a thirty-four-year-old Harvard graduate. She started by reminding me that we had spoken about this concept two years prior.

Huh?

"We were in Henry Lehr on the Upper East Side, trying on jeans," she said. "You were struggling to get yours up, and you looked at me and said, 'Hi, I'm Donna Karan, and I hate you.' Then you told me how you were determined to open a company that would feature jeans designed for a woman."

"That sounds like me!" I laughed.

Then we talked sales strategy. For such a small and proper woman, Denise had balls. She wasn't afraid to ask for anything. Her bravado was just what we needed. The only issue was that she didn't wear DKNY, something that I pointed out and she didn't deny. As president, she wanted to look professional. I guess when you're blond and petite in the business world, you need the heels and authority of a Donna Karan New York. But I still kidded her about it.

Denise hired the best team imaginable: Stefani Greenfield (who later founded Scoop), Brigitte Kleine (who went on to become president of Tory Burch), and Paula Sutter (who headed up Diane von Furstenberg), as well as Mary Wang (who eventually became Denise's successor). The same year we hired Denise, 1989, we hired a very young Angela Ahrendts to be our new president of sales at Donna Karan Collection. Angela went on to lead Burberry with Christopher Bailey and now works at Apple, leading their retail and online sales. We had a knack for catching rising stars.

———————

Our DKNY shows exploded with energy. The first one was held in the Donna Karan New York showroom at 550 Seventh Avenue in the fall of 1988. Our windows framed the skyline, and we had the DKNY logo emblazoned in skywriting above it. (We also blanketed the streets with our logo tees, handing out hundreds to messengers, taxicab drivers, and street vendors.) Seventy-five models stood on platforms of every height, like the buildings of the city—moving, dancing, and hanging out to the beat of the music. Like the streets of New York, the room was ridiculously overcrowded, with photographers clamoring to get their shots. The collective spirit said it all.

A few seasons later, in 1991, the theme of the show was family. We had all the supermodels, but we also had my daughters Gabby and Lisa, now ages seventeen and twenty-six, who walked down the runway together. Stephan came out with our first granddaughter, Mackensie, on his shoulders. Lynn's young son Sam was there, and he and Mackensie became the poster kids for DKNY. Two future stars (and child models at the time), Lindsay Lohan, five, and

Kirsten Dunst, nine, were also in the show. (Lindsay also starred in one of our ad campaigns.) We had dogs, including a bulldog owned by Linda Beauchamp, who eventually headed up our menswear. I wanted to express that DKNY was all about family, friends, and fun.

Though we launched at Saks, I was anxious to get into Bloomingdale's, the quintessential New York store. (Even the queen of England had thought so, remember?) At first, Marvin Traub wanted to give us a fourth-floor space with the other bridge collections. "It's dead up there," Denise told him. "We want the energy of the third floor's East Ender, and we want to be the first thing you see when you get off the elevator—a celebration of New York via DKNY." More than twenty-five years later, we're still there.

We launched in seven major U.S. cities, including Los Angeles, Dallas, and Chicago, and each time we brought a bit of New York flavor with us, like an actual hot dog cart or popcorn machine. We went global at the same time, opening in Japan (thanks to Tomio), Harvey Nichols in London, Trudie Goetz in Switzerland, and Joyce in Hong Kong. From day one, revenues poured in. Frank called it "our rocket," and it was. Within two years, we were constantly creating and launching new divisions: DKNY Jeans and DKNY Accessories. Then DKNY Hosiery (but of course), DKNY Shoes, DKNY Kids, DKNY Eyes, and eventually DKNY Men's, DKNY Active, DKNY Watches, DKNY Fragrances, DKNY Swim, DKNY Underwear, DKNY Home, DKNY Infants and Toddlers, and DKNY Men's Tailoring. We even did DKK9 for dogs.

———————

I'm often asked what it takes to be successful. My answer is, don't think about success. Do something you believe in, something that speaks to your needs, your lifestyle, and your passions. The minute you focus on what you think will make money, you're sunk. Donna Karan New York and DKNY were answers to what I needed. If I had ever sat down with a business strategist and said I wanted to create a collection around a bodysuit and a wrap skirt, they would have thought I was crazy. Over the years I've clashed with many an executive, and now I realized why: they look to the past. *We did really well with this, Donna. Can you give us an updated version? Maybe in a new color?* Designers look to the future. They give you what you don't have—or didn't know you need. When Denise's sales staff would worry that they couldn't sell one of our edgier looks, she'd tell them, "God didn't make you a designer. You're a salesperson, so sell it." Exactly.

DKNY launched many iconic styles, including the sexy neoprene scuba dress, the "FedEx paper" dress, and my favorite, the Cozy. The Cozy was originally designed by Jane and Lindsay Ackroyd for Pure DKNY, a division that embraced the Zen side of DKNY with cotton and cashmere yoga-inspired clothes. They created the Cozy as a half sweater, half scarf that a woman could tie in different ways or just let hang loose. No one quite got it, and like the Cold Shoulder, it was shoved to the back of the discards. One day Anjali Lewis, who worked in marketing, pulled out the sample and wore it to work. (Maybe she was cold—who knows?) DKNY's president, Mary Wang, noticed it, loved it, and put it in the main line. The minute I saw it, I wanted one in every color—okay, really just in black and in white cashmere—and since then, we've sold tens of thousands of them. Maybe we should be going through our discard closets regularly.

DKNY was born in NYC and lived on its streets. Our ads were shot in Central Park, on the Brooklyn Bridge, in front of Broadway theaters, going into a subway, standing *on* a subway train. Early on, we featured our signature model Rosemary, but always in a family context or with her "husband" Peter. Later, we used other models, often in groups, to show this wasn't just one look or one woman.

Our message was out there, but we wanted something even bigger. Peter Arnell came through once again. "A seven-story-high bill-board in SoHo," he said, showing us a prototype. "It'll be fantastic, huge. Just the logo with a montage of the city within the letters. We'll put it in other locations, but this will be the big one, the one they remember." And it was. That mural became our flag. Just recently, when we collaborated with the ever-gorgeous Cara Dele-vingne on a capsule collection for DKNY, she told us, "When I first came to New York City and saw the DKNY mural on Houston Street, I was wowed. To me, DKNY *was* New York."

Ironically, we opened our first DKNY flagship store in London. In 1994, Christina Ong, the global hotelier and fashion retailer, came to us with a London store opportunity for Donna Karan New York. But the minute I saw the raw Old Bond Street industrial space, I knew that it wasn't right for Collection, but it was perfect for DKNY. This was our first freestanding retail store, so we obsessed over every detail. We installed a floor-to-ceiling glass storefront and packed the interior with color and personality.

The most surreal moment came the night before the store's opening, when everyone was making last-minute tweaks. "Patti, why does this place feel so empty?" I asked. "Did we not bring enough clothes?" Then it hit me: the sidewalk-style café bar was missing! It was supposed to be a focal point of the store, a slice of New York in London. A whole corner of the store was empty! Fortunately, the bar showed up at five in the morning, and went on to be famous for serving the best salad in London.

DKNY stores quickly multiplied. With Christina and other retail partners, we opened in Manchester, England; Istanbul and Ankara, Turkey; Dubai, United Arab Emirates; Jeddah, Saudi Arabia; Singapore; Hong Kong; the Philippines; Bangkok, Thailand; Tokyo, Japan; Montreal, Canada; and, in the States, in Huntington, New

York; Las Vegas, Nevada; Costa Mesa, California; Cherry Creek, Colorado; and Short Hills, New Jersey. I could go on, but you get the idea.

We finally opened our DKNY Madison Avenue flagship in 1999 on the corner of 60th Street. Up until this point, we had been very focused on the wholesale business, selling to stores like Bloomingdale's, and this would be our first wholly owned and operated store. I wanted the shopping experience to be as eclectic as our brand, so in addition to clothes, the 16,000-square-foot space housed a marketplace with a café, a flower stand, and a vintage shop. We sold books, furniture, and baby strollers, and even had a Ducati motorcycle as a prop. We put a mirrored wall up in the store to reflect the traffic and bustle of the street. And most dramatically, since it was a corner store, we cut the entrance of the building on the bias to create a sense of welcome and openness. By now, I was also deep into my "woo-woos" (more on that later) and had a feng shui expert come and clear out any bad energy. He didn't like the front door and suggested we hang a cluster of sage above it, as well as soften all the sharp edges with greenery and introduce some essential oils throughout the store. Patti rolled her eyes, of course.

Everyone thought we were nuts to open up across from Calvin Klein and all the other luxe designers on the street, but I didn't care because our store was so different. It was fun and over the top. I remember seeing salespeople from Calvin looking out their windows and staring, as if they were thinking, *What's she up to now?* or maybe *Now she's really lost it.* Once again, I was following my instincts. DKNY was home at last on the streets of NYC, and everything about it felt right—and *was* right. I couldn't have been happier.

16 | NEW YORK STATE OF MIND

My life those days was 99 percent work, 1 percent play. I still tried to run home to make dinner every night, but more often than not, Stephan, Gabby, and I would meet at our favorite Italian restaurant, Sette Mezzo on Lexington Avenue at 70th Street, just a block from our apartment. (That's assuming Gabby hadn't already had lunch there with friends. She used to take her whole high school there on our credit card, right after they'd all raided our closets.)

Stephan and I tried not to let anything interfere with our weekends with Gabby, Lisa, and Corey. We were still renting on Fire Island in the summer, and we'd go on ski trips at Christmastime. But otherwise, we were working around the clock.

It was a challenge to keep up with our success while still trying to plan ahead. The year we introduced DKNY, our sales more than doubled, jumping from $40 million to $100 million. A year later, in 1990, the CFDA once again named me womenswear designer of the year. I was thrilled, but I was also scared to death. In my mind, the higher you climbed, the further you had to fall. My answer, as it always had been when I felt out of control, was to work, work, work.

The company culture was shifting. We had more "suits" walking around than ever. One night Beth, my executive assistant for the past six years—the one who observed the Sabbath—came into my office and resigned. We had long since hired someone to supplement her on Fridays and Saturdays, but we still couldn't keep her. She found an executive position at Hadassah, the Jewish women's organization. "Beth, you will always have a job here," I said, hugging her. "I mean it. If you ever get bored at Häagen-Dazs, just call me." (I've always had trouble with names.)

As my co-CEO, Stephan was the brand's creative visionary. It was his idea to change our name from the Donna Karan Company to Donna Karan International. He never saw us as just a Seventh Avenue label; he saw us as a far-reaching global brand, similar to Chanel, Inc. But we still needed to operate the day-to-day business, and operations were not Stephan's focus.

Right before launching DKNY, we approached Steve Ruzow to be our chief operating officer. Steve had been running the active-wear division at Warnaco, the American corporation known for underwear, sportswear, and swimwear, including licensees such as Calvin Klein, Chaps, and Speedo. We'd met him when he was at Gottex, where his wife, Miriam, was president of Gottex NY and principal in its parent company. The four of us had become friendly. Stephan and I loved his mixture of warmth and professionalism. We wanted to keep a family atmosphere, however big we grew.

"Steve, the world wants us. They're lining up every day," Stephan told Steve the night we set out to recruit him. "But our back end isn't keeping up with our front. We can't make the clothes fast enough, and we're delivering practically in season instead of in advance." Steve took the job and proved perfect for us because he was organized, strategic, always thinking ahead, and very no-nonsense. He was also a big-picture type, taking us from one warehouse in New Jersey to five. Steve established global production and distribution channels for Collection, DKNY, and our accessories. To streamline our Asian business, he set up Donna Karan Hong Kong, Donna Karan Japan, and Donna Karan Korea. Next he established Donna Karan Italy and a distribution center in the Netherlands. Steve traveled all over the world, making sure our offices were consistent and that the right people were in place. It was mind-boggling to think about all the pieces in this puzzle.

I was especially excited to have a company home in Milan. So was Stephan, because I had been using a suite at the exclusive Villa d'Este hotel in Como, north of Milan, as my base of operations, and the bills were astronomical. As it was, Julie Stern was still screaming at me about my extravagant fabric bills. Fabrics remained my drug of choice, and now I had a lot more money to spend.

Success also freed us up to explore all the parts of a woman's wardrobe. Donna Karan Toners, our shapewear hosiery introduced in 1990, was a huge hit, and another innovation born out of a personal need. I called them "the sixty-second workout," because all you had to do was pull them on to look slimmer and firmer. We also introduced Donna Karan Intimates with Wacoal, where we could do modern versions of the foundation pieces my mother wore (one generation's girdle is another's body shaper), along with supportive but sexy-looking bras. (I may not have worn them, but I appreciated that most women did. And I learned that making a bra was almost as complicated as nuclear science—this was serious stuff!) Because I was known for body-conscious jerseys, I felt I had to provide the right undergarments to suck everything in and smooth every inch while still being comfortable. I didn't want my customers to ever have to sacrifice comfort to look good.

My friend Sonja Caproni who, after leaving the luxury department store I. Magnin, had gone on to work for Paloma Picasso and

Karl Lagerfeld, joined us to head our accessories division. I drove her crazy, of course. Once we were working on a fall collection and all the jewelry was gold. A week or so before our show, I started feeling more silver.

"No problem," she said. "We'll switch it."

Then at nine o'clock on the night before our show, I changed my mind back. Sonja thought I was joking, until she saw that I wasn't laughing. She paused, swallowed, and said, "Okay. Let me see what I can do."

She called up her suppliers, and they opened their studios that night to dip the silver pieces. By the time we showed the next morning, the accessories were gold—and probably still wet.

It was the winter of 1990, and Stephan and I were sitting on our vicuña suede sofas, having the same old argument. He was determined to build a business far bigger than our fashion one. Stephan wanted a legacy, and he felt that fragrance was the way to do it.

"Donna, hemlines go up and down, but fragrance is forever. Look at Chanel!" he said with great impatience.

"But I hate fragrance. Hate!" I said. I truly did. It was always too strong, too fake, too old-lady-ish. I loved essential oils or the clean, fresh scent of shampoo and soap.

"I promise you, Donna, we will make a fragrance you love. We will create and control everything about it."

"Good luck," I said, and rolled my eyes.

"You like Casablanca lilies, right?" he said, pointing to our foyer table, which always had a giant bowl of lilies on it. "Let's start with that. What else do you like?"

"Vicuña suede." My hand caressed our sofa.

"Okay, what else?"

"The back of your neck," I said, leaning into him, rubbing my nose in his neck, and inhaling.

He smiled. "That might be hard for me to smell, but I'll work on it."

That's all it took. Stephan was off and running. Like me, he loved a creative challenge, and this was a doozy. And also like me, when Stephan was in the creative zone, he became obsessed. Our bedroom was transformed into a laboratory, with my mad-scientist husband constantly mixing essences in tiny vials—a drop of this, a hint of that. He tried them on me and every woman he ran into, from friends to employees to women in our building. No one was safe. I couldn't keep the samples straight, but he did. I went to sleep smelling of them.

One morning he put three vials in front of me. "These are your choices," he said. "Choose one."

I picked an intoxicating blend of exotic flowers, patchouli, amber, and sandalwood. I loved how personal it was to me in every way—dark, sensuous, and evocative—and unlike any traditional fragrance I'd ever smelled. But I couldn't let it be, of course. I said to Stephan, "You need to give me a beauty company, not just a fragrance. I want hair care, body lotions, soaps, deodorant—everything a woman actually uses. And candles!"

First we approached Chanel to partner with us, but the company didn't want to take on an outside beauty business. So, fearless as ever, Stephan hired Jane Terker, a beauty executive from L'Occitane, as our new division's president, and the two of them forged ahead. Tomio, Frank, and Steve did not want to open a beauty business. They wanted us to go the traditional route and license it to an established company. *Stephan, we don't have the capability to do beauty. We can hardly produce and distribute our clothes,* protested one. Another objection was, *No one does their own beauty company—the startup costs alone will bleed us.* Yet another was, *Established beauty companies have the machine in gear. We can't reinvent the wheel.*

But Stephan wouldn't back down. He and Jane traveled the world to develop our products. They worked with perfumeries, visited glass-making factories, and researched every last detail that affected the business. The one thing we had that no other beauty company had was an in-house sculptor to create our bottles. Stephan wanted them to be evocative and abstract, and to feel good in a woman's hand. He loved curves, especially the curves of a woman's back, and he was very into mixed media and pairing opposite materials. That's how he came up with our trio of bottles made out of matte black metal, brass, and glass. Like our clothes, they were curvy, sensual, and modern.

Creatively, Stephan and I were so connected. Over time I've come to appreciate that more and more. He'd always say art was creating something from nothing. His artistic process was based on string theory in modern physics—or, as he put it, "connecting the dots." He'd scatter dots on a page and then connect them with fast, lyrical strokes. A figure would emerge, and he'd translate that into a drawing, a painting, a sculpture. Similarly, my hands follow the lines of the body when I'm draping, and I re-create those curves with a seam. The beauty bottles were the place where his two worlds came together: the businessman he had become and the sculptor he had always been.

When he moved on to ancillary products (cleansers, creams, and so on), I put my foot down once again. "I don't want to wash my hair or clean my face with my fragrance! Let's make the bath product scent subtler, cleaner, and softer." It sounded so reasonable, but what I was asking for was revolutionary. Once again, Stephan delivered: He took a few notes from the fragrance, and we named the bath and body collection Cashmere Mist. The body lotion was its star. It sold five times the amount of any other product in the line, and almost the same amount as the original fragrance. I wore it morning, noon, and night.

One day two years later, I came across a beautiful frosted bottle with the name Cashmere Mist on its label. *Excuse me?* I grabbed it, stormed into Jane's office, and screamed, "What is this?" I may have thrown the *f*-word in there.

"Stephan didn't tell you? We're making a fragrance of Cashmere Mist."

"No, my loving husband didn't tell me," I said, furious. But it's a good thing he didn't. Cashmere Mist remains our bestselling fragrance.

We also developed a skin care line named Formula for Renewed Skin with Dr. Patricia Wexler, the famed dermatologist and my good friend, and Mark Potter, a Texan chemist Jane had met through a reporter. Mark had worked on skin products for the troops during Operation Desert Storm, so we knew his formulas would be innovative and effective. Beauty editors loved our all-purpose gentle cleanser, exfoliating mask, and moisturizing SPF face tint. It's a crime these products no longer exist.

We tackled men's fragrance next. Because Stephan was a race car and motorcycle fanatic, I wanted it to smell like race cars. When he and Jane met with International Fragrances and Flavors, they visited a garage with the engines on so they could smell the exhaust. It could have killed them all! But that was Stephan, passionate and committed. He even created a bottle that looked like a stick shift.

I wanted to call the fragrance Thrust. I loved that it evoked the *vroom* of driving, and yes, that it was sexual. But our friend Hal Rubenstein, the fashion editor, said, "Don't you dare, Donna." We settled on Fuel for Men as the name. Next we did a women's fragrance called Chaos, for which Stephan created a bottle shaped like a crystal shard, and one called Black Cashmere, with a bottle re-

sembling a smooth and glossy river rock. We also offered bold, geo-
metric scented candles, one called Calm and another called
Invigorate.

Stephan was still very much involved with the main business.
His office was adjacent to Steve's, and at the end of the day they'd
open a bottle of scotch and close the door to review what was what.
Stephan had my back, which gave me such peace of mind. If I
wanted something, assuming it was reasonable, he'd insist I get it.
He was also the calm, approachable one. He wore a ponytail, in
part, so businesspeople would think he was an artist and underesti-
mate him. But Stephan had the last laugh. He proved far more
business-savvy than even I could have dreamed.

By now, circa 1991, our creative needs were too big to keep working
with an outside agency like Peter Arnell's. We had more divisions
than I could keep track of, and every division required everything
from in-store boutiques and ad campaigns to shopping bags and
hangtags. I wanted what Calvin had: a dedicated in-house ad
agency. Calvin's was called CRK Advertising, and it was legendary.
He and his creative director, Sam Shahid, had made an indelible
mark in fashion and beauty advertising, beginning with Brooke
Shields and her Calvins and right through to Kate Moss and Marky
Mark. I called Trey Laird, who knew our brand well from working
with Peter. Trey was now working at GFT, an American licensee to
European brands such as Armani and Valentino. I asked Trey to
work on a project that would show me creatively what he would do
for my upcoming collection, inspired by the romance of poets and
artists.

Trey is a proper southern gentleman, with a shy, charming, boyish quality. Creativity comes in many packages, and his was the

calm, contemplative kind—the opposite of mine. The first time he met me, he entered my typical whirlwind of a day. I was fitting on Doreen and Gina. Patti was holding the phone for a reporter who was about to interview me. I was trying on one shoe, talking to the shoe designer, and, yes, taking off my top (no bra, as usual) to try something on. If he was freaked out, Trey didn't show it. For our next meeting, he found me mid-pedicure in my office. But by then, nothing surprised him.

Trey and I had connected way back when he was a junior assistant. He had this unique ability to put everything back in place after I made a mess of it. I would rearrange presentations in several combinations, and he would quietly recall the order of, say, the fifth version I liked. He could follow my thinking and help organize, enhance, and express it as well. These were invaluable qualities that I had never forgotten.

Now Trey returned to my office with his assigned project. He was wearing an Armani suit—and not just any Armani, but a black label Armani. "Let's talk about this suit, Trey," I greeted him. "The fabric is Bartolini. I know because I just saw it at Première Vision. I think of you as a polo shirt kind of guy. How do you, a boy from the South, come in here looking so amazing in an Armani suit made of Bartolini fabric?" He blushed. Before he could answer, I said, "Wait, I have one more thing to tell you—your fly's open."

Trey's presentation was totally on point. He was nervous about taking on a company as big as ours; after all, he was only in his late twenties. But I believed in him. When I sense that someone is talented, age or lack of experience doesn't faze me in the least. Trey was instrumental in designing our DKNY London store, and he had never done a store before. Early on he brought in Hans Dorsinville, who was just out of design school, maybe twenty-two years old, and we had an immediate connection as well. Hans is a soulful Haitian

Canadian with the kind of even temperament suited to riding creative waves. (Years later, Hans came with me to Haiti to shoot our ad campaign, more dots connected.) Trey and Hans both got me.

They also take my sometimes impulsive decisions in stride. God knows I've sent them on many a wild goose chase. For the spring 1994 collection, we did outerwear pieces—trenches, ponchos, anoraks, balmacaans—made from a reflective fabric by Mectex, which we found at Première Vision, the huge annual fabric fair in Europe. In natural light, it looked chic and matte in mineral colors like icy blue, jade, and gray. Yet in a direct, focused light, it glowed almost white. Very cool. I only discovered this a couple of days before the show. I realized that you couldn't appreciate the fabric's glow without some kind of eye-level light. "Trey!" I screamed. He and his team somehow sourced fifteen hundred miner's headlamps with batteries and had a hangtag printed to explain the reason for the hats placed on each seat. (Before signing off on this idea, Patti called the office of *Vogue*'s Anna Wintour to make sure she'd wear one, and the answer was yes.) We had the models come out twice: first in the dark with the audience's headlamps as the only light, and again after we turned on the house lights. The effect was sensational and totally worth the last-minute scramble.

———————

Thanks to our DKNY flagship store, I was going to London every chance I got. My first stop there was always Egg, a store on Kinnerton Street in Knightsbridge, created and owned by one of my dearest friends, Maureen Doherty. A blond Brit, Maureen is my polar opposite. She is the minimalist of minimalists, a purist who edits everything down to the essential. Egg is a whitewashed former carriage house, and the clothes there are architecturally simple, mostly in white linen, maybe accented with natural, black, and gray. Maureen has an eye for artisans and introduces me to all sorts of people, from great knitters to potters. I wish I had even an ounce of her ease—she's a spirit in a rocking chair, sipping tea (which she always serves). Once I asked her if I could open an Egg in New York City, and she laughed. "Donna, I'd love you to open a chicken soup store—a nice Jewish girl selling chicken soup, brilliant—but your first question would be, 'How many kinds of chicken soup can I serve?'"

Our DKNY London store (as un-Egg as it gets) was doing fabulously, and we were anxious to open its Collection counterpart. I found the perfect corner store on Bond Street, but it wasn't available. The one next door came on the market, and Christina Ong nabbed it for us. I loved it because it had a basement, which I envisioned someday turning into a club or restaurant. We hired legendary architect Peter Marino to design it.

Creating a store an ocean away can be a challenge. I wanted a dark environment, but the idea wasn't translating. Patti and I flew to London and met Dominic Kozerski, a young, London-based associate of Peter's. On the way to the store, we stopped at the Saatchi gallery, where we saw the British artist and sculptor Richard Wilson's "20:50" installation, the floor of which was flooded with recycled engine oil. I was mesmerized by how the oil reflected the planes of the room. When we arrived at our new store's raw space, it was still too white. I had asked for a black store with touches of white, but they gave me a white store with touches of black. Then it hit me: It should be a black shiny jewel box like the exhibit we had just seen. In the corner sat a pile of black trash bags. Dominic immediately slashed them open, and we started taping them all over the walls, then the ceiling. Brilliant! I realized we needed a floating wall to break up the space, and that it should be placed on the diagonal to give the rectangular room the off-kilter shift it needed. So we had the workers hold more plastic bags in a straight line, which I placed at the right angle by directing some of the men to move forward and others to move backward.

Creatively, the London store, which opened in 1996, was a seminal moment for me. It was a gorgeous showpiece, with a gold-painted wall and hints of light everywhere. To celebrate its opening, we threw an over-the-top party, which Trey staged with the fashion show producer Alexandre de Betak. The event, held at a warehouse in Shepherd's Bush, did a few things. First, it rocked London, which had never seen anything like it. Celebrities like Richard Branson, Boy George, Liam and Noel Gallagher from the band Oasis, photographer Mario Testino, Yasmin Le Bon, and Gwyneth Paltrow, whom we'd recently outfitted for the film *Great Expectations*, danced into the night. The media dubbed it the "Party of the Century." Second, it cemented my relationship with (and trust in) the young architect Dominic, who went on to work with Trey designing all our brand stores. In 2000, Dominic would establish his own company with his partner Enrico Bonetti, and the two would help design and build my homes, including my city apartments, my East Hampton houses, and our family compound in Parrot Cay, in the Turks and Caicos. But most notably, that party established my future décor and entertaining aesthetic. From that moment on, I wanted all my environments to be black and ivory, with low banquettes, touches of gold, candles everywhere, and the sexy vibe of a nightclub.

A few years later, I took this to an extreme. Stephan and I were looking to leave East 70th Street, and we found a perfect apartment at the prestigious San Remo on Central Park West. Unfortunately, it was a rental, so I couldn't do any construction. Instead, I said to Dominic, "Let's paint it black!" And we did, from the waxed walls to the chandeliers to the floors to every stick of furniture; I really let loose. We installed black and gold banquettes and—the most fabulous focal point of all—a water wall lit from below. It looked sensational. I was smart enough to leave our bedroom ivory, and to leave Stephan a back room to do what he liked with.

When Stephan came home, well, let's just say he didn't appreciate the drama as much as I did. "Donna, we have black clothes, black furniture, black rugs, black tables, black dishes, black everything!" he yelled. "How are we supposed to find our keys?" To make his point, he bought a hard hat with a miner's headlamp and wore it every time he came home, including while he ate his dinner.

Even Barbra hated it. One time she hit and bruised her shin on the corner of a black coffee table on a black rug. "This is ridiculous!" she cried, rubbing her leg.

———————

Stephan wanted to ride his motorcycles, so we had to leave Fire Island (which doesn't allow most motor vehicles), our summer getaway for so many years. We found a quirky, far-from-fancy three-bedroom house in East Hampton, high on a bluff. What was supposed to be a modest renovation turned into a nightmare when we discovered the builders had knocked down far more of the original house than expected; in fact, all they left was a bedroom and the fireplace.

Stephan was secretly happy because he got to play architect. I offered opinions here and there, but he made it clear this was his domain. He let me do the bathrooms and decorate (just not in black). I called my old friend Ilene Wetson and asked her to do a white house, and I drove us both nuts by insisting that all the whites match. Finally, I brought in a color expert who patiently explained that matching whites was virtually impossible, especially when natural light hits different textures in different ways. So instead, I channeled my obsessive-compulsive tendencies into shopping for the house. Bring on the antiques! Here's what I love about an antique: it's had a life before you. You don't know where it's been, what it's seen, or what energy it holds. Also, it's a one-of-a-kind. So I'd see something, and I'd absolutely, positively have to grab it; God forbid I missed my chance. I bought giant, ornate mirrors, whitewashed wood tables and chairs, Italian marble statues, and distressed concrete benches. Everything had to be white.

"Welcome," Stephan would say to the pieces being wheeled into our house. "This is where antiques come to die."

So now we were renting a modern black apartment in the city and owned an antiques-filled white house on the bay in East Hampton. Stephan and I were a good team. Our friend Pearl Nipon, who with her husband created the line Alpert Nipon, had a great line about us: "One's the head and the other's the neck, but the neck controls where the head goes." I was never sure which part I was, but it worked either way.

17 | WOMAN TO MAN

From the day I met him, Stephan was never a suit kind of guy. He was strictly jeans, a T-shirt, and leather jacket. We went to a fancy Chinese restaurant on one of our first dates, and he had to borrow one of the restaurant's jackets. Not long afterward, I was sleeping over at his place and he woke me up to say goodbye before leaving on a business trip. There he stood in a brown plaid suit, tan shirt, and wide tie, and I almost died. If anything could have made me fall out of love with Stephan, that was it. I felt like I'd woken up to a stranger, a man who bore no relationship to the sexy jeans-wearing guy I'd gone to bed with. Thank God for his cute face. A lifetime later, when our business required him to wear a suit, I took charge. I bought all his tailoring at Armani. He looked fabulous in Armani suits.

Early in 1992, I noticed a young man sitting in the reception area of our offices. He didn't have an appointment. "I'd like to speak with you, if you have a moment," he said to me. He was very proper and spoke with what I later found out was a Dutch accent. (I'm glad I was fully clothed.)

"Sure, sure, come on in," I said.

"My name is Michael Hogan," he said. "I'd like to work on a menswear collection with you."

"Listen, my husband only wears Armani. Unless you can do something better than that, I have no reason to go into menswear."

"I think we can. I'd like to introduce you to the custom tailor Martin Greenfield." I didn't know who Martin Greenfield was, but he said the name with reverence. Since my father had been in the custom tailoring business, I was intrigued. A few days later, Michael returned with an elegant, gray-haired man in a perfectly tailored suit: Martin. I immediately connected with his old-school manner.

I picked up a photo of my parents and told him, "If you can make my husband a suit with the quality of my father's tailoring, but with the sensibility of my design"—I pointed to my design room, right outside my office—"then I'm interested. Stephan's a 54 long. It has to be in crepe. Blue or black, I don't care."

A few days later, Martin returned with a 54 long suit. It was a heavier crepe than we used in womenswear because it had to hold structure and padding. He skipped the pant crease for a more fluid, easy look. I called Stephan in to try it on. He looked hot, no doubt about it. "How does it feel, Stephan?"

"Amazing. Really comfortable," he said. After the shock of that brown plaid so many years ago, I knew not to ask him how he thought it *looked*.

Michael and Martin got to work making samples. Istvan, my women's creative director at the time, was dying to jump in and help. "Forget it, Istvan," I said. "I need you worrying about womenswear. Do I have to remind you we have a show in a week?" And then a lightbulb went off. I called in our model booker, Ray DiPietro, and asked, "Can you hire us a few male models for Friday?" Ray raised an eyebrow. "I'm perfectly serious," I assured him.

The night before the show, as we were putting the finishing touches on the menswear looks, I stopped cold. *Maybe my partners should know about this,* I thought. I told Frank, Tomio, and Steve Ruzow I had a surprise for them and asked them to meet me on the fourteenth floor right away. The three men entered the small, airless room where I had the men's suit samples lined up. In my sweetest voice, I urged each of them to try one on.

"Sensational, Donna," Tomio said, admiring himself in the mirror.

"I agree, these are great," Frank said. "I'd love to own something like this."

"You do. We do," I said. "And I'm putting them in tomorrow's show with the girls." This is how I've always done things: jump in and figure it out later.

"Donna, wait, slow down," Steve said. "Let's think this out."

"Don't worry," I said innocently. "I'm just giving them a taste of what's to come. A preview, that's all."

But when a major designer shows ten or so menswear looks during Fashion Week, you're in the menswear business. Even I knew that.

———

Our handful of menswear looks were the buzz of the industry. Photos appeared in every publication, and when reporters asked about our plans, I told them the truth: the show was an exploration. We had no actual business to speak of. Nonetheless, stores were clamoring to be the first, offering us the world for an exclusive.

Linda Beauchamp, the men's fashion director at Saks Fifth Avenue, approached Steve about launching our menswear at her store. Linda had long red hair, a curvaceous figure, and a direct, no-nonsense manner that radiated power. My kind of woman. She even had a New York accent like mine, only she was from New Jersey. I invited her to my apartment to make the pitch, and by the end of the meeting, I asked, "How do I get you to be our menswear president?"

We didn't have an office for Linda, so she worked out of mine at first. I'd be talking on the phone, trying on a sample with my free hand, and nodding approval on fabrics while someone else placed a salad in front of me and another staffer lit candles. "How do you work like this?" she marveled.

"Like what?"

Multitasking is like breathing to me, so I just folded menswear into the mix. I quickly discovered, however, that it held a special place in my heart because of its discipline (tailoring is so precise!) and how it connected me to my father. I thought about him constantly. The process was invigorating, and my designers loved it as much as I did. We took many leads from our women's clothes in terms of flexibility, luxury, comfort, and, of course, a seven-easy-pieces approach. If I was going to do menswear, it had to say something new, but I also appreciated that men are resistant to change. Our biggest challenge was striking a balance between classic and modern.

A MAN'S SEVEN EASY PIECES WARDROBE

1. **The black crepe suit.** This was our foundation. Together, the jacket and pants were a classic suit; separated, they were two pieces of sportswear. That seems obvious now, but in 1992 a suit was a suit and a sports jacket was a sports jacket. The secret was in the crepe and molded construction, which gave it a stretch-like comfort. It was also seasonless and perfect for traveling. This was a major departure from the average worsted-wool suits men were wearing at the time.

2. **The white shirt.** Every suit deserves an elegant white shirt. Ours were made of the finest, smoothest cotton and had hidden snaps to keep the collar down. Add a black tie and you could substitute the black suit for a tuxedo.

3. **The knit T-shirt.** The right knit can turn a suit into a casual, day-into-evening look. Our fine silk and cashmere knits came in polos, crews, and high Vs.

4. **The cashmere sweater.** You could replace the jacket with a chunkier, luxurious cashmere pullover or cardigan. Ribbed, cabled, or leather-buttoned, these were the kinds of sweaters women would steal. We also did a cashmere sweatsuit: ultra-luxurious.

5. **The sports blazer.** The suit jacket doubled as a sportswear jacket, but we also offered a classic blazer for variety. Our signature style was in vicuña or bright red cashmere (quite a statement at the time). We also served up tweeds and classic menswear patterns like glen plaid, herringbone, and houndstooth (referred to as novelties in the business).

6. **The leather jacket.** Thanks to Stephan, I knew my way around leather jackets. This one was sleeker, smoother, and softer than a biker jacket but exuded the same masculinity. Robert Lee Morris did the zip pulls in our signature gold.

7. **The tailored coat or trench.** Every man needs a dress coat or a great trench. Our cashmere dress coat echoed our jackets with its molded shoulders and clean lines, and our trench was a classic: simple, belted, functional.

Stephan was our critical eye when it came to function. He'd ask for two-way zippers and pockets that wouldn't let things fall out. He told us to make sure the buttons stayed on because men don't replace them. And he really chimed in about the label. "I'm telling you, Donna, no man in his right mind is going to wear a suit with a woman's name on it."

"So what should I call it, Don Karan?"

Stephan thought DK Men sounded good, and that was the label

we shipped with our first collection. Soon after, Istvan got his wish and moved to menswear (by then Michael had left) with Alan Scott, a talented British designer who became our design development designer, and Wallis Shaw, a Scotsman who gave our knitwear a feeling of authenticity. It was the perfect team, and Linda ran her small division like a family. Also, she was married to Bob Beauchamp, a fashion editor who worked at *GQ* and then *Esquire*, so we had an insider track to the menswear industry. Everything was falling into place. We launched at Barney's New York, where I assumed I could work with the customer in the dressing room as I always had. But they stopped me from going in. How was I supposed to sell the clothes?

Then a miracle occurred—big-time. The phone in my office rang, and the voice on the other end said, "Donna, please hold for President-elect William Clinton."

His drawl was unmistakable; I had met him briefly at a fundraiser at Barbra's Malibu house the previous summer. "Hi, Donna, it's Bill. Our friend Barbra says you're the only one I can trust to make me a suit for the inauguration." My first thought was, *Oh my God, I'm being asked to dress the president of the United States.* My second thought was, *The inauguration is two days away!* He called on a Friday, and Martin, like Beth, honored Shabbat. But I'd worry about that later.

I inhaled. "Of course I can help you out, sir. What size are you?"

"54 long."

"You mean 54 extra long, right?" I remembered that he was much taller than Stephan.

"No, 54 long."

It was a mad scramble, but we pulled it off—and in the process, I learned how to make a tuxedo. I sent along a 54 extra long, too, just in case.

Stephan and I attended the inauguration with Barbra and music producer Richard Baskin, and then we went to the Arkansas ball at the D.C. convention center. This was no fairy-tale ball. We were starving and spent the whole time looking for food. We stupidly thought there'd be a sit-down dinner or at least snacks in the VIP room, but there weren't. As we were congratulating Al Gore on his vice presidency, someone came in and said that the president and first lady had arrived. The Secret Service immediately started pushing us toward the stage.

So there we were: me, Stephan, Barbra, Richard, and Barbra's friend Ellen Gilbert and her husband, all up on the stage next to Chelsea and the president's mother, Virginia. Hillary and the president strode onto the stage and with a sweep of his arm he said to the crowd, "I'd like to introduce y'all to my family." His arm was pointing at us! All we could do was smile and wave. When the president came over to greet us, instead of congratulating him (like I meant to), I asked, "So what are you wearing, a 54 long or a 54 extra long?"

He smiled. "A 54 long."

That's when I realized the president is never wrong.

Martin Greenfield and I dressed President Clinton throughout his presidency; we made him some twenty suits in all. More important, he and I began a lifelong friendship that later included philanthropic ties through our work in Haiti.

That same year, we were awarded the CFDA Menswear Designer of the Year. My menswear hero Giorgio Armani presented the award, and in my acceptance speech, I thanked my father in heaven for sending me Martin Greenfield.

Despite Stephan's belief that "no man in his right mind would wear a suit with a woman's name on it," a nonstop parade of testosterone wore Donna Karan New York Men. Our clothes were especially beloved in the sports world: Fox network announcers for the Super Bowl and the World Series wore them, as did NBC sportscasters for the Olympics in Nagano and guys from the Knicks, the Nets, the Giants, and the Yankees. One of our favorites was Patrick Ewing, whom we put on the cover of our made-to-measure brochure. If we could dress Patrick, we could dress anyone. The musician Sting wore our clothes, too, and I became good friends with him and his wife, Trudie Styler, both dedicated yogis and philanthropists. And on the spiritual front, my friend Deepak Chopra, the author and holistic healer, also wore our clothes, and he looked particularly good in the dark suit.

Design-wise, I pushed the envelope too far a couple of times. Once I did a man's bodyshirt (a shirt and boxers in one, which kept the shirt tucked in). I thought it was a great idea, but no one else did. Then I did a men's sarong, inspired by my love for how men dress in places like Indonesia. We got another firm no from the press and retailers. One of my more surreal menswear moments was when Jack Nicholson came to see me. Jack had met Linda through a mutual friend.

"I need some golf shirts," he told me after we said hello.

"We don't do golf shirts, Jack. We do a lot of other shirts, but not golf shirts."

"You really need to do golf shirts. In colors."

As if, I thought. (Sarongs are much more my speed.) But hey, stranger things have happened. Like having Giorgio Armani present me with the CFDA menswear award the first year I did menswear, and dressing the president of the United States for his inauguration.

18 | INWARD BOUND

Business was great. Every day presented a new challenge, a new problem to solve, a new plan to put in motion. In 1993, just a year after being named the CFDA's Menswear Designer of the Year, we received the Fragrance Foundation's FiFi Award for best fragrance, the most prestigious in the industry. I was thrilled for Stephan and incredibly proud of him. With the continued rise of Donna Karan New York and DKNY, and our ever-expanding global presence, I was being heralded as the "Queen of Seventh Avenue."

But personally, I didn't feel like the queen of anything—least of all my own destiny. I was too busy being the Donna Karan the world thought I was and expected me to be.

In the spring and summer of 1992, I spent more time than ever at our house in East Hampton. One day I went down the winding wooden staircase to the shore, and there, right at the bottom of the steps, something caught my attention. It was a rock the size of a baked potato, with two "eyes" (brown spots). A real Mr. Potato

Head. Out of tens of thousands of rocks, it had stopped me. Or called out to me to stop. So I did. I sat and looked at it for a while. It was perfectly still, so content. My body relaxed. The noise in my brain quieted. I heard a knock, a whisper from within.

Donna, Donna. Remember me? The rock wasn't speaking, of course, but deep inside I heard a faint voice. It sounded lonely and longing. The voice belonged to the real me. I had stopped talking to her a long time ago. I didn't have time for her; I didn't even know her anymore. Like the rock, she just was sitting there, waiting for me to notice. But she was also hurting, silently pleading with me to make time for her. "Who am I?" I wondered. "Where have I gone?" The rock looked back as if in understanding, and, crazy as it sounds, I felt like I had a friend. The rock became my touchstone. I didn't try to move or "own" it in any way. Instead, I just looked forward to seeing it every weekend. It was the first stop I'd make after the two-hour drive from the city. The ritual was calming, grounding, and centering. I loved that while my life in the city whirled round and round, my rock sat still, waiting.

On the surface, I had it all: I was with the love of my life. I had a daughter I treasured beyond anything, and I was even a grand-mother, thanks to Corey and Lisa. I was a highly acclaimed designer and financially very comfortable. But something inside wasn't being fulfilled or nurtured. I just couldn't find inner peace. Despite all the therapy I had, I was always searching, searching, searching—for what, I didn't know. I was so busy being Donna Karan the designer and the brand that I'd lost *me*. I had given myself away to my busi-ness and to the public at such a young age. Where was Donna Karan the woman?

I had been so afraid of being left alone my whole life that I had always kept myself busy. I became my mother (someone I swore I'd never be) and went to work, where I was surrounded by people. I was thriving professionally, but personally, I still didn't feel good enough. I'm not alone, I know. So many of my women friends, even the famous ones, tell me the same thing—that they are always working hard to prove they are worthy of being invited to the party. At work I had to be a leader and make decisions. The minute I walked in, I switched it on: showtime. But inside, I was still the girl with the crazy mother and the insecure, outsider feeling. I looked in the mirror and saw the girl they sang about at camp: "spaghetti legs and a meatball head."

Sitting with the rock, I was sitting with myself. I was getting to know Donna Karan the woman, listening to her, reflecting on where I'd been and where I was going. It felt good to sit and just be.

One day, after a few months of visiting this rock, I returned on a Saturday morning and it was gone. My heart jumped. I frantically walked up and down the beach. I searched and searched, turning over every rock even remotely its size. I couldn't accept that it was gone. Was it a sign, another death of some sort?

That same day I chose a new rock—this time a boulder poking out of the water that was so huge you could sit on it. Nothing was going to move it. I said out loud, "Now *you're* going to be my rock." I climbed onto it, turned to face the ocean, and was still. I kept my eyes open, took in the expansive view, and listened to the rhythmic sounds of the lapping water. I saw how small my problems were in comparison—how small *I* was in comparison. By being still, I became open. I could listen with my mind, body, and spirit to myself and to what the world was telling me. Most meaningful was that the boulder became my connection to the other side, to people in my life who had passed. It's where I talked to my father, my mother, and, years later, to Stephan. Interestingly, I always felt my parents' presence in front of me, out at sea, but Stephan's was always behind me, as if his spirit hadn't quite left me.

———————

When in doubt, I turn to nature. It doesn't ask anything of you other than to observe and appreciate it. For a problem solver like me, it's a relief to surrender and inhale the beauty. The beach is my greatest escape from the madness of my life. The magnificence of the ocean awakens me to myself. It's larger than life and gives me perspective. I can be alone on the beach without being afraid. The shoreline is open and embracing. It's a big smile. I can't tell you how many color stories I've created from my beach walks. But more than a place to find inspiration, the beach is my sanctuary, my personal temple where I can reflect, regroup, and recharge.

———————

Over the years, I've come to realize that I willingly gave away my identity. That's what women do. We take on so many roles: mother, wife, sister, daughter, designer, leader, philanthropist, caregiver, and on and on. We give it away every day, never saving a piece for ourselves. It's easier to solve the daily problems at work and home than to face ourselves. My quest has been to let go of the ego—this brand called Donna Karan—and find myself. To empower the real Donna, the one who is lost, afraid, unsure. Being famous takes you away from working on yourself.

My spiritual teachers have helped me appreciate that you know who you are deep down inside, but people want you to be something else. You can be powerful and vulnerable at the same time. The right hand can be strong, and the left hand can be hurting. One hand is always giving, but the other doesn't know how to receive. Life is full of dualities, two sides of the same coin.

My journey to reconnect with myself has made me open to any experience that teaches, heals, or helps me grow. Therapists, psychiatrists, psychics, astrologists, yogis, channelers, tarot card readers, drummers, acupuncturists—they all have something to offer.

I'm a seeker. Of course, there are quacks out there, but if you assume everyone is a quack, you'll never experience the possibility of enlightenment, and to me that's the worst fate of all. I don't pretend to have any answers. I'm on the path. The more I ask, the more there is to learn. I'll never arrive, I'll never have it all figured out. It's a private road, but I haven't had to travel it alone. From the start, I had a trusted companion.

It wasn't Stephan. He was far too rational. He believed in therapy, especially when it came to communicating better with his children or with me. But he wasn't interested in my "woo-woos," as he called them. He was even-keeled and calm, and he really enjoyed being with himself, whether he was riding his motorcycles, sketching, or sculpting. He patiently tolerated my spiritual search, rolling his eyes playfully. "What's my wife up to now?" he'd ask. I was a source of endless amusement for him.

Gabby is more like Stephan, though maybe not as patient. She's linear, organized, very grounded, and black and white—the opposite of me in many ways, but exactly like me in others. I've tried to get her to join me in my various pursuits, but her answer is always the same: "When you figure it all out, then we can talk."

So neither my husband nor my daughter shared the path with me. Nor did Patti, though we connect on other "out there" things (more on that later). No, my fellow explorer is my friend Barbra Streisand. She is my spiritual sister. Fashion may have introduced us, but our parallel lives and shared hunger for something deeper and more meaningful have been our glue. When I first saw *Yentl*, Barbra's 1984 film (and without question her most personal project), I had tears in my eyes. But when I read the final credit, "Dedicated to my father," that was it. I knew we were destined to be close friends. Her father had died when she was a baby, just like mine. We'd both grown up with difficult mothers, which made the loss of our fathers that much harder to bear because we both fantasized that they would have protected us. And we shared fame. Barbra and I were both successful at an early age. It's hard to remember when we weren't public people.

So when Barbra called me one day in the early 1990s to invite me to a Brugh Joy workshop, I jumped. Dr. W. Brugh Joy was a Mayo Clinic physician who, after being diagnosed with pancreatitis, transitioned into alternative healing and spiritual therapies. He led powerful self-development workshops. Barbra brought her son, Jason, who was around twenty-five at the time and a real sweetheart. I loved the whole experience. Trust me, it was hard work—lots of facing fears and exploring darkness. Through dreamwork, meditation, and other exercises, Brugh taught us about the destructive force of the ego and showed us just how universal these issues are. There were some twenty-odd people in our group. He would focus intensely on one person and his or her story, and we would all have similar emotional reactions. We realized that we all had the same vulnerabilities.

After that, Barbra and I, two nice Jewish girls, were up for anything. We drove upstate to see the Guru Mai at her ashram in the Catskills and then to a Deepak Chopra retreat at the Maharishi Ayurveda Health Center in Lancaster, Massachusetts. Deepak, a medical doctor who has long embraced a mind-body-spirit approach to well-being, gave me my first mantra and introduced me to Ayurveda's holistic healing system, developed thousands of years ago in India. At the retreat, we learned that Ayurveda identifies three kinds of *prakriti*, or "natures." There's *vata*, which is the active, restless, energetic type—that's me. There's *pitta*, which is more cerebral, insightful, and decisive—that's Barbra. And there's *kapha*, which is serene, calm, and tolerant—neither me nor Barbra, not by a long shot. This became clear when it came time for the hot oil treatments, called *pizhichil*, which involve a four-hand massage while you lie in a tin pan filled with hot oil. Barbra and I were in separate but adjacent rooms. The goal was to transport us to a place of calm, but she was horrified by the oil and complained the whole time. "This is my idea of bliss, Barbra," I called to her. I was in heaven, loving all the warm liquid pooling over my body.

"You know what?" she shouted back. "You're really crazy!"

Years later, after Stephan died, Demi Moore called with an idea. She and I had become great friends after meeting in the midnineties at her then husband Bruce Willis's club, Mint, where he would perform with his band. Demi knew I was having a hard time after Stephan's death and asked if I wanted to join her and her friend Eric on a trip to Dr. Nonna Brenner's Healing Center in Austria for leech therapy, which supposedly rid you of toxins and negativity. It took place in a private house in the mountains—not luxurious, but very quaint. We had an enema every day. We took mountain walks. We journaled, and Nonna, a trained psychotherapist, took us into her "soul room" for one-on-one therapy. It was one-stop body cleansing and spiritual healing. And yes, every day we had leeches (four, five, or more) put on our toxic or stress points in order to suck out all the crud. Mine were mostly on my back and neck, with a few on my chest. I was scared the first time and squirmed as they placed them. But then, nothing—I didn't feel a thing. They'd sit there for a half hour until they were so blown up with blood they practically fell off, leaving pink rings on my skin. I felt a little light-headed. For days afterward, I felt emotionally lighter, too.

I'm also addicted to silent retreats, which force you to tune out the exterior world, look deep inside, and speak with yourself. This may surprise you, since I'm not exactly the quiet type. But the truth is, I'm not very social. I like to talk and connect, but I also love quiet, as long as I have the comforting presence of others around me. I liked to be *guided* through my silence, not abandoned into it. I learned this the hard way. Once, just after finding out that Stephan was sick, I went away on a silent retreat in the middle of the woods in Colorado. You've heard of Outward Bound? This could have been called Inward Bound. It was conducted by a couple with whom I had already done a lot of spiritual work. They picked me up at the airport, and we went grocery shopping. Then they left me in a cabin for three days. I did my own cooking and cleaning. There was no phone, computer, or television. It was just me and my journal. I was truly alone, and I felt abandoned. Not only did it conjure up feelings of my childhood, but it foreshadowed what I would feel like if Stephan was gone. I had no one to cry to, and I spent more time sobbing out of loneliness than I did reflecting. There was nothing therapeutic about the experience; I didn't emerge a different person. I was just relieved not to be alone anymore.

Disastrous trips aside, I love getting away, clearing out the baggage, and searching within myself for clarity, self-acceptance, and self-love. I don't care about luxury as much as I do about authenticity. I want to experience every interesting thing I can.

———————

As great as you feel after a spiritual retreat, it's hard to sustain the benefits. That's why I love yoga. You can practice it anywhere. When I was in high school, I loved yoga because it was expressive, freeing, and flowing, like dance. I had long legs and loved to stretch them and feel the energy that moved through my body from pose to pose. As time wore on, my practice became spiritual as well as physical. When you're always working, you need to settle down and find a moment of peace. Everyone thinks it's all about getting your leg over your head, but it's much more a communion of mind, body, and spirit. There are lessons to learn over and over, physically and spiritually, which is why it's called practice.

I practice at Yoga Shanti in Sag Harbor with Rodney Yee and Colleen Saidman Yee. I love the energy of a class. I'm late for everything in life, but never for yoga. I show up and do what I'm told. On the mat, my mind doesn't wander. I don't do anything but the pose at hand. It's such a relief not to think. Despite all my years of practicing, I'm far from the best yogi on the planet. I'm extremely flexible, which is great, but my challenge is one of containment. As in life, I need to learn not to give it all away, to hold on to myself and create a sense of stability. My channels are always open, with energy flowing in and out. It's depleting to live that way.

Practically speaking, there's the issue of posture. I'm a very physical designer: My head is always cocked when I work, my hips jutted out to one side or the other. Yoga helps me center and realign my body.

My yoga journey has been long and full of good teachers. In the mid-1970s, when I first moved to the city, I had a teacher who spoke slowly and deliberately, and sounded like my psychiatrist, Dr. Rath, which I found comforting. Once or twice a week he and I would practice in a corner of my bedroom, often with a very young Gabby nearby. Later, I took up Ashtanga yoga with Danny Paradise, who worked with my friends Trudie and Sting. Danny was the textbook yogi: a hippie with long hair and a bandana around his head. Ashtanga is a set series of progressive postures that produce intense internal heat, encouraging sweating and detoxification. Some people call it power yoga. I loved practicing with Danny, but he was a true nomad, always off traveling around the world. Then Gabby turned me on to Jivamukti Yoga, a studio founded by Sharon Gannon and David Life. Gabby was going to New York University and living downtown near the studio on Broadway, and I started going with or without her every Saturday and Sunday. I adore Sharon and David, who trained my current teacher, Colleen.

In Los Angeles, I've studied with Tara Lynda Guber, whom I consider the Donna Karan of LA. Like me, she's out there, and spiritually open to new ideas. Through Tara Lynda, I met Ken "Tesh" Scott, who practiced Contact Yoga, also called partner yoga. I loved the quality of the stretching and how our body weight worked with and against each other. I found Tesh a studio in the Hamptons (a rustic old barn on top of a hill) where he taught me and my friends. I also practiced with Jules Paxton, another yogi versed in both traditional and Contact Yoga. I'd give gift certificates for private sessions with Jules to all my loved ones. Even Gabby was a fan. Despite all my attempts to get Barbra into yoga, and God knows I've tried, it doesn't speak to her the way it does to me. She loves aerobic exercise, Pilates, weight training, and machines. Best friends can't share everything.

My spiritual quest intensified in the summer of 1994, thanks to my new friend Pam Serure, the owner of Get Juiced, a juice bar in Bridgehampton. A friend had given me one of Pam's juice "boxes," and as soon as I finished it, I called Pam to introduce myself. Anyone who could make juices like that was someone I needed to know. Small and forceful in a New York way, Pam was a natural healer—a "Jewish juicer," as I called her. She practiced body purification through various channels of detoxing and meditating and offered a whole menu of spiritual and bodywork methodologies, including aromatherapy, dreamwork, journaling, breathwork, and primal screaming. "I need it all," I told her when we met. "A total reboot. The stress in my life is too much, and it's affecting my health, my sleep, my everything."

"Give me three days," she said. And she meant it. No phone calls, no talking, no interference.

"Can I bring a friend?"

"Of course."

We created a three-day retreat at my house with my new friend Linda Horn, whom Patti had introduced me to a few months back. Linda is the essence of bohemian chic and was fast becoming my favorite partner in escape. She produced television commercials and was no stranger to stress. And like me, she was up for anything new and adventurous. It helped that Stephan loved her husband, Steve, so we often went out as a foursome.

Our first three-day silent retreat was fabulous. Pam brought the nutrition, the yoga, and other bodyworkers, including an amazing New Zealander named Kamala, who worked on breathing and meditation. We got really into it. We journaled, recorded our dreams, screamed at the waves, and swam nude. We created an altar out of beach rocks and shells. We practiced yoga and got massages. At the end of three silent days, I felt like a new person—I'd stopped the music and tapped into myself in a deep and peaceful way. I was feeling the power of self-care. Linda and I were expected at a fundraising cocktail party that evening. "Bring your juices, you'll be fine," Pam said. So off we went, our faces glowing.

Patti Cohen isn't woo-woo like me, but she has a real weakness for psychics, astrologists, and card readers. She introduced me to the amazing astrologer and psychic Maria Napoli, who sees things no one else can. I've consulted her before hiring almost every senior executive in our company.

Psychics have saved my life, no doubt about it. Once, my fashion director, Peter Speliopoulos, my design associate and "second daughter," Bonnie Young, and I were headed to Florence, Italy, for a fabric meeting. Right after we took off, the pilot discovered the plane had an electrical problem so we returned to the airport. Both Peter and Bonnie, who was hugely pregnant, wanted to get off, but I felt we should wait out the repair. They grew more and more impatient as the night wore on.

"Donna, I have a child at home and I'm pregnant. I just don't feel good about this," Bonnie said.

"Let me call Molly," I said. It was 2:00 a.m. when I called one of my favorite psychics and gave her the tail number of our plane.

"It's a bad number right now," she said. "Don't fly it under any circumstances."

The next morning, I called Molly to ask if anything had shifted. It had. "You're good to go," she said, so we did.

———————

While I explored my spiritual side, Stephan worked in his art studio or planned motorcycle trips—anything to avoid my in-home re- treats. That's how we came to buy my "spa house" next door.

At first Barbra thought she wanted to buy it as a Hamptons re- treat close to mine. "Let's go over and see it," she said excitedly one day.

"But it's not for sale," I told her. Besides, I'd never met these neighbors.

"You never know. Let's go and introduce ourselves."

So Barbra and I walked over and knocked on the door. A middle- aged woman answered, and we watched the shock register on her face. I tried to break the ice.

"Hi, I'm your neighbor Donna, and this is my friend Barbra. I know this sounds odd, but we were just admiring your house and wondered if we could take a look inside."

Still stunned, the woman nodded, and warmed up a bit as we walked around.

When we got back to our house, I got a call from Lisa, Stephan's daughter. I could hear the outrage in her voice. "Donna, what did you just do?" It turned out that the husband of the woman next door worked on Wall Street with Lisa's husband and told the whole floor how Donna Karan and Barbra Streisand had just invited themselves over for a house tour.

Next, we visited neighbors down the beach from us. A whole

family was home, and the mother had her hair in rollers. This time, Barbra spoke. "Hi, I'm Barbra, and this is my friend Donna, who lives down the road. We're curious about homes in the neighborhood and would love to see yours. Would you mind?"

Eventually the first house we saw went up for sale, and Stephan bought it for me. Not us, *me*. He was tired of people coming into our home, chanting, and stepping over him—or, worse, me hosting weekend sanctuaries and kicking him out. I told Stephan I wanted a Balinese-inspired space with a yoga studio, a massage area, and huge, open rooms with little separation between indoors and out. I repeated over and over that the floors between the deck and living room had to be flush for a seamless transition. "I got it, I got it," he kept saying. But someone measured wrong, and all the custom doors came in an inch or so too short. To this day, I bump my toe on the door saddles every time I walk from the living room onto the deck. And each time I do that I say hello to Stephan, who must be smiling from above.

One day a woman who worked in our sample room asked me a question: if I could meet anyone in the world, who would it be? "His Holiness the Dalai Lama, no question," I told her. I've always revered his love, his kindness, and the beauty of his teachings, and I've joked that I was a Bu before I was a Jew. It turned out that she, too, was a devotee. The next day, she came in and said she'd found out that His Holiness would be in New York for a fundraising reception being held at a hotel, and I could buy an invitation to meet him. I jumped at the chance—not just for me, but for Stephan as well. We had just learned that Stephan was sick, and I desperately wanted him to receive a blessing. I also invited Jane Chung, who was a new mother and wanted a blessing for her son, Dylan.

Our tickets included a private meeting for us with him and his entourage. I was so intimidated, I couldn't look up or speak. All I could do was cry. There is a photo of me in the Dalai Lama's arms, and I am weeping. You might think, "But you've met countless heads of state, royalty, President Clinton!" But for me, meeting the Dalai Lama was ten times more overwhelming. His Holiness represents the sacred world of kindness and peace. I've since been privileged to have a handful of audiences with him, and I can still barely speak.

Even Stephan, who had resisted every spiritual path I explored, felt the powerful energy of being in the Dalai Lama's presence. The photo I have of the two of them is one of my most cherished possessions.

I won't say I found myself through all these journeys, because that may never happen, and anyway that isn't the goal. I was learning to *be* with myself and explore my feelings. I was giving birth to the seeker within and realizing there was more than one path to self-enlightenment. In the summer of 1992, I lost my most trusted guide. I was taking one of my solitary morning beach walks when my cell phone rang. The name Rath appeared on the caller ID, but it wasn't Dr. Rath. It was a woman, a family member—his wife? A daughter? A sister? I don't remember. It was so jarring, because as stupid as this sounds, I thought of him as *my* Dr. Rath, not a man with a family of his own.

"Donna, I'm sorry to tell you Frederick died yesterday," said the voice. "He'd been sick for a while. We wanted you to know as soon as possible." She may have told me about the services or where to make a donation, and then I thanked the woman, who clearly had more calls to make, and hung up.

I looked at the water and inhaled and exhaled deeply. My father, Anne Klein, now Dr. Rath . . . with a snap of the fingers, someone is gone. I hadn't seen Dr. Rath in a while; since moving to the city,

I no longer saw him every week, and we took a break in the summer. But we'd built a powerful bond over my twenty-plus years of treatment. He was a father figure, a confidant, and a dumping ground for all my personal relationships. I met him when I was Donna Faske, right before my marriage to Mark. He came to every show he could, and his stately gray hair, beard, tweeds, and pipe were a comforting presence in the crowd. People would often ask who he was, since he clearly wasn't part of the fashion scene. He would say he was my friend.

Now I was forced to continue the journey without him.

19 | LOSING CONTROL

Where I loved nature's calm side—its beaches, snow, sunrises, sunsets—Stephan loved its chaos. He adored the lightning, the roar, and the unpredictability of thunderstorms. He even enjoyed flying in turbulent air. For these reasons, we nick-named him "Storm."

Stephan loved racing because it was all about riding into the crazy wind. This passion went way back. In his early twenties, a long-haired Stephan drove a 1957 convertible, which he complained was "all show, no go." Then he got a racer, a 1950s Allard (a British roadster), and modified the body and the engine for racing by adding a roll bar, oversized cylinders, milled heads, and a blower (supercharger). Stephan raced the Allard at the Westhampton Drag-way in Long Island, as well as the racetrack in Lime Rock Park in Lakeville, Connecticut. At one point, he had a BSA motorcycle with "ape-hanger" handlebars (picture *Easy Rider*). My husband loved speed almost as much as he loved storms.

Stephan's fifty-sixth birthday was approaching, and for gift ideas I called our friend Jann Wenner, the co-founder and publisher of *Rolling Stone*. "I have to make it really good, Jann, because Stephan's not talking to me," I said. This wasn't unusual; Stephan was often not talking to me because of something or other I'd done.

"If you want to blow his mind," Jann said, "I know the perfect gift: a Ducati. That's his dream bike." Jann and Stephan shared a love of motorcycles. With Jann's help, I bought a fire-engine-red one and had it delivered to our beach house.

"Are you kidding me?" Stephan shouted when he saw it. "Oh my God, Donna!" He was ecstatic and couldn't wait to race it. It was more for me to worry about, but at least he was speaking to me again.

This was 1995, right around the time Stephan's cancer was discovered. He had a spot on his lung that had to be removed in what's called a sectionectomy. He made it seem simple and straightforward, like it was an average doctor's visit, no big deal. I was like a child with Stephan—he let me think everything was okay, that he had it under control. I believed that if anyone had the strength and power to control something, even cancer, it was him. Jane Chung, my DKNY daughter-in-design, was getting married, so we put off the surgery by a day to attend her wedding.

"I'm confident we got it all," the surgeon reported to me, the kids, and Patti and Harvey, who were with us in the waiting room at Memorial Sloan Kettering hospital. He told us that it had been a non-small-cell tumor and assured us there was no need for follow-up treatment. We cheered and high-fived one another. I was so relieved. My husband and I could get back to life and work. We didn't have time for a drawn-out illness. We had other problems to tackle.

———

Two years earlier, in 1993, Tomio and Frank had requested that we have lunch together at the Four Seasons Hotel. Our monthly partner meetings, usually held in my apartment, were stressful and antagonistic. Maybe a restaurant would set a different tone, I hoped.

"We are bleeding money and need to take action," one of them began.

It's going to be about selling the beauty company again, I thought.

"We can raise money in one of three ways," Tomio said. "We can take on another partner who can invest in the company, but I'm sure you don't want that any more than we do."

I shook my head. "Another partner is the last thing we need."

Tomio continued, "We can raise our debt by issuing corporate bonds, which has its own problems, including a very high interest rate."

"Or we can take the company public," Frank declared, as if it was all decided. "That would be the best course for all." He didn't say it, but it was obvious he wanted out, and going public would be a smooth and profitable way to break the partnership. Like Stephan, Frank was weary of the infighting.

Stephan nodded in that cool, confident way of his and said, "I've been talking to Bear Stearns myself to explore our options." Finally, it appeared, they agreed on something.

But I didn't. I felt like a child, stomping my foot. "No, no, no. We're not ready," I said. "This is way too premature." But no one was listening to me.

After a false start that year (we withdrew due to poor market conditions), we renewed our public offering in 1996 with Morgan Stanley leading the charge. I desperately wanted to maintain control over the company, and I learned that the way to do it was by getting super voting shares, which would give Stephan and me, the original owners, superior voting ability even as minority shareholders. But our bank said no. So instead of voting control, Stephan negotiated that we would receive royalties from the company for the continued use of my name. When we first opened the Donna Karan Company, we had created Gabrielle Studio, a separate entity, to protect my name, and when DKNY was founded and trademarked, we added that to Gabrielle Studio as well. From a business perspective, this was a very savvy move, as it gave us control over our labels, the most valuable part of our business. You couldn't have a Donna Karan New York or DKNY product unless it bore the name, which we owned, regardless of the IPO.

I learned in 1996 that an IPO involved a "road show," which was a traveling sales tour to introduce our company and product. We would be spending three weeks on the road—two weeks in the United States, one in Europe, twenty cities in all. I hadn't ever heard of such a thing, and besides, what did I know about talking to investors? So I did it my way: I took my Seven Easy Pieces and demonstrated the founding principles of our company, literally. We had a black velvet coat stand with my seven pieces hanging on it, and using myself as a model, I'd show how the system worked. I had practiced this demonstration on my personal trainer beforehand, and even he got it. I'd start with the bodysuit and hosiery, add a pant, then toss on a jacket. Or I'd try a skirt and a coat. Or I'd switch in an evening element for a nighttime look. The investors were captivated—in Paris, they even applauded. It was pure theater, and it was crazy. At one point during our travels, I got something stuck in my eye and had to wear an eye patch for a while, but I carried on with the demonstrations nonetheless.

Stephan didn't come with us, but he called constantly, yelling at me from afar. "Donna, stop being Donna. This is serious. We need you to be on point." Someone must have called him about my antics, like the time I sat alone on one of our planes and wouldn't open the doors, swearing I had had it and was going to take off without the rest of the group. I can be bratty when I'm tired or pushed to my limit, and this tour was driving me nuts. But I also had a huge revelation on that trip, which was that my system of dressing really worked! Here I was, traveling around the world, having to look polished and pulled together each and every day. And I pulled it off with just my seven or so easy pieces. I was a walking, breathing advertisement for my clothes.

On May 6, 1996, almost two months before we officially went public, *New York* magazine published a cover story entitled "Donna Karan: Corporate Goddess." In the picture, I looked like I was praying. The inside title was "Donna Karan Sells Her Soul," and the subhead read, "As her company is offered to the public by Wall Street for a second time, the New Yorkiest designer peddles spirituality as the essence of Karanism." The article claimed that many fashion critics thought my fall 1995 collection was dreary and peculiar, and worried that I was getting "weirder" just as our company was set to go public. People around me took huge offense, but I loved the cover. I thought I looked great, and I was proud to put my spirituality out there. I was owning my truth.

Also, that particular fall collection, which I called Modern Souls, remains one of my very favorites. Yes, it was mostly black, but it was as classic and sexy as it gets, featuring long ribbed cashmere tank dresses; simple, chic tailoring; and sequined evening pieces. I knew the real reason for the less-than-glowing reviews: the shoes. I'm not kidding. I had shown all flats—big mistake. If I pair something with a high heel, the press is happy. Flats, I'm in trouble.

I'd deliberate for hours over the shoes. After Dr. Rath died, I was seeing a therapist and healer named Anna Ivara. I would go into Anna's office with a tote bag full of shoes and muse about what kind of collection I wanted to do. Was I feeling more for a boot? A sandal? Or should I sex it up with a high heel? "You think this is easy?" I'd ask her. To me, shoes are the soul of a collection.

There I go again—anytime you use the words *soul* or *spiritual*, you get labeled a woo-woo. I was using those words a lot in those days (still do), and I didn't understand other people's resistance. Spirituality is life. Most people brush their teeth every day, and we can talk about that. And many if not most people pray every day, too, so why not talk about *that*?

But the marketplace is uneasy with a professional in search of spirituality, so I had to zip it up, however unnatural that felt. The irony was that I needed faith more than anything at that moment. Still, once a yogi, always a yogi. I am flexible and can do any pose asked of me—including breathing and standing still in the face of adversity.

The big day finally arrived: June 28, 1996. It was a Friday, which made sense—all my fashion shows were held on Fridays. I was excited, as it was the first time I'd ever been on Wall Street. A black-and-white Donna Karan flag hung outside the New York Stock Exchange to welcome us. Stephan, Frank, Tomio, Steve, our kids, my sister, and I all crowded onto the balcony of the exchange and took in the energy of the trading floor. I was scared I wasn't going to ring the bell correctly, but I did, at exactly 9:29:59 that morning. The sound reverberated in the room, igniting a frenzy. I bought the first hundred shares of Donna Karan International at $24 a share. We were off and running.

To celebrate, we rented a fabulous yacht and turned it into a floating party with our families, executives, and bankers—somewhere between fifty and seventy-five people. The champagne flowed, and we toasted ourselves, our future, and New York City.

That's the last good memory I have about going public.

Life had forever changed. The company was no longer my baby; it belonged to everyone else. Every quarter, we had phone calls with analysts and the financial press, in which we had to explain every bump and difficulty. Once a year we'd hold a shareholder meeting, where people all but threw rotten tomatoes at us. To make matters worse, everyone was angry about the money we were earning through Gabrielle Studio and the use of my name. My family and friends had all bought the stock and were watching its value slip while I was receiving royalty checks. Even Barbra was pissed at me, as she, too, had invested. Stephan and I had never felt so alone. We were living in a nightmare with no place to turn.

My biggest heartache of all was that my creative freedom had been stunted. From our very first seven easy pieces, our success was born out of following our gut, not following a strategy. I wanted to design menswear? I tried it out and put it on the runway. My friends were having babies? We created a kids' collection. Jane had an idea for DKNY? We ran with it. Creatively, we were very spontaneous, and that gave us the space to see what worked and what didn't. That's how we innovated. When you're playing with your own money, you can take chances. When you have shareholders, no one wants you off message.

In 1997, with a new corporate structure in place, we licensed DKNY Jeans, Active, and Juniors to Liz Claiborne. Next we sold the beauty business. Puig and Estée Lauder were vying to be our exclusive global licensee, and Estée Lauder made the offer we couldn't refuse. Transferring our beauty division to other hands was a hard one for Stephan, but we knew we were too young, too small, and too inexperienced to keep going. Being public didn't give us the time we needed to grow up properly. Estée Lauder understood the business better than anyone, and I knew we'd made the right decision, but we were giving our baby up for adoption, and that hurt.

Through all the turmoil of being a publicly held company, our design team was on a roll. Peter Speliopoulos had joined us as Collection's fashion director in 1993. A perfectionist, he had become my right arm, keeping the room and my design vision going. He loved classicism and artistry as much as I did when it came to fabrics and embellishments. Collection was getting fabulous reviews, and our advertising was hot and sexy: Demi Moore and Bruce Willis starred in our much-buzzed-about 1996 fall campaign. It featured one of my most treasured icons: the handcrafted velvet dévoré dress. That dress was a pure artistic expression and a joyful relief from all the negativity. It was a moment where I could revel in doing what I love best: creating.

I had another such moment in late 1996. We were invited to participate in the first Biennale di Firenze, a three-month exhibition fusing fashion and art that took place in nineteen museums across Florence. It was an amazing honor, as I was the only American included. Ingrid Sischy, the writer and longtime editor of *Interview* magazine, who became one of my closest friends, was one of the three curators. The exhibit would be called "Time and Fashion." Fashion designers were asked to collaborate with artists: Miuccia Prada with Damien Hirst, Helmut Lang with Jenny Holzer, Gianni Versace with Roy Lichtenstein, Jil Sander with Mario Merz, and Rei Kawakubo with Oliver Herring. I was given a historic charitable site, the Museo del Bigallo, across from the Duomo.

I worried I couldn't pull off an appropriate connection, but the minute I saw the Madonna and Child at the altar, I wanted to create angels floating from above, dressed in clothes that transcended the moment. My final statement was a trio of beautiful dévoré gowns, softly lit from the stained glass windows. Suspended from the vaulted ceiling, they cascaded down to fuse with the raw stones the chapel was built from. Even Stephan, who never felt fashion quite rose to the level of art, was impressed. That meant the world to me.

Business demands constantly brought me back to earth. In 1998 we introduced the Donna Karan Signature Collection—a less-expensive line of classic Donna Karan pieces produced in Italy. It was a huge hit, and it allowed us to take more risks on the designer side while giving our loyal customer the tailored work clothes she wanted from us. But it also meant that we had another design staff and business to manage.

Still, despite all our moves inside and out, the stock never regained its value. The figurative tomatoes kept coming at every annual meeting.

Emotionally, the period from 1996 to 2000 knocked the breath out of me. The company was reeling from changes. The press was attacking me left and right. I had to keep up appearances while still designing and producing collection after collection. I was constantly putting out fires and didn't have a moment to stop and reflect, let alone catch my breath. Patti kept having dreams that I was driving us down Fifth Avenue at high speed in a car with no brakes.

Of course, everyone pointed to the money Stephan and I were making. How could we not be thrilled? Who were we to complain about anything? But trust me, the cliché is true: money doesn't buy happiness. Of course I appreciate the money, and it offers a certain kind of freedom, but it's never been my motivation in my work or my marriages. The first time around, I married for security. Mark made me feel safe, not alone. I married Stephan for love, plain and simple. Now we had money to take extravagant trips, live in beautiful homes, and invest. We could help our children and relatives and not sweat our financial future. But I swear I would have traded this newfound wealth to go back to where we were: building our company and legacy on our own.

Once the beauty division was sold, Stephan had less to do at the company. He served on the board of directors with me and protected our interests. But Donna Karan International's legal and licensing divisions, which had been Stephan's domain, now reported to John Idol, our CEO since going public. It was the perfect time for him to return to his art.

Shortly after the IPO, Stephan had bought a two-story former refueling and repair building in Greenwich Village and turned it into the ultimate studio. The first floor, where he worked, featured an open space with twenty-two-foot ceilings; the second floor was an apartment loft we could escape to. The studio had a huge working brick fireplace and a dramatic arched panel window. The loft had a floor-to-ceiling paneled glass wall and doors that gave onto a magical rooftop garden with mature trees, also conceived and designed by Stephan. The studio was his haven, where he went every day. He was incredibly productive there.

But all was far from well. Cancer struck again, just three years after the first time. It was another small spot, but this one was on the other lung, and a primary cancer, meaning it was unrelated to the prior cancer. Surgery was scheduled to remove the spot quickly and effectively. We wondered if Stephan's cancers had been caused by his early cigarette smoking or by the asbestos he was exposed to at his family business. (In those days, theaters had asbestos curtains that would come down in the event of a fire to isolate the front of the house from the stage and backstage. Stephan told me he'd spent many hours rolling out, cutting, and sewing large panels of asbestos cloth.) Later, as an artist, he worked with Plexiglas, casting resins, and solvents that generated fairly toxic dust and fumes. Or maybe it was all his pot smoking. Who knows? Stephan had once had double pneumonia and a collapsed lung, so he was vulnerable to begin with. The cause was irrelevant; he had lung cancer, pure and simple.

For the second surgery, Stephan brought a zipper to his doctor and joked, "Close me up with this so you can save on all the stitching next time."

The night before, Stephan went out on his bike. His son Corey, his wife Suzanne, and their children, Etan and Maya Rose, were staying with us at the apartment. Maya Rose was a baby, and we had an intercom in their room. It must have been turned on, because all of a sudden I heard Stephan talking, probably to Corey. "I swear, I didn't see the car coming."

"Stephan? What are you talking about?" I yelled. I raced into the room, and there was Stephan with a leather jacket draped on his shoulders. He was trying to hide his injury from me, but I noticed the arm sling.

"I took a fall on the bike," he said by way of explanation. "They took me to the hospital, and it turned out I broke my collarbone and arm."

Rodney and Colleen Yee, Gabrielle Roth, and Christina Ong

With His Holiness the Dalai Lama

My Kabbalah teacher, Ruth Rosenberg

Meditating on my rock

Kabbalah leader and dear friend, Karen Berg

In Israel with friends Lisa Fox, Ruth Rosenberg and her husband, Moshe, and their daughters

With Sonja Nuttall in Indonesia

Renewing our vows on Parrot Cay—with Corey, Lisa, and Gabby

A family portrait from Gabby and Gianpaolo's wedding

Gabby and her bridal party

Me and my "baby"

With Gail and her family, from left: Barbara, Glen, Hank, me, Gail, Dawn, and Darin

With Gail, circa 2000

Lisa, Mackensie, and me after I broke my knee in Sun Valley

In Sun Valley, between broken knees

Our whole clan celebrating Corey's and Glen's birthdays in 2013

Corey, Gabby, Lisa, and me on Stephan's Larger than Life Apple sculpture

Gabby and her father, Mark Karan

Practicing yoga with my grandson Miles

My granddaughter Stefania in Parrot Cay

Celebrating Stephan's Dressage Horse

My favorite Annie Leibovitz portrait

Stefania and me taking a bow on the DKNY runway

My weekend joy: watching Stefania ride

Like father, like son

Sebastian on his way to Haiti

The Francis Bacon
painting I bought
for Stephan

In my East Hampton
spa house

A typical yoga class in the city (I wish)

The interior
of my
819 Madison
Avenue store

With architect
Dominic Kozerski
and a "Breath" chair

My bedroom in Parrot Cay

In my all-black city closet

With Gabby in Parrot Cay

The view from my bedroom

The Urban Warrior campaign,
shot in Morocco, fall 2001

Jeremy Irons and Milla Jovovich
in Vietnam, spring 2001

A dress with a Bill Morris
glass buckle, fall 2004

Demi Moore, fall 1996

A Black Cashmere fragrance ad

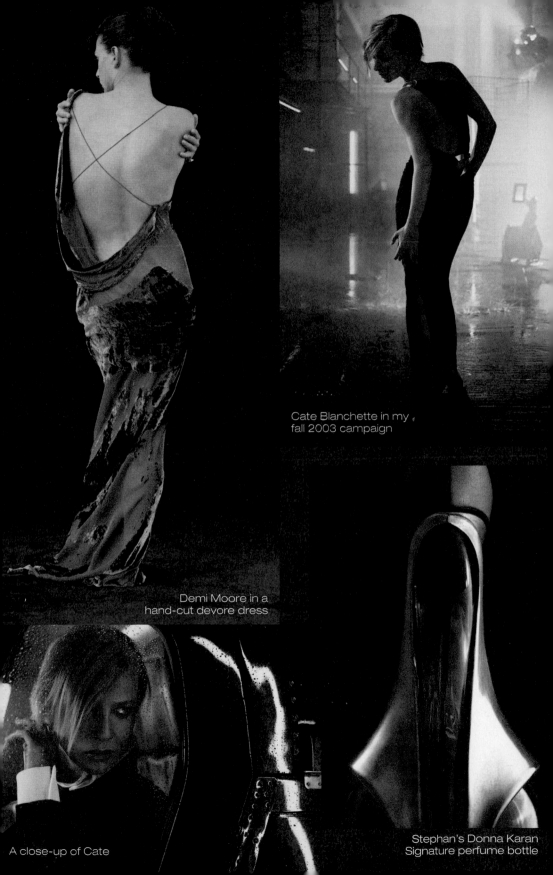

Cate Blanchette in my fall 2003 campaign

Demi Moore in a hand-cut devore dress

A close-up of Cate

Stephan's Donna Karan Signature perfume bottle

Rodney and Colleen teaching at Urban Zen

Rodney Yee, Colleen Saidman Yee, me, and a patient with Dr. David Feinberg of UCLA

The launch of Urban Zen

Cutting the ribbon at Beth Israel with Dr. Woody Merrell

Healer Ruth Pontivanne, who inspired the UZIT program

Urban Zen
clothes,
spring 2014

Balinese furniture at Urban Zen

An iconic Urban Zen
down-filled suede jacket

Haitian objects of desire
at Urban Zen

. . . inspired by robes in Bhutan

Donna Karan
dresses,
fall 2000 . . .

Making a friend in India

In India with a
matching cow

With John James (JJ) Biasucci

With BS Ong and Gabby in Nepal

Arriving in Jacmel, Haiti, to shoot a Donna Karan New York ad campaign

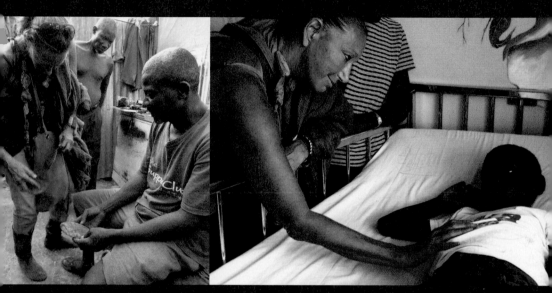

Working with a horn artisan in Haiti   Visiting St. Damien Pediatric Hospital in Port au Prince

With Sebastian in Haiti   "The Glossy Posse of Haiti," from right: Shelly Clay, Caroline Sada, me, Pascal Theard, Marni Lewis, Isabel Encinias, and Paula Coles

With Haitian artist
Philippe Dodard

With my close friend,
photographer Russell James

Ad campaigns shot in Haiti by Russell James

With Kevin Salyers
of Urban Zen

A sweet girl at
Caroline Sada's school
in Cité Soleil

With filmmaker and humanitarian,
Bryn Mooser

My dear friends
Sandra Brant and Ingrid Sischy

Zainab Salbi, founder of the
philanthropic organization
Women for Women

Lisa Evans and me wearing our
Not One More bracelets

With Uma Thurman at the
Stephan Weiss Apple Awards

Anna Wintour at the Apple Awards

With Deb and Hugh Jackman

President Clinton
accepting the
Stephan Weiss
Apple Award

Patti Hansen and Keith Richards

Stephan's Apple sculpture
in Hudson River Park

I was trying not to scream or cry, as I wanted to do both. But Stephan made me laugh instead by continuing with his story: "They took X-rays, and the doctor on duty comes in and says in this very serious voice, 'I don't know how to tell you this, sir, but while we were looking at your X-rays, we discovered—' So I interrupted him. 'Oh, that. That's my cancer. We're taking care of that tomorrow.'" Classic Stephan.

The next day, we "took care" of the cancer. The surgery was long and difficult. His oncology surgeon, Michael Burt, told us, "We got it all," but I couldn't, wouldn't, didn't, trust that it was true. When Stephan woke up in the recovery room, I was sobbing by his side. "What are you crying about?" he snapped. He hated it when I cried, maybe because it reflected his own fears. After he was fully awake, he told me that he had passed to the other side at one point and had an out-of-body experience. That put the fear of God into me, but I did my best to be cheery around him. I even brought a photo of his beloved Ducati to the hospital so he'd feel right at home.

We were still painting the black apartment in the San Remo at this point, so Stephan came home to our old place on East 70th Street. There, in front of our building, I had a present waiting for him: a fire-red Lamborghini Diablo.

"You have the bike," I said. "I figured you want the car, too."

I know, I know, it was over the top, and totally ridiculous. But I kept thinking, *What can I possibly give him to compensate for what he's going through? What will make him light up?* I did what I always do when I want to comfort: I switched into mothering mode. I spoiled him. Money can't buy health any more than it can buy happiness, but it can make a childhood dream come true. (Actually, the car of his dreams was taxicab yellow, so he exchanged it.) They say the difference between men and boys is the size of their toys. I planned to shower Stephan with big toys and all my love for as long as I could.

20 | SEEING THE WORLD

Stephan loved big toys, but I've always loved big experiences. My greatest luxury is traveling the world. The farther away, the more exotic, and the more ancient the culture, the better. I could easily spend the rest of my life going from one new place to another, exploring and discovering. This is a relatively new passion for me. For most of my adult life, I was busy raising a child, building a business, working around the clock, and then, after our company went public, answering to shareholders. I was lucky to take a week off. But I was determined to change my ways. None of us knows what the future holds. That's one thing Stephan's cancer taught me.

––––––––––

Like New York, Europe was a place for work. As much as I loved my fabric-buying trips to Germany, Italy, France, and England, they were for business. In and out was the name of the game. I was always on a tight schedule, rushing from one fabric house to the next, one city to another. If there was time, I'd check out a hot store, hit a flea market or an exhibit, and then grab a nice dinner and jet home.

The one time we would take it easy was when we visited my friend Andrea Pfister and Jean-Pierre Dupre, his life and business partner, in Italy. Andrea and I had become extremely close when he designed shoes for me and Louis at Anne Klein. The couple lived in a cliffside villa on the Amalfi coast. You've never seen such a glorious place, and since they were such dear friends, we'd stop there regularly when in Europe. Stephan gave me my engagement ring on their balcony overlooking the sea. Over the years, we've visited them with friends including Patti and Harvey and Barbra Streisand. Years later, Gabby met her future husband, Gianpaolo de Felice, at a seaside restaurant on the island of Ischia while styling a story about Andrea and Jean-Pierre's home for the *New York Times*.

Our travels in the United States were pure fun and relaxation. Sometimes we'd motorcycle up the West Coast, just the two of us. After a show, we'd go to Canyon Ranch in Tucson, Arizona, where we'd sign up for eight-hour hikes in the mountains with our favorite hiking instructor, Molly Elgin. They were tough walks at high elevations, and I loved being outside and breathing fresh air after weeks of intense stress. Nothing beats the quiet, the physical challenge, and the perspective you gain when you look up at an enormous tree and realize it's been there for hundreds of years, majestically growing taller and taller. Did I mention I'm a tree hugger? My juicing friend Pam introduced me to the concept on a hike in Sedona, Arizona. I will stop and literally hug a tree to feel its calm and comfort. I have a tree in Central Park that calls my name, kind of like my rock on the beach. Nature humbles you. It reminds you that you're only here for a little while, and that each day is a wondrous gift to enjoy.

In the '90s, we took lots of vacations with the kids and grandkids (by now Corey and Lisa had given us five: Maya Rose, Etan, Mackensie, Miles, and Mercer), mostly out west, where we'd go paragliding and whitewater rafting. For the holidays, we'd rent an enormous house in Aspen or Vail, Colorado, and later in Sun Valley, Idaho. Gabby's longtime boyfriend, Kenny Thomas, who designed for Ralph Lauren, would come as well. We brought many friends on these getaways, too, including Barbra and her friend the composer and producer Richard Baskin, Patti and Harvey, Bernadette Peters, and Lynn Kohlman and her husband, Mark Obenhaus. Susie Lish, our fabulous chef and caretaker, who has been a part of the family since we started the Donna Karan business when Gabby was ten years old, would go in advance to set things up so it really felt like home.

We made wonderful friends on these trips. Demi Moore and Bruce Willis, of course, whom we met in Sun Valley at Bruce's club, Mint. Arnold Schwarzenegger and Maria Shriver, who had a huge holiday party in Sun Valley every year. (Once Susie sent us with a coconut cake, and Clint Eastwood had a slice and asked, "Who made this cake? I want to marry her!") Sometimes Jamie Curtis would stop by, and we'd all wind up in the kitchen cooking dinner together. The mood was always friendly, warm, and easygoing, and the scenery was magical: snow, snow, snow, and more snow, with amazing mountain views and huge moose wandering outside our windows—surreal stuff for New Yorkers. We'd ski all day, then come back to the house and collapse in our long johns, drink hot chocolate, sit around the fire, and sing. The only person not singing, of course, was Barbra. She never sings in public, and that includes in a house full of people. You can't even play a recording of her music if she's there.

"Oh, come on, Barbra, it's no big deal," I said one time.

"You think it's so easy? Why don't you sing?" So I serenaded her, along with Liza Minnelli.

On this trip, Liza had called from Aspen and asked if she could come stay with us. There were demonstrations going on in the town (who knows about what) and she was uncomfortable there. She arrived with Billy Stritch, her good friend and accompanist, who played the grand piano while Liza and I sang "My Funny Valentine," teasing Barbra. She didn't care. Instead of singing, Barbra and Richard performed card tricks for the group. We had a blast that week. Stephan spent the whole time wearing a sarong and a garrison (military) belt because the *New York Times* had made fun of me for putting them in our menswear show. I remember laughing nonstop— until we got a phone call from Kenny. Gabby was in the hospital with a ruptured cyst on her ovary, and she needed surgery.

I ran to the hospital, which was somewhere out in the boondocks, raced into Gabby's room, and all but threw myself on top of her. Barbra and Liza, all bundled up in ski clothes, followed me into the room looking very concerned. By that time, seeing Barbra and Liza together was perfectly normal to me, but not to the average hospital nurse or attendant. Hushed crowds gathered, straining their necks to get a better view.

My fiftieth birthday was coming up, and Stephan suggested that we take a boat trip to Greece. Boats are my idea of heaven. (Barbra introduced me to the indulgence, along with my other ridiculous addiction: private planes.) Why boats? They're like floating hotels. You never have to unpack, put on makeup, or even wear clothes. Slip on a swimsuit and you're done—the freedom of that alone! There's also a feeling of getting away from it all, something I'm great at once I leave New York. For my fiftieth, Barbra and her husband, James Brolin, joined us, as did my spa and travel buddy, Linda Horn, and her husband, Steve. Talk about a wonderful memory. Stephan's cancer was under control (or so we thought), and we could really relax and enjoy ourselves, island-hopping and having leisurely lunches and dinners at sea.

Not long after that, we were in Cabo San Lucas, Mexico, with Barbra and Jim at some over-the-top luxurious villa. One morning Barbra took a sip of coffee, leaned back, and said, "Boy, do I love vacations, especially when I'm not paying for them."

"What do you mean?" I asked. I was genuinely confused. I thought we were splitting everything.

"Our investment paid for this one."

"You mean *my* investment?"

"Exactly. The one that *I* made for you."

"What investment?" Stephan asked, alarm rising in his voice.

I should say here that Barbra is an excellent investor. She has a real talent for day trading, and her returns are incredible. One day I'd had an idea: "Barbra, let me give you $1 million to invest, and see what you can do." Don't ask me how I got the million without telling Stephan, but I did. And now, in front of Stephan, Barbra was luxuriating in the profits ($800,000 in five months, she made sure to point out).

I yelled at Barbra, and Stephan yelled at me. All while on a fabulous vacation in Mexico.

Barbra is my BFF, my soul sister. We're like Lucy and Ethel, connected on some deep level. We love to hang out in each other's closets, shopping, playing, and dressing up. We can disagree, but I don't see her often enough to be mad at her. Besides, we're too busy planning our next adventure. Our vacation styles are polar opposites. While I can let everything go, Barbra is constantly plugged in, calling her office, sending emails, and reading scripts. And as I've said before, her fans are *everywhere*. One time we were on a boat in the middle of the Aeolian Islands. There wasn't another soul in sight except for a couple in a small fishing boat. Within two seconds, they were pointing to us and saying Barbra's name. And when we go out for dinner? Forget about it. I could be wearing pink pajamas with elephants on them, and no one would care. All eyes, ears, and conversation are directed at her: "Barbra, Barbra, Barbra!" In any language, it's exhausting to be Barbra.

You'd think I'd pack light on all these trips, throwing my swimsuit and sandals in a bag and hitting the road. But no. I bring everything, just in case. I'm famous for FedExing my luggage to my destination and then not opening it once I'm there (Patti can attest to this). My overpacking drove Stephan nuts. He was forever making fun of my "Seven Easy Pieces of Luggage" or my "Seven Easy Trunks." I think of him every time I zip up an extra bag or nearly throw my back out trying to close an overstuffed suitcase.

After all this vacationing—a week here, ten days there—I still hadn't taken on Asia, not really. We had gone on many business trips there over the years. Having Japanese-born Tomio Taki as a partner gave me, Stephan, Patti, and Harvey a front-row seat to the wonders of Japan and its neighboring countries. But I never had time to immerse myself in far-flung cultures just to soak up inspiration.

I'll tell you who *did* have the time: my alter ego Bonnie Young. Bonnie joined us in 1992 as Collection's director of fabric development, which meant she was in charge of sourcing and innovating fabrics. I had met Bonnie through Gabby, whose boyfriend, Kenny, had worked with her at Ralph Lauren. About four years into working with us, she came into my office and said she'd been offered a position at Prada, one that would give her a lot of travel opportunities.

"But you travel here," I said, not understanding.

"To Europe, yes. But I want to travel the world and be inspired."

"You and me both," I said, laughing. This was right after the IPO, and I longed to be anywhere but where I was. So maybe I was projecting my own wanderlust onto Bonnie, but I also didn't want to lose her talent and unique, creative eye for fabrics and details. So I came up with what would be *my* dream job. "I'll tell you what. Do it for me. Travel the world and bring it back to New York. Be my eyes and ears. Source what you can, and come back with boards to inspire us."

"Seriously?"

"Seriously."

Bonnie signed on immediately as director of global inspiration, and her first trip covered Tibet, Nepal, and China. She brought her boyfriend, Rudy, with her, as it was safer at the time to travel with a man, and he helped schlep her bags and carry her various finds.

I know, I know, *she* should have been paying *me*, right? But most design houses have some version of a Bonnie, and to be fair, this was incredibly hard work. She still sourced fabrics and was on the front line for our next collections. Fashion is insane that way. Designers work on many seasons all at once. You're preparing for your spring runway show at the same time you're publicizing fall's deliveries as they're going into the stores. Somewhere in there you're also creating mood boards for summer and purchasing fabrics for resort. It's totally schizophrenic.

Bonnie brought back a treasure trove of ideas and set up her office like a flea market filled with Tibetan monks' robes, ancient jewelry, hand-sewn leather, ceremonial wigs, embroidered fabrics, and photos everywhere. She also made a film, so we could see and experience where the many artifacts in the room came from. Her eye was extraordinary.

Gabby had recently graduated from New York University and started assisting Bonnie on her trips. They went to Asia, West Africa, the North Pole, and Papua New Guinea. All this inspirational traveling was paying off. Every time they returned, the design elements they found would work their way into the clothes by way of colors, textures, shapes, or embroideries. Not in a literal sense, mind you. I don't like costumes. I design modern clothes for modern lifestyles. To me, inspiration is the inhale: you breathe in the beauty, the richness, the culture. And the clothes are the exhale: the real-life translation into pieces you can wear to work or walking down city streets. In most cases, you would never have a clue what inspired me. It could be anything from colors found in a Moroccan spice market to a handwoven Balinese basket to a particular stitch on a vintage jacket found at a Paris flea market.

Bonnie's presentations only intensified my own desire to travel, so I called Christina Ong, my London and Asian retail partner, for ideas. Christina lives in Singapore and travels the world. She and her husband, Beng Seng, whom everyone calls "BS," had been helping Bonnie and Gabby on their trips. Without missing a beat, she told me I must see Bali. "I'll take care of everything," she assured me.

I had very romantic notions about Bali and kept humming "Bali Hai" from the musical *South Pacific* as Stephan and I packed. After the twenty-four-hour journey, we arrived at the beautiful airport in Denpasar, Bali's capital. We had no sooner left the airport when we hit bumper-to-bumper traffic, with billboards and storefronts everywhere you looked. It was Bali LA, not the Bali Hai from my childhood dreams. I was so disappointed.

I called Christina. "I had this whole other vision of Bali—one of natural, unspoiled land," I said. "Does that not exist anymore?"

She got it immediately. "I'm sending you up to Ubud," she said. "That's the place for you, I promise."

Stephan and I took the two-hour drive high into the hills of central Bali to the private villas of Christina's friend Amir Rabik, which were part of his home. It was nighttime, so I couldn't see anything. I went into the bathroom, where I discovered a tarantula on the floor and screamed. "Where's my nature girl now?" Stephan kidded me. I could hardly sleep. But the next morning, when I looked around at the peaceful green hills and smelled the fresh, fragrant air, I knew I'd landed in paradise. That's when my real journey began.

This was in 1997, and my connection with Bali was immediate and visceral. I felt like I had come home. I still fantasize about moving my family there and calling it a day. I could carry on about the lush peaks and rice paddies as far as the eye can see, but it's the people who speak to my heart. They're warm, wonderful, hospitable, and lovely. And, just as impressive, they preserve their culture through creativity and commerce in the most seamless way. Their land is part of their lifestyle and export businesses, from agriculture to artisan furnishings. The culture awakened something in me. I didn't start Urban Zen until years later, but a tiny seed had been planted.

My connection to Bali was meant to be. The karma was everywhere: Bali's license plates all begin with DK (I even saw a DKCK, which I photographed to show Calvin). The clincher for Stephan was that Bali is motorcycle heaven, as bikes are the primary means of getting around on the island. "Tell me we aren't meant to live here permanently," I said to him as we rode past rice paddies on a borrowed bike one afternoon. He was just as smitten as I was.

Christina and BS soon joined us and insisted that we see the Begawan Giri Estate, which overlooks the Ayung River. A man named Bradley Gardner had created this luxurious hotel on a hill, with five houses inspired by the elements: air, water, earth, wind, and fire. When I saw it, I felt once again like my soul had come home. It was pure nirvana. We walked down the 140 steps to the river, passing many ponds along the way. At one point I found myself floating in a pond, enveloped in endless greenery, and a remarkable calm came over me. I'd never experienced anything like it before. I felt as if I was being held and caressed by God—it was that spiritual a moment. I was so at peace I couldn't get out of the water.

While we were there, we found out Begawan Giri was for sale. I wanted to invest, but Stephan put the kibosh on that immediately. Fortunately, Christina and BS bought the place themselves. Today, the estate is a wellness resort called Como Shambhala, and it's my absolute favorite place in the world. I try to go there every year or two.

Since that trip, Christina has become one of my closest friends. We couldn't be more different: she's soft-spoken and reserved (words never used to describe me, that's for sure). But we're both Libras, so my theory is that we balance each other: East meets West, yin and yang. Like me, Christina is a creative businesswoman who loves her family more than anything. She also has a passion for artisan culture that takes her to every corner of the world. She's had a profound influence on my life. Not only did she introduce me to Bali, but she introduced me to Parrot Cay, as well as to my yoga teacher, Rodney Yee.

Quiet as Christina is, my outgoing personality doesn't faze her at all, and I'll tell you why: her husband, BS, is a bat out of hell. A global entrepreneur and utter genius, he never stops for a minute. In him, I have met my ADD match. Honestly, he makes me look relaxed and focused. I have been on planes with BS where he changes his mind about which country to land in. Stephan adored BS, and the group of us—Christina, BS, me, Stephan, Bonnie, and Gabby—started to travel together in various combinations.

BS took us to Nepal, Vietnam, Cambodia, Singapore, the Philippines, Burma, and Bhutan. BS is such a crazy traveler, he'd have us visit North Vietnam in the morning and South Vietnam in the afternoon. His tours were impressionistic and passionate; he wasted no time, knowing just what to do in each and every place. With each stop, I fell deeper and deeper in love with the East and its serene spirituality, aesthetic sensibility, and artisan craftsmanship. It spoke to me on a very deep level.

Bonnie calls BS a one-man travel boot camp. Every morning he gave us an itinerary. Here first, there next, and then over there. Once Bonnie, Gabby, and I planned a trip to Bhutan with BS, and here's how it unfolded: the girls and I flew from New York to London and then to Delhi, India, where we stopped to do some furniture shopping, then on to Nepal, where we met BS and Christina. We were in Nepal for what felt like just minutes, though we managed to buy some fabric and silver for inspiration. Then we were off to Bhutan, the most beautiful country imaginable. The next morning, we climbed an hour up a hill to see these amazing prayer flags. As soon as we reached the top and looked at them, BS said, "Okay, time's up. Gotta go. Plane's waiting." I'm exaggerating, but not by much.

Then we flew back to Milan, Italy, where we caught up with Bonnie and Gabby's new boyfriends at the time, Luca and Gianpaolo. We spent the night doing a fashion show for them at the Hotel Principe di Savoia with all the dusty, musty ethnic pieces we'd picked up in various village markets, and they thought we were crazy. This entire trip happened over a matter of days, not weeks. But Bonnie and I were good at cramming it in. We once went on a forty-eight-hour shopping spree in Istanbul because we had a weekend to kill between fabric meetings in Milan.

My first trip to India was with Bonnie and Gabby in November 1999. We arrived in Delhi, and once again I was disappointed. It looked like Miami or some other modern urban mecca. We went into a fabric store (one of the most remarkable places I've ever been—it was like Première Vision, the legendary semiannual fabric show in Paris, but all under one roof), and I groused to the owner that my first impression of India did not live up to the more romantic, cultural mecca of my mind. "Where is the magical India I've imagined my whole life?" I asked this chic-looking Indian man.

"You need to go to Varanasi," he said matter-of-factly. "Go there, and I'll meet you." His name was Babba, and we didn't know him from Adam, but that didn't stop me.

"Let's go now!" I said enthusiastically before Gabby or Bonnie could object.

Varanasi, an ancient living city on the banks of the Ganges, was surreal in every way, and it far, far, far surpassed my imagined ideal of India. It is a spiritual destination for Hindus, who flock there in great numbers because they believe that bathing in the polluted waters of the river will absolve them of their sins. It's also a place to die. More than two hundred bodies are burned daily in cremation ceremonies, which I found fascinating—and a bit macabre. (I called Patti in New York to describe what I was seeing, and she said she was getting sick just from hearing about it.) I couldn't stop photographing everything I saw. Bonnie snapped a picture of me wearing all white and talking to a white cow. That night, Babba treated us to the most magical evening I've ever experienced on a trip. He took us by boat up the Ganges, which was lit with floating candles because of a festival going on. We arrived at a temple with roses strung from ceiling to floor and a lavish dinner set up just for us. Flutes played Indian music. I think there was even a snake charmer and a couple of men standing on their heads. You would have thought an Indian princess was getting married.

"You wanted authentic," Babba said. We also wanted his fabric, and returned to his Delhi store and practically bought out the place. He was no fool, this businessman.

Try as we might not to stand out when traveling, we always do. Especially when we're loaded down with luggage. Once Bonnie and I had to dash to make a train in Tokyo. In Japan, everything is neat and orderly. There was this nice, single-file line for the train, and no one was carrying packages of any kind; women just held their little purses. Cut to me and Bonnie juggling five enormous suitcases, boxes, and God knows what else, with porters trying to help us. It took forever to explain to the conductor that, yes, we needed *all* of it with us in our seats. We later found out that everyone thought we were making a movie. But that's the thing about traveling: you are on an adventure, but you still have to get your work done. Train and plane time is working time.

My passion for the East thoroughly transformed my design aesthetic. My clothes had always combined American and ethnic elements, but now they became more streamlined, with origami folds and other Asian accents. My mission was to infuse the ancient beauty of the East with the modernity of the West, and that's where the name Urban Zen came from. For me, it's as much a way of life as it is a design vision. At that moment, I had no idea just how far I would take it.

———————

Now that I was venturing outside of New York, I wanted the Donna Karan woman, my customer, to do the same. My design was still urban in spirit and function, but I wanted to show that, like me, this woman was on a journey of passion and inspiration. So for spring 1997, we shot the ever-amazing Iman in Red Rock Canyon National Conservation in Nevada. I wanted to convey a sense of artisan simplicity connected to the earth. The palette was tribal and tactile, the silhouette long, lean, and timeless. That collection was full of body-conscious jerseys that could fold up into nothing in a suitcase and be dressed up or down, the kind of easy, versatile clothes I personally needed more and more (not that they made my suitcases any slimmer).

On the other end of the spectrum, for fall 1999 we did dramatically sculpted and molded felted clothes with shapes that stood away from the body. Full skirts with nipped-in waists. Cocoon coats. Strapless dresses. The landscape in the ads needed to complement these strong silhouettes. Trey and Hans, our creative directors, were all set to photograph the clothes in the salt flats in Death Valley National Park in California. But as with our presidential ad campaign in 1992, inspiration struck me late at night. Just a few days before the scheduled shoot, I called Trey. "I'm feeling for frozen, not desert. You know, icebergs. I think it will make a lot more sense for these clothes. What can we do?"

Trey took a deep breath—starting with Stephan, that's how the smart men in my life have always handled my big ideas—and said, "Let me get back to you." And he did, with creativity and enthusiasm. Trey and Hans canceled the Death Valley shoot and took the clothes to Greenland instead. You've never seen such inspiring photos. The landscape was lunar and starkly beautiful—the perfect backdrop.

My fall 2000 collection was inspired by red Bhutanese monks' robes, and the clothes were so sexy, so body-conscious—so un-monk-like—that we photographed the ads in Paris with Milla Jovovich, an actress and model I love, and the sexy, edgy British actor Gary Oldman. It was a sizzling campaign showing a hot couple driving in the rain, Milla in a soft red dress and Gary in a black jacket and open-collared white shirt. A year later, in one of my all-time favorite campaigns, the Donna Karan woman went to Vietnam for spring 2001, with Milla Jovovich looking sultry in chiffon bias slip dresses and Jeremy Irons in easy linen suits and cotton shirts.

The very next season, our woman went seductively native in a collection I called Urban Warrior, featuring earthen-colored raw-cut shearlings, handknit sweaters, and bias-cut body jerseys, all accented at the hip with Robert Lee Morris low-slung belts with antiqued brass hardware. For that campaign, we photographed the actress and model Amber Valletta in a tented camp in the Moroccan desert with, once again, Jeremy Irons (I had a huge crush on him). I was desperate to bring our woman to other parts of Africa, but it never happened, despite a fun-filled casting call in Cape Town—more on that later.

My imagination was soaring. I was living in the world now and constantly seeking my next adventure, but always bringing it home to New York City in a real and urban way.

The only time I had trouble unplugging from my life was in the summer, because I knew the European fashion shows were right after Labor Day. This was frustrating, mostly because we Americans were always accused of copying what had just come down the Paris and Milan runways. (As if it were humanly possible to design and sew a copycat collection in a week!) So I was always a little anxious at this time of year. Then in 1999, Helmut Lang, an Austrian designer based in New York City, launched a movement to have the U.S. market show first, and got enough support to make the switch. Yes, it killed our summer vacations, especially August. We had less time to design, and even less time to get our fabrics delivered. But the great news was that I stopped worrying about what the French or Italians were doing. I now had permission to rent a boat with Barbra and not so much as open a newspaper. That was a vacation in and of itself.

On the surface, all these trips were a form of escape. Helming a public company was one of the most challenging things I had ever done. I lived in fear of Stephan's next scan, even though his cancer had been quiet for a few years. And Gabby was grown up and out of the house and didn't need me in any real sense. But my travels were about so much more than escaping. With each new adventure, I was sinking deeper and deeper into myself. That's what happens when you go to a place where no one knows you or your brand. You're not performing for anyone but yourself, and you remember how to be a child with a sense of wonder and discovery. You experience awe in the most profound sense, and it's the most addictive drug of all. I still had so much traveling ahead of me—multiple trips to Africa, Israel, the Middle East, Indonesia—and I've barely touched my bucket list, which includes Russia, China, Tibet, Cuba, South America, and the North and South Poles.

To this day, my favorite trip is the one I haven't taken, and my favorite moment is the one when I arrive.

21 | CREATE, COLLABORATE, CHANGE

To explain my passion for philanthropy, I have to jump back to the mid-1980s. Nothing prepared any of us in the fashion industry for the AIDS crisis. All of a sudden young, vibrant men were getting horribly sick. You'd see a lesion, hear a cough, watch someone get skinny and old before your eyes, and within months, if not weeks, you'd be attending their funeral. Assistants, designers, executives, editors—everyone was impacted. It was terrifying, and we couldn't ignore it. The majority of the country at that time considered it a "gay" problem, so help was slow on the national front. But to me, fashion was the ultimate gay community. If we didn't do something to raise consciousness and money, who would?

Every problem has a creative solution, and I had an idea. In 1986, I called a meeting with Perry Ellis, then president of the CFDA. I liked Perry. He was young, gracious, and lovely to deal with, and I admired his clothes and the fresh energy he brought to fashion. I knew he was going through a rough time—his partner, Laughlin Barker, had died in January of that year, and many speculated it was from AIDS. As I sat in Perry's impressive wood-paneled office, I couldn't help noticing the lesions on his face.

"Perry, are you okay?" I asked gently.

"I'm allergic to cucumbers," he said, pointing to his face. "Can you believe it?"

I paused, then let it go. We were friends, but not close enough for me to press the point. Instead, I jumped into my idea.

"Perry, this AIDS epidemic is everywhere," I said. "It's literally killing our industry. We've got to do something as a community to show our support." I started to talk faster because I could feel him shutting down. "I have this idea. Let's open a shop. We all have so much stuff in our design rooms, so much extra stock. All the money can go to AIDS. We can start with a prototype in New York and open up several across the country."

He looked at me without expression. "AIDS is a private issue, Donna," he said. "I don't think we should be putting it out there." His clipped voice signaled that the discussion was over.

Perry died a couple of months later. Two weeks before, at his show on May 8, he had been too weak to walk the runway. His office would not confirm that his death was related to AIDS. He was forty-six years old.

Meanwhile, men continued to die all around us. I didn't lose anyone particularly close, but I went to many a memorial. These were young men in their twenties, thirties, and forties—they had no business dying. It was making me crazy.

After Perry died, I took my fundraising store idea to Carolyne Roehm, the newly appointed president of the CFDA's board of directors (I was on the board). I also went to Anna Wintour. After countless conversations, Carolyne and Anna called a meeting and explained that they saw it more as an evening than as a store. Fine with me, I told them; whatever it took. "Let's do this!" Anna said, slapping her desk. We'd call it Seventh on Sale. The CFDA and *Vogue* would sponsor, and I would co-chair. We'd have a dinner—we had to feed people—but we agreed it would be more about the shopping, a flea market of the highest order, with all designer clothes, all at a discount, and all proceeds going to the New York City AIDS Fund to benefit HIV/AIDS organizations.

This was 1990. Donna Karan New York was flying high, DKNY was being born, and every day at work brought a drama of one sort or another. I needed a major event like I needed a hole in my head. But I threw myself into Seventh on Sale with all my heart, and so did everyone around me. The generosity of spirit and resources was astounding. Every American designer asked how he or she could contribute. *Vogue* brought in the European designers, who were just as generous. Even the stores—which, let's face it, had a lot to lose with this shop-till-you-drop event—signed on. There was no push-back.

The CFDA and *Vogue* served as command central. We picked a Thursday in November and secured the 69th Regiment Armory on Lexington Avenue between East 25th and 26th Streets, a huge space. We decided to create a market environment around the center of the space, where we would do the dinner. Robert Isabell, the premier party planner of the time, was in charge of the design, and came up with the brilliant stroke of hanging drapes around the dining area, which we would raise after all the shopping. We wanted to stress the shopping first and foremost.

Egos were put aside, and we had fun. Ralph Lauren was extraordinary. Among his many contributions, he handled the entire back end and retail logistics (because no one understands retail better than Ralph). Alfredo Paredes, the creative genius at Ralph, was particularly remarkable with his vision and management. Everyone was engaged and passionate. The day before the event, Stephan came with me to see the space. I was unpacking clothes in the DKNY booth when he ran over to me, alarm on his face.

"We've got a serious problem," he said. "The curtains are not fire-retardant, and you have candles on every table. This is a tinderbox.

The Fire Department will shut us down." Given his experience with his family theater-curtain business, he knew what he was talking about. Stephan wasn't prone to hysterics, but he looked pretty hysterical then.

I went straight to Robert Isabell. Robert was a smooth operator—he'd have to be, given all his high-end clients. In a rush of words, I explained the problem.

"Have you told anyone else?" he asked.

"No, I came to you first. But we have to do something immediately. The whole fashion industry and every big name in New York is coming here tomorrow night."

A sneer formed on his handsome face, and he stepped in close to me. "Listen to me," he said in a dark voice. "*Leave it*. Just leave it alone." Robert's voice was so menacing that I shivered. Who knew the boogeyman of my childhood would come to life in the form of a high-society party planner? I backed away from him, but not from the problem. I told everyone. Someone suggested I call Ian Schrager, the hotelier and former co-owner of Studio 54. He would know about parties and fire prevention. And he did. I don't recall the particulars, but we flew up some guys from Texas who sprayed the curtains with fire retardant just in time for the event.

The event was perfection. Guests were dressed to the nines, and the cash registers rang all night. Personally, I had a blast. I was going through a short phase—my hair was short and I wore a platinum sequined mini dress. Most unexpected for me was the fun of shopping other designers. Bill Blass personally helped me at his booth, steering me to a black frou-frou dress (he knew my color). I tried it on and bought my first Bill Blass original.

After the Thursday dinner event, Seventh on Sale opened to the public. We sold tickets for three-hour shopping slots spread over the next three days. The lines went around the block to Park Avenue. Designers and retailers replenished their stock, so there was a constant influx of new merchandise. More than anyone, Anna Wintour, a true leader, was there day and night, night and day, personally overseeing details big and small. We raised $4.2 million in three and a half days.

Now I was juiced. This was my first taste of philanthropy and conscious consumerism. A world of possibility opened to me. Up until then, charity events had been self-congratulatory affairs. You bought a table, got dressed up, and listened to speeches as you ate rubber chicken. At Seventh on Sale, the dinner was the least of it. To see people rolling up their sleeves and physically moving—well, it just warmed my ADD heart.

Thanks to Anna Wintour, three years later I had the pleasure of getting involved with Kids for Kids, the NYC street carnival to benefit the Elizabeth Glaser Pediatric AIDS Foundation. Elizabeth Glaser was the wife of the actor Paul Michael Glaser. In 1981, she contracted the HIV virus through a blood transfusion after giving birth to the couple's daughter Ariel. The virus was transmitted to Ariel, who tragically died in 1988. Elizabeth and her two close friends, Susie Zeegen and Susan DeLaurentis, created a foundation to support pediatric HIV/AIDS research, as little to no research was being done at that time.

I so admired that Elizabeth was unafraid to be a face for AIDS, which in the late 1980s was as much a stigma as it was a disease. For a prominent wife and mother to come forth that way completely changed the perception of AIDS. It was no longer a gay issue; it was an everyone issue. I loved Elizabeth on a personal level, too. She was from Hewlett, one of the Five Towns, and so was Susie Zeegan, one of her co-founders. We were the same age, but we had never met. We were determined to create the coolest street fair this city had ever seen, with loads of things to do, eat, and buy, and fun activities for every age.

On a Sunday in April 1993, we set up our carnival in front of Industria Studio in Greenwich Village. Once again, thanks to Anna Wintour's passion and influence, everyone showed up with a generous spirit. Famous artists like Roy Lichtenstein, Francesco Clemente, and Red Grooms painted with kids. Photographers organized by Fabrizio took portraits. Coach Pat Riley of the Knicks brought basketball players to shoot hoops with kids. Fashion designers and celebrities like Richard Gere, Susan Sarandon, and Tim Robbins manned the booths, and we all wore the colorful T-shirts our company contributed. I can still see Stephan walking around with alternating grandkids on his shoulders. That's what I loved most about the day: it brought families together to raise money and encouraged children's involvement in helping others. We raised about $1.2 million that first year (Kids for Kids has gone on to raise $26 million to date). In the process, I made so many new friends, starting with Elizabeth and Susie, my new buddies. After that first carnival, I sent each a photo of the three of us with a caption that read, "Amazing what three girls from the Five Towns can do."

While Anna Wintour was the first co-chair for Kids for Kids, Liz Tilberis, my friend and the editor in chief of *Harper's Bazaar*, co-chaired the second. Liz was one of the kindest, least pretentious women I've ever known. We first met in London at a dinner party where Liz, then editor in chief of *British Vogue*, was seated next to me and Patti. In 1992, Liz came to New York with her family to shake up *Harper's Bazaar*, which she transformed with her usual flair. The first issue announced, "Enter the Era of Elegance," next to a striking shot of Linda Evangelista wearing one of our black sheer and sequined dresses.

Liz was good friends with Princess Diana, whom I had only seen once in Australia for the Bicentennial Wool Collection. Through Liz, I got to sit next to Princess Diana at a luncheon. She was the most elegant woman I'd ever met, exuding grandeur and eloquence. She was also as lovely and regular as anyone else, and that was her real charm.

The year before Liz joined us in Kids for Kids, she had been diagnosed with ovarian cancer. Liz believed it was caused by fertility drugs she had taken in an effort to get pregnant. Not surprisingly, she took on the disease with her usual grace and humor. Having always battled her weight, she was delighted with her newly slim figure, calling it a result of "the cancer diet." She cut her hair super-short and chic. Liz had always been great-looking, and now she was a knockout. But she was also very sick. By this time, Stephan had had his two cancer surgeries, so Liz and I had something else in common: that uneasy combination of hope, fear, and the desire to make a difference. In 1997, Liz became the president of the Ovarian Cancer Research Fund, determined to raise consciousness and money to help battle this silent disease.

Liz came to me looking for a corporate sponsor. Patti and I sat in my office with Faith Kates, an OCRF board member and co-founder and owner of Next Models, and Jeannette Chang, senior vice president and publishing director of Hearst Magazines, which publishes *Harper's Bazaar*.

"We have to do something, Donna," Liz said urgently. "Unlike the Pap test for cervical cancer, there is no test for this disease. By the time it's discovered, that's it. You're at stage three or four. We need to invent an early detection test at the very least."

"I'm happy to be a sponsor, Liz," I said, "but this is a woman's disease, and we are a woman's industry." We agreed that the Seventh on Sale concept was great, but we wanted to do something smaller in the Hamptons, where we all had homes. That would mean introducing a Kids for Kids element of fun, because if it's summer and you're in the Hamptons, chances are you have kids and/or grandkids with you. Everyone loves a barbecue, we reasoned. Liz and her husband Andrew's home was on a huge piece of property on Gardiners Bay, not far from my East Hampton house. Perfect. We grabbed our Rolodexes and called up all our fashion friends. "Come empty out your personal closets of clothes, books, art, whatever, and help us raise money for ovarian cancer," we told them.

Held in 1998, the first Super Saturday was a far more intimate affair than Seventh on Sale. We installed an outdoor dance floor and hired a DJ and a caterer who served burgers and steamed lobsters. Eighteen fashion designers contributed, including Ralph Lauren, who set up a wooden hutch filled with sweaters. The *Vogue* fashion editor Grace Coddington propped up a bunch of black-and-white fashion photos against a tree. La Mer offered a table of luxe products. And per our ask, people literally emptied their personal closets—this was a true tag sale of the chicest order. There were design books, Chanel bags, vintage pieces. I wanted to buy everything but held back to give others a chance. About four hundred people attended, and we raised $400,000. We gave each guest a tote filled with fabulous donated swag, not realizing we were setting a precedent for years to come.

Sadly, Liz could only come out to say hello, after her assistant helped her get dressed. We had created something so fabulous, but Liz was only around for another year to enjoy it. She died at fifty-one. Just like Kids for Kids, Super Saturday lives on, and eighteen years later, it's a Hamptons institution, which I still co-chair. Now it's held at Nova's Ark Project, a vast nature preserve and sculpture park. Hundreds of companies have booths, thousands attend, and we consistently raise well over $3 million. Every year, I take my whole family—and carry Liz firmly in my heart. I know she's cheering us on from above.

———————

In 1999, Stephan and I established the Karan-Weiss Foundation to carry out our many philanthropic pursuits. Two of our favorite undertakings were artistic: New York City's Dia Center for the Arts and the first fundraising event for Robert Wilson's Watermill Center. Both organizations support and exhibit contemporary and emerging artists. It was great to see Stephan engaged in his passion for art. Things had not been going well: the cancer was back.

This time was especially scary. Michael Burt, Stephan's oncology surgeon, had died a year earlier in a motorcycle accident, and when Stephan's cancer reappeared, we felt lost without him. But Dr. Burt was a surgeon, and surgery was out of the question because this time the cancer was too close to the lining of the lung. We began seeking opinions from new doctors; once we got three in one week. At first, the cancer was considered stable, but a few months later, it was shown to be "active" and therefore spreading. We'd have to introduce a mild form of chemo, which meant that Stephan couldn't ski or be active. Try telling him that.

I knew not to buy him any lavish gifts. He was still smarting from my last one. Just a few months after the Lamborghini, I had given him the Christmas gift of all Christmas gifts: a painting by his favorite contemporary artist, Francis Bacon. That one really got me into trouble. We had a deal now: I wouldn't spend over a certain amount without clearing it with him first. But we were living in the black apartment at the time, and after doing my research, I found the perfect Bacon: a mostly red and orange, floor-to-ceiling piece with a yogic-looking figure in the center. I thought, *How perfect, how us.* Mind you, I didn't see it in person. I bought it based on a photograph from Germany. And yes, I broke our deal. I called the bank to get my second secret million—or so (I got my first one for Barbra to invest).

When the painting finally arrived, I had it hung and waited for Stephan to come home. When he walked in, I wrapped my arms around him. "I have a surprise for you," I sang after kissing him. There was no hiding this huge surprise, and his face lit up with wonder. "Oh my God, Donna, is that Francis Bacon?"

I nodded with joy, delighted that my great idea was working.

"It's amazing." He stood back, then walked up to view it closely. "Where did you get a poster this good?"

"It's not a poster," I chided. "It's the real thing."

His smile vanished. *"Are you out of your mind?"* he yelled. "You're not allowed to do this. Where did you get the money?"

I tried to placate him. "Honey, it's not about the money. It's about the art. And it's so beautiful. Look, see the yogi?" But the only yogi he was looking at was me, and I wasn't making him any calmer. We kept the painting, of course, and I know Stephan loved it. I'd catch him staring at it, probably marveling that it was in our home. For that alone, it was worth every single penny.

He had his first treatment in February 1999, and he said it made him "ache to the bones." Unfortunately, just a few months later, in April, the doctors felt the cancer wasn't responding and switched to Taxol, a stronger chemo drug. Stephan started to have horrific muscle cramps in his legs, neuropathy (degeneration of the nerves) in his feet, and some hair loss. He also had severe hiccups. We now had a supply of oxygen tanks at home, which he needed more often than I liked. He didn't complain at all; he suffered quietly—but I could tell how uncomfortable he was. Ironically, my pot-smoking husband couldn't smoke when he needed it most, so we started baking pot cookies and brownies. (Once Gabby's boyfriend Gianpaolo came to our house in the Hamptons and ate five of our "special" chocolate chip cookies. He got so stoned we worried he wouldn't wake up. I started feeding him ice cream, figuring the sugar would sober him up, only to have Gabby scream at me, "Stop, Mommy. You'll choke him!") Sadly, the cookies weren't enough to alleviate Stephan's symptoms, and he continued to suffer quietly.

So naturally Donna the Woo-Woo Queen got busy. By now, Ruth Pontvianne, the Brazilian healer, was living with us and administrating frequent therapeutic massages with essential oils and aromatherapy. We took him to see an acupuncturist. Lindsey Clennell, an Iyengar yoga teacher, came to Stephan's studio to work on poses that would help with his breathing. And I practiced Reiki on him every day. We also used a slant board at home to drain the fluid building up in his chest. Maybe we couldn't cure this damn cancer, but we could make him more comfortable.

I wanted Stephan to have some fun, too. I love renting boats, so in September 1999 I threw Stephan and Barbra a joint party in New York Harbor. It was his birthday, and Barbra had just finished a series of concerts in New York. The timing coincided with Rosh Hashanah, so Barbra's friend, the late great composer Marvin Hamlisch, led the floating dinner party in prayer. The evening was a bit schizophrenic, as we then alternated between the soundtrack from *Star Wars* (Stephan's favorite film) and Barbra's songbook. At the end of the night, the sky lit up with fireworks I had arranged. Other times, we had to accept Stephan's health limitations. For New Year's 1999 (ringing in 2000), we had plans to go with Linda and Steve Horn to see Barbra's special Las Vegas concert (the one she later turned into her album *Timeless*). At the last minute, Stephan realized he just wasn't up to it, and the four of us rang in the New Year in East Hampton.

Stephan still went to the studio and always had his sketchbook on hand, as well as little clay models he was preparing to turn into sculptures. As uncomfortable as he was, the artist within was feeling just fine—still engaged, still creating. His essence was intact.

———————

The lease on our black apartment was running out, so I started dragging poor Stephan to see dozens of new places. Every one had something wrong with it: not enough windows, the ceilings were too low, or I hated the block. My list of rejects was endless. One day he called me at work.

"We're done. I bought us an apartment, and I don't want to hear another word about it."

"Excuse me?"

"You heard me," he said. "You were never going to decide on one, and we need to get moving. Want to see the one I chose?"

This was a classic Stephan move: indulge me for a bit, then take over. He'd chosen one of my rejects, a space on Central Park West with a wraparound terrace. The ceilings were low, and it needed a ton of work, as it was three apartments we'd have to combine into one. But he didn't care. It was bought and paid for. "Call Dominic and get creative," he said. Dominic was the architect who worked on all our stores and East Hampton homes and who helped paint the black apartment.

While we renovated, Stephan found us an interim rental in SoHo at 42 Wooster Street, near where Gabby lived on Broome Street. I loved living downtown. The whole vibe was so me: young, carefree, unpretentious, artsy. Whenever I proposed to Stephan that we should consider buying in the area, I got a don't-even-think-about-it look.

———————

Dominic and I got to work on the new place. The timing was good, because we were also creating our first Collection store in New York

City, at 819 Madison Avenue, so he could source for both at the same time.

For years, it had killed me that our only Donna Karan New York store was in London. I wanted one in New York, the city where the label was born. Given our stagnating stock values, the board of directors refused to consider financing one, so I did it myself, against everyone's counsel, including Stephan's. He had a cow every time I brought it up. Trey and Dominic found a great location, a limestone townhouse on Madison Avenue at 68th Street, the former Versace store. Maria Napoli, one of my favorite psychics, tried to talk me out of it because she didn't like the street address, but my gut told me to keep going. The good part about paying for it myself was that I got to do what I wanted. The awkward layout required a total gut renovation. Once the demolition got going, they discovered there was an outdoor space that had been walled off from the store— a garden! I envisioned a serene oasis, a place where you could leave the city behind. Design-wise, I wanted air, light, and water, so we installed an indoor-outdoor water garden, with bamboo for privacy. I loved that you could hear the ripple of water in the middle of the city. Dominic and Trey went to work on the interiors: lots of limestone, floating black walls, gold accents—all our signatures. (I envisioned a café, too, but to my frustration, we found out that regulations prohibited it.)

I planned to sell clothes and accessories, of course, and have a cashmere shop. But I was most excited about the artisan market: a place to sell the handmade treasures I found around the world, plus gorgeous vintage pieces and capsule collections from designers I believed in. Sadly, Stephan couldn't physically share in my excitement because the construction dust was too much for his compromised lungs. (If he knew how much I was spending, it probably would have been too much for his heart, too.) I took photos of everything and reported back to him every night at Wooster Street.

––––––––

"You must come to San Francisco." It was Dominic on the line, the excitement in his voice palpable. "There's this exhibit you'll love—the Japanese master sculptor Izumi Masatoshi. I promise it will be worth the trip."

He was right. I was moved to tears by the beauty of Masatoshi's stonework. Two chairs, titled "Breath," spoke to me in particular. I desperately wanted them for the apartment and bought them on the spot. When I got home, I showed Stephan photos.

"Beautiful," he agreed, "but how do you expect to keep them in the apartment?"

"What do you mean?"

"They're solid stone," he said, his voice rising. "They will literally crash through the floor!"

I hadn't thought of that. "Okay, let's put them into the new store."

"And how do you plan to get them into the store?"

They must have weighed a ton each, so we had to have a crane hoist them over the building and into their new home in the rock garden, where they were the perfect centerpiece.

"Once you get them in there," Stephan warned, "they'll never leave." Never say never. Sad to say, the store closed in 2014; now those chairs sit in my East Hampton yard. I'm still miffed I can't have them in my apartment.

––––––––

There's a phrase, "living with cancer," and that's exactly what Stephan and I were doing. He was holding up surprisingly well. We adjusted our lifestyle: no more trips to Canyon Ranch or out west skiing, and we ditched a plan to buy a home in Sun Valley, as the altitude was too high. We traveled to Parrot Cay instead, staying at our friend Christina Ong's Como Shambhala hotel, the Turks and Caicos version of her resort we loved so much in Bali. Stephan worked just about every day at his studio on a series he named, appropriately, "Living on the Edge," composed of seven bronze figures, each perched on construction beams, captured in a moment of suspense. Our lives felt like that, though I did my best to suppress my anxiety about the future. But one morning I just couldn't hold it in, and so I let the tears flow. Boy, did Stephan get mad. "Why are you crying?" he yelled. "Because I'm sick? So what. None of us know what the future holds. You could get hit by a truck tomorrow. I'm here now, Donna, right in front of you." And he was. But so was my worst fear: losing the love of my life, my rock.

That night, he came home with two new watercolor paintings he'd made for me and placed in the bedroom, at the foot of our bed, so I would see them first thing in the morning. One was a plus sign in sunny yellow, the other a minus sign in black. "You can look at life either way, Donna," he said. "It's your choice, remember that." Those paintings are still the first thing I see when I wake up.

———————

During this whole period, Stephan was busy planning the future of the company. Ever since we'd gone public and he got his diagnosis, I was constantly saying to him, "You can't leave me with this," referring to the shareholders, the board of directors, and the other headaches of running a public company. David Bressman, who had been Donna Karan International's general counsel, was now our lawyer, working for Stephan directly. David brought in Gail Zauder, a managing director at Credit Suisse First Boston, and the three went to work, looking for a solution to our public company problem.

"It's the kind of problem," David would say, "that requires surgery, not medicine."

I wasn't part of the negotiations that led to us being acquired by LVMH Moët Hennessy–Louis Vuitton, but I was thrilled. LVMH was the holy grail of luxury goods, with the expertise, resources, and global scale we needed to take our company forward. On a personal and creative level, I couldn't help remembering that one of our first photo shoots had had Rosemary coming off a plane loaded down with luggage. All I could think was, *Yes! Finally, we'll have a proper luggage collection!*

Stephan had me flying to Paris for so many meetings that my friend Bonnie Young was convinced I was having an affair because I refused to say *why* I needed to leave our Milan fabric trips for quick, overnight jaunts to France. The minute I met Yves Carcelle, the president of LVMH Fashion Group, I was hooked. He had this amazing Buddha in his house, and I was convinced our partnership was destined. At one point, to ensure that our discussions were private, we brought Yves to Como Shambhala in Parrot Cay. We were all sworn to secrecy. Even me, with my famous lack of filter, understood that you didn't mess around when it came to a public company. I didn't tell a soul, not even Patti.

When I returned to New York, Patti came into my office and said, "Donna, I had the oddest experience. I went to this new psychic named Susan King. She told me that a good friend, wearing a similar ponytail to mine only with dark hair, was on the beach with a sick man, a Frenchman, and a short Italian man with glasses. She said there were papers involved. I kept shaking my head, no, no, no, but the psychic was certain about it." The Italian man with the glasses was not in Parrot Cay with us, but he was clearly Pino Brusone, the managing director at Armani, who was set to join us once LVMH took over. I had met Pino through Christina Ong a few years back. I adored him and desperately wanted him to work with us, and now that dream was coming true.

"Wow, that's crazy," I said, stunned at the psychic's accuracy. "Did she say anything else?"

"No," Patti answered. "But I have to say, I'm tired of paying psychics who only want to talk about you."

After the LVMH deal was fully revealed, Susan King became our go-to psychic for all matters big and small.

―――――――

Operation Karma—that's what I called our covert negotiations. There were many parts to LVMH buying our company, and they unfolded over four months. First, they bought Gabrielle Studio, the most valuable component because it held our trademarks, for $450 million. The second stage was to buy Donna Karan International stock for $8.50 a share. There was also a provision to buy our 819 Madison Avenue store, which made me sigh in relief because I had insisted on paying for it, and now a huge financial burden was lifted. I would be chief designer and maintain creative control. There were several other clauses and conditions, but those were the ones that stood out to me at the time.

When I went to sign the final papers at the offices of Skadden, Arps, Slate, Meagher & Flom, the law firm that represented Gabrielle Studio, there was a conference room full of executives, lawyers, and bankers. Piles of documents were neatly stacked in rows around a long table. Stephan had already signed everything and wasn't there. I was a little late and wearing my usual ten pounds of cashmere layers.

"Good morning, everyone," I said brightly. "Listen, I just got off the phone with my psychic, who told me that Mercury is in retrograde, which means this is a terrible time to enter any kind of contract. Can we put this off for a while?" (Thank God Stephan wasn't there!) The room was silent for a minute. Finally, Eileen Nugent, our powerhouse mergers-and-acquisitions lawyer, who had been working with Stephan, Gail, and David, cleared her throat. "Donna, may I speak to you in private?"

She put her arm around me and led me to a corner. A minute later, I picked up a pen and signed each and every paper put in front of me.

"What did she say to you?" David asked afterward.

"She told me, and I quote, 'This is the best fucking deal I've ever seen in my whole career. Now sit down and sign the papers. *Now.*' I swear she was channeling my husband."

That night Stephan and I were in our Wooster Street apartment reviewing the press release and other details about the deal, to be announced the next day, when Bonnie Young, who lived nearby, called. "Donna, may I come up? I need a favor."

"Any other night but now, Bonnie. I'm so sorry."

"It has to be tonight. I'm getting married tomorrow and you are the only witness I want on our marriage certificate." Bonnie was marrying the photographer Luca Babini, the father of her baby, and she was due to give birth any day. I quickly let her up, signed the certificate, and rushed her out the door.

The next day, December 17, in front of hundreds of employees, we made two announcements: Bonnie Young was married, and we had a deal to sell the company to LVMH.

The press release went out, and not surprisingly, the directors and shareholders were furious. By selling Gabrielle Studio, the holder of our trademarks, the stock would surely plummet. One shareholder sued. No one was happy about LVMH's offer of $8.50 a share. It took almost a year (and Stephan would be gone by then) for LVMH and shareholders to agree to $10.75 a share, which finalized the deal. By November 2001, more than four months after Stephan died, the acquisition was complete. LVMH now owned Donna Karan International lock, stock, and barrel.

Yves Carcelle, who negotiated the deal with Stephan (and who died from kidney cancer in 2014) later wrote the most beautiful note describing this time:

I've never enjoyed negotiating so much as I did with Stephan Weiss. That's strange to say, because negotiation is never easy. People come to the table with different agendas, different degrees of ego, and of course, expectations about money. But my negotiations with Stephan for the trademark to Gabrielle Studio and then the acquisitions of Donna Karan International were the highest quality I've ever experienced.

Stephan was a man of intelligence, and at the same time, he possessed a great respect for other people. He was an extraordinary negotiator because he took the time to truly hear the other person, to understand their point of view. I remember sitting in a room with him, reviewing a list of five or ten points drawn up by the lawyers and bankers. "Stephan," I'd say, "these are the points they've issued." After each point, his response was always the same: "Give me a minute," followed by 30 to 40 minutes of concentrated silence. Finally, he'd say, "I think that's fair." Or else, "Look, I see your point, but I have a problem with it. Let's find a solution." And we would. This was the exact opposite of most negotiations, where passions flare, people jump to conclusions and the shouting begins. . . . My life's one regret is that I did not know him longer.

There was a lot to celebrate, of course. But there was something bittersweet about the LVMH deal. Stephan was doing what he did best: taking care of his family. He saved me from the public company nightmare and gave our children long-term security. He was, in effect, putting his affairs in order before saying goodbye.

22 | THE LAST CHRISTMAS

With the LVMH deal settled and announced, we could turn back to our lives. Christmas was coming. This would be a year of big gifts.

That spring, I had sat with the designer Donatella Versace at the Met Gala, the huge, celebrity-studded annual ball for the Metropolitan Museum's Costume Institute Exhibit. "Donna, what is zat on your hand?" she asked in her sexy Italian growl.

"My ring," I said proudly, and put forth my oversized topaz ring, which I loved.

"Darling, zat is not a ring," she said. "*Zees* is a ring." She extended her hand and flashed the biggest diamond I'd ever seen in my life. I went home and told Stephan, who clearly made a mental note. Right before Christmas, he presented me with a little black felt bag. Inside was a stack of five or more slim, diamond-encrusted eternity-style rings. I was thrilled as I slipped each one on my finger.

"There's more," he said.

I fished in the bag, and my hand hit a rock. Literally. Out came a ring with what looked like an ice cube on top—14 carats, I later learned. I nearly screamed—not with excitement, but with fear. It was ridiculously big and so not me. For years, I'd try to cover it with long sleeves or turn it inside to face my palm. I couldn't seem to make peace with owning something so ostentatious. But at that moment, Stephan's happy smile erased any doubts, and I was nothing but grateful.

Of course, I had to be bratty, too. "I got something bigger than you did. I'm going to top you," I sang around the house. But I would wait until Christmas to give it to him.

The whole family went to Parrot Cay for Christmas, and we stayed in our usual villa, Bungalow 118, at Como Shambhala. Gabby brought her boyfriend Gianpaolo, whom Stephan adored (even though he questioned how they could make their relationship work given that Gianpaolo was a pilot for Alitalia and the two of them were separated by the Atlantic). And Yves Carcelle came down with his family. We had a ton of fun, celebrating and relaxing under the sun.

Then I gave Stephan his gift. I took him to a spot on the beach that backed up to an expanse of undeveloped land. "Merry Christmas," I said, my arms spread wide.

"What am I looking at?"

"Ten acres. The site of our future home." I smiled brightly. "You said to be positive."

He was awestruck. "How did you pull this off?" he asked. But then he shook his head and said, "Forget it, I don't want to know."

I was so proud of myself. "Told you I got something bigger than you got," I teased.

"Promise me something, Donna," he said, wrapping his arms around me. "We'll build a house here for the family. One big enough to hold everyone, including future grandkids. Gabby and Gianpaolo look pretty serious to me, despite their little geography problem." For that one minute, I let go of my worries and imagined that everything was going to be fine.

Como Shambhala always has an incredible New Year's Eve party with dinner, dancing, and fireworks (now I host the dinner at my house), and 2000's event (ringing in 2001) was no exception. Bruce Willis and Keith Richards duked it out for DJ duty. At some point, George Harrison of the Beatles brought out an old record player and took over. Stephan and George had become friendly and realized they were engaged in a similar struggle: George had had throat cancer, which had returned, this time to his lungs. The next day, the two took a long and soulful walk down the beach together. I can only imagine the conversation. Neither man lived to ring in another year.

————

From the moment we returned to New York, Stephan grew sicker and sicker. More of his hair fell out, and what was left was white. His breathing worsened, so we needed the oxygen with us at all times. Ro Cappola, an oncology nurse whom Stephan had become close with after his second surgery at Memorial Sloan Kettering, stayed in touch and would stop by and hang out. An Italian American brunette who was always battling her weight, Ro (short for Rosemarie) is a real New York character, with a tell-it-like-it-is sense of humor. Stephan trusted her implicitly and did anything she said or advised, and she was deeply comforting to all of us.

Still, I was a nervous wreck. Corey, who went to every doctor's visit with his father, told me his primary doctor said there was nothing more to be done. What an asshole! Who would ever tell someone to give up hope? In my fury, I called my friend Evelyn Lauder. In 1992, Evelyn had established the Evelyn H. Lauder Breast Center at Memorial Sloan Kettering. She was wonderful and compassionate, and immediately put me in touch with the head of the hospital. We were instantly assigned a new doctor.

Not that a new doctor could make the chemo work better. The difference was that he treated us like people. That's what you need when you're sick and afraid: Compassion. Dignity. Partnership. Support. Stephan knew the chemo wasn't working. We didn't talk about him dying, but it was happening in front of my eyes. It hurt me to look at him. He'd aged fifteen or twenty years in no time at all. He'd shrunk. The energy was draining out of his body. He wasn't my Stephan anymore.

Gabby, who lived just a block away from us downtown, spent her days at his side. He was her dad, her rock of Gibraltar (as opposed to her mother, yours truly, who constantly traveled and worked around the clock). Gabby would lie on the bed with him, keeping him company as he watched *Star Trek* and old movies. If Stephan was strong enough, Gabby would walk him over to his studio. Gianpaolo, who came to New York every chance he got, spent time at the studio, too, allowing Stephan to really get to know and love him.

Stephan came to my fall 2001 show, held in February of that year. Our friend the dancer Gabrielle Roth stood in front of him for protection as he made his way carefully into the crowded room. I came out at the end of the show for my bow, and I literally didn't recognize him. Against all the health and color in the audience, he looked like death.

Yet, to his credit, he insisted on living. He was very excited about a new sculpture series he was working on, called "Larger than Life" (a collection of two-ton brass sculptures of a shoe, an apple, a horse, a roll of film, and so on) and was traveling upstate with Corey to the foundry that would eventually produce them. And he continued to spend all his free time with Gabby, who wouldn't leave his side.

At one point, there was a horrific fire a block away from us, and the local firemen needed to use our apartment to get close with their hoses. Stephan and Susie, our friend and chef, let them in and then insisted on feeding all the guys. The whole department— those very same men—were killed on 9/11.

In early 2001, Stephan and I decided to renew our vows. Since we wanted the whole family with us, we waited until spring break, in mid-April. We rented a plane and brought a very intimate guest list: the kids, Barbra and Jim, and Jane Chung and her husband, Mack. On the flight, Barbra taught our grandson Etan to play gin rummy.

We held the ceremony on our property at sunset. We all wore white, and a very tall, very funny island man officiated. It was a hike to get to the spot, so Stephan had his oxygen tank with him. We kept the ceremony short and full of love; it was a celebration of the life we had created together, hand in hand. Everyone was hysterically crying, me most of all.

When we returned, I went to Susan King (the psychic who was eerily accurate with Patti) to ask her how much time I had left with Stephan. She told me the upcoming Memorial Day weekend would be his last at our home in East Hampton.

During the first week in June, Stephan's breathing got a lot more labored. Our home oxygen was no longer sufficient. We thought he had a cold and wanted to get it under control, so we checked him into Memorial Sloan Kettering. He brought his sketchbook and his little clay models. The VIP room on the nineteenth floor was like a studio apartment, with plenty of space for family visitors; there was even a small room for someone to sleep in. Ruthie, our healer, came with us to administer massages and anything else either Stephan or I needed. Ro was there around the clock as our private nurse, and she refused to go home, regardless of the long hours. Ann Culkin, the primary nurse on staff, was wonderful, too. Stephan was so nice to them, always joking, laughing, and flirting. He'd always tell me, "Whatever you do, take care of the nurses, Donna. They're the heroes here."

But of course, I was in the middle of designing resort. Day one of Stephan's hospital stay, I had the clothes brought up to the hospital room and modeled them for him, voguing it up. He especially loved the sexy leather and suede jackets.

Each day Stephan became a bit weaker. He was adamant that he only wanted me and the kids in the room. No business associates, no friends, no extended family. We called Gabby, who was in Brazil working on a story for *Travel + Leisure* magazine about an Ashram Adventures retreat. She flew home immediately. When she arrived, Gabby began organizing our meals, calling in for sushi platters and dinners from Sette Mezzo. She's got that same Jewish mother instinct I have: when we're nervous, we just want to feed people.

At one point, Stephan's mother called to say she was driving in from Long Island to visit. (I can only tell this story because she's no longer with us.) "I don't want to see her," he said to all of us. It wasn't for any bad reason; he loved his mother, but she could drive him crazy. "Stephan, it's your mother," I reasoned. "We can't keep her out."

"I've got an idea," Ro piped up. "Stephan, you're not feeling well, right?" He shrugged. "Well, if you really needed a sedative, I could give you one. A strong one that would last a while." We all smiled.

Sure enough, Stephan's mom came in and sat by the bed. He was out like a light.

"Hilda," I said gently, "he's going to be asleep for a while."

"I don't care," she answered. "He's my son. I'll wait."

"You'll be waiting for a long time," Ro said. "He's really knocked out."

Hilda stayed for a while longer, but when she realized he wouldn't be waking up anytime soon, she left. I still feel a little guilty about it, but it was his mother, and his wishes.

Stephan let all his wishes be known—and loudly. Once Ro and Anne were washing him, and he was out of it. Barbra's music wafted through the stereo, and all of a sudden he spoke lucidly. "I'm not dying to Barbra's music," he said. Don't get me wrong, he adored Barbra and loved her voice (he said she had a "Stradivarius" in her throat); he just didn't want hers to be the last voice he heard. It would be too weird. Stephan briefly perked up again when Luca, Bonnie's husband and a fellow bike rider, brought Stephan's helmet to us, which I placed at the end of his bed. Stephan was on morphine and becoming less and less responsive, but he seemed to recognize the helmet. For a minute, anyway. Then he slipped away again. Maybe I was delirious with grief, but I knew in my heart where he'd really gone: on a motorcycle joyride. I saw his energy leave the room and just felt it in my bones.

"Great," I said to the kids. "We're all just supposed to sit here while he vrooms around the world?"

"We could dress him up and bring him home," Lisa said amid a fit of giggles. (Did I mention we were punch drunk from sleep deprivation?) "You know, like that movie *Weekend at Bernie's*, where they dress the dead guy and bring him everywhere?" Everyone laughed.

Except for me. *Wait*, I thought, *she's on to something. Why not just bring him home? What's the difference?* I tried to find a doctor to release him, but there was no one around. I took matters into my own hands, grabbing his clothes and tugging at his hospital gown.

"What are you doing?" Ro asked.

"Taking him home. It's crazy to sit here while he's off riding. Who knows when he'll come back?" I was perfectly serious. Why should we all hang out in a hospital room when he could be in his own bed? But moments later, I felt him slip back into his body, and Corey, Lisa, Gabby, and I continued to sit vigil with him around the clock. We read letters that we'd written to him, and I couldn't stop kissing him.

At thirteen, Lisa's daughter, Mackensie, was the only grandchild old enough to visit, which she did briefly. Stephan and she wore matching paw print necklaces, each engraved with the other's name.

The paw print was a reference to "the black bear," a.k.a. Stephan's Range Rover, which they would take out on adventures, just the two of them.

Stephan was failing rapidly, and we all knew it. One of the doctors told Gabby they didn't think Stephan had enough oxygen for his brain to continue to function. She stood by his bed, sobbing and holding his hand, and wouldn't you know it—he squeezed her hand, opened his eyes, and said, "Don't cry." Even in his darkest hour, Stephan took care of us.

That Saturday night, we sent Gabby and Corey home to get some rest. Lisa and I would hold down the fort. Stephan was deep into a coma by then, and Ro told us that the end was near; his organs were shutting down.

The next morning she woke us up. "It's time."

Lisa and I went to his bed. Lisa put her hand on Stephan's chest to feel his heartbeat. I just kept caressing him, whispering, "I love you, I love you, I love you." And then he was gone.

I didn't want to leave him. That was the hardest part of all. Ro told me to take all the time I needed, that I could stay for a good hour or more. As far as I was concerned, they'd have to cart me out of that room. We called and broke the news to Corey and Gabby, who were both on their way. Corey said that as he drove across the George Washington Bridge he had felt something pass through him, and he knew. Gabby, who returned with Gianpaolo, was grateful she'd had that moment with him right before he slipped into a coma.

We held the memorial in the upstairs garden of Stephan's Greenwich Street Studio. It was a gorgeous sunny day in June, and about seventy people attended. The family all wore white. Two white doves were set up in the garden. Barbra flew in, as did many of our friends. Richard Baskin led the ceremony. Rabbi Sobel, the man who'd married us, spoke, as did I, Corey (with his wife, Suzanne, and son Etan), Lisa, Gabby, David Bressman, Patti's husband Harvey, and the editor Ingrid Sischy, who had become a great friend of Stephan's as Village neighbors. Outside, a dozen of his motorcycle racing buddies and their Ducatis all lined up next to his empty bike with his helmet placed on top. When the ceremony was over, the guys all revved their bikes in tribute. We released the doves and said goodbye to Stephan.

All of us were hugging and crying when the most remarkable thing happened. The beautiful sunny sky suddenly turned black as night, and a thunderstorm erupted. *Stephan*. He was with us that day, for sure.

We had him cremated, and I gave each of the kids a part of him in a small package they could transfer into whatever container they wished. Later that summer, we brought his ashes to our beach in East Hampton and gathered by my huge rock. We were about to toss them when we noticed Lisa rubbing some into her skin. Suddenly we were all doing it alongside her, wanting to physically absorb a piece of Stephan. It was a beautiful moment.

I had reserved a portion of the ashes to travel with so he'd always be at my side. I scattered a bit in Parrot Cay by our property. Gabby and I took a bit of him to Europe to scatter outside Andrea and Jean-Pierre's cliffside home. At one point I said to Gabby, "Quick, get Daddy out of the sun"—I had left him outside on a patio chair. On the way back I stopped in Paris, and I swear to God, I left him in a hotel room! They FedExed him back to me, but all I could think was, *Stephan is going to kill me!*

I still have some of Stephan left. I'm trying to find a way to send him on the ultimate journey, to space. Nothing fascinated him more. But the truth is I'm not sure I can let him go, even now. As I sit in his studio writing these words, I know he's here in *this* space, *his* space . . . and forever in my soul.

23 | FREE FALL

With Stephan gone, I didn't know what to do with myself. There were no more hospital visits, no more memorials to plan; I had nothing to fix or make better. I couldn't go back to our old life, nor did I want to move on to my new one, whatever that was. I was in limbo, suspended, and everything felt pointless and overwhelming. Stephan had been my rock. He'd made everything okay. He'd allowed me to be *me*: creative, ditzy, disorganized, crazy. Could I be me without Stephan? I was in free fall.

Stephan died in June, and I holed up at the beach with Ruth and Susie for the rest of the summer. I never socialized. The last thing I wanted to do was find myself in a situation where I had to act like I was okay when I wasn't. But as fate would have it, I was far from alone. It's amazing how life sends you what you need just when you need it. Three special women entered my world that summer: Jill Pettijohn, Colleen Saidman, and Sonja Nuttall.

Jill was an emotional godsend. I had met her months before in LA through friends; she had worked as a personal chef for Nicole Kidman and Tom Cruise as well as Drew Barrymore. At the time, I told her I was trying to go on a diet—the story of my life—and she said she could help me. But then her father died, so she postponed her trip to see me; she eventually ended up coming to East Hampton right after Stephan passed. A New Zealander with blond curly hair, Jill had the perfect quiet temperament for my household. Also, we were both grieving. She put me on a raw food diet, modeled on LifeFood, a nutrition regime created by Annie and David Jubb, Ph.D., whom Jill had studied with. It's simple: You only eat food that has its life force intact, such as greens, nuts, seeds, grains, and fruits. It has to be organic and in its whole state. And to keep enzymes in place, you never heat anything over 108 degrees. I also gave up "whites," as in bread, rice, wheat, pasta, potatoes, and corn, as well as sugar and dairy. I lost twenty pounds (no wonder—just look at that list!), and was back in my tightest jeans. But more than that, my energy was renewed, and it started to pierce through the thick black cloud around me.

Colleen Saidman was another angel that summer. Colleen owns Yoga Shanti in Sag Harbor, and a friend of mine had stopped in to ask if she knew anyone who specialized in grief yoga, if such a thing even existed. Colleen said she'd be happy to work with me herself.

A gorgeous and successful model, Colleen turned to yoga to cope, as she said, "with being judged completely by my skin." She'd studied with my old friends Sharon Gannon and David Life of Jivamukti, and like me, she was on the path. Her spiritual journey had taken her to India for a year, where she worked with Mother Teresa to help the poor, sick, and dying. Colleen and I also had master yogi Rodney Yee in common. Christina Ong had introduced me to Rodney a year earlier. He lived in California and had taught a private lesson in my office during a visit to New York. Colleen confided in me that she had a huge crush on him, but they were married to other people, had children, and couldn't pursue it. Thanks to my life with Stephan, I believed that sometimes the road to true love is messy. "Let's bring him here!" I said, never hesitating to interfere in other people's lives. So we flew him in, and I later learned that their first real kiss occurred right outside my house.

The energy between them was unmistakable during our practice. Finally, I joined their hands together and pushed them into a bedroom in my house. "Go. This is meant to be," I said, closing the door behind them. And it was. Fourteen years later, they're married and as in love as ever. You have to trust your heart, no matter the circumstances.

I met my third angel through my friend Maureen Doherty, the owner of Egg in London. Her designer friend Sonja Nuttall was moving to New York, and Maureen asked if I could meet her, so I invited Sonja to East Hampton. I instantly loved her Zen-like presence. She was dressed all in white, which contrasted beautifully with her olive complexion. She spoke slowly, in a deep, soothing, melodic voice. I didn't have a job for her, but we had a karmic connection and began making plans. Unlike my married friends, Sonja was free to travel with me, whether to Parrot Cay so I could check on the property, Europe for inspirational shopping, or Bali, my spiritual home. After we'd become close, Sonja went to a psychic who told her she was related to Stephan in a past life and was sent to help ground me after he left. Whether you believe it or not doesn't matter; the fact is, she *did* ground me. And I had someone to pal around with.

It was nice to have friendships with girlfriends that did not involve spouses. When your husband dies, you feel awkward and sad being with the couples you knew together. With Jill, Colleen, and Sonja, Stephan wasn't missing because none of them had known him. It was a summer of healing. I was as close as ever to Barbra, Patti, Lynn, Linda Horn, and Gabrielle Roth. But I was also forging a new life and learning to be Donna without Stephan—words I had never thought I'd have to say.

Going back to work was hard. Our shows were scheduled for the first week in September, which meant I was in the design studio in the city for most of August. I was fine during the day, but the evenings were horrible. I sketched and tinkered late into the night because I didn't want to face our empty Wooster Street apartment. I became obsessed with our new store on Madison Avenue, set to open later that month. I was also drawing up plans for my future home on Parrot Cay and overseeing the finishing touches on the new place on Central Park West. In the meantime, I had two shows and a store opening to plan. My survival plan was to keep busy, busy, busy.

————————

We all know what happened on September 11, the day of the DKNY show. The world changed, and I changed, too. With all the death and tragedy that hit New York, I came to appreciate the long goodbye I had had with Stephan. He had cancer for almost seven years, and that time was a gift. The 9/11 families said goodbye to their loved ones that morning and never saw them again. Before letting go of Stephan, I had so much time to talk to him, plan with him, spoil him, and even remarry him. I also appreciated that he was spared 9/11; we lived so close to the towers that his lungs would have been unable to cope with the dust.

We showed the spring 2002 Collection in our showroom. Inspired by Stephan's fluid sculptures, we called it The New Structure. We created wired, 3-D shapes that defined and liberated the body by stretching aerodynamic sheer and matte fabrics over a thin wire structure to give dresses, skirts, and coats a floating effect. The jackets, in canvas muslin, were body-articulated, with visual seams and exposed zippers. We also introduced the Flag Dress, an off-the-shoulder, sheet-like piece that came alive on the body. It was one of Louise Wilson's last collections with us. She had been our creative director since 1998, when Peter left to design for Cerruti in Paris. Louise was an enormously respected professor of fashion at Central Saint Martins in London (she helped launch the careers of Alexander McQueen and John Galliano, among others) when I asked her to join us. Fashion has produced many larger-than-life characters, and Louise was one, with a razor-sharp wit and take-no-prisoners critiques. She stayed with us for two years and then shuttled between New York and London, where her partner and son lived. But the commute was too much. I was going to miss her horribly. She ran our design room like she did her schoolroom. She told us all what to do, which I needed both while Stephan was sick and now that I was in shock from his death. Sad to say, Louise passed away in 2014. She was fifty-two, the same age as my father when he died, and just two years older than Anne Klein, and one year older than Liz Tilberis.

———————

With our new owner, LVMH, came a new president, Pino Brusone. I loved Pino personally, but he wanted me to be more like Armani. "Why must you do so much black?" he once asked. How could I even answer such a question? It would be like me asking him, "Why must you speak with an Italian accent?"

Pino moved to the States for our company, but he was never really happy to be here, and I understood. He left a year later, and in 2002, Fred Wilson, who had been president and CEO of LVMH Fashion Group America, took over. I thought Fred was wonderful, a true sweetheart of a man. But it was yet another change, and I was facing too many changes at that moment. I even had a new executive assistant: Marni Lewis, who had toured with Christina Aguilera and Britney Spears. She still works with me today at Urban Zen. When I interviewed her, she asked a question that threw me: "What do you most value in life?"

"Huh?" I said, nonplussed. "What do you mean?"

"What things are most important to you?" Marni said. "I've done some work with Tony Robbins, and he suggests we ask that of anyone we're about to work closely with."

I liked that she thought that way, but I needed a minute to think about my answer. Then my list came right out: Creativity. Freedom. Love. Family. Health.

After working with me for a few months, Marni made an observation. "I can see why you love work so much, Donna," she said. "You've had a lot of obstacles thrown in the way of your values." She went through the list. Love: My husband was gone. Family: Mine was grown up and spreading out. Freedom: I was answering to new bosses. Health: Stress was literally making me sick. "That leaves creativity," she concluded. "And work gives you that."

She was right. Our new store was my only source of pure joy at the moment. It was my home away from home. I loved spending time in the dressing room with my customers, and I loved my "marketplace" area, where we sold objects from my travels. It was my first Urban Zen statement, and in my LVMH agreement, that's exactly what we called the non–Donna Karan portion of the store. Stephan had put in that provision. He knew what a shopper I was and how much I loved innovating new products, and he didn't want this section to be tied into the store's finances. It was yet another gift he gave me before leaving.

———

I returned to Sun Valley in late March 2002 with my good friends Linda Horn, Lynn Kohlman, and Lynn's husband, Mark, and their teenage son, Sam. We were set to stay at Richard Baskin's house while he was gone, and he had asked his friend Steve Reuther to pick us up at the airport. I had never met Steve, so I was intrigued by this friendly, handsome single guy with long gray hair. He was a film producer, and I loved that he had an LA connection. Unfortunately, he wasn't into me in the way I'd hoped. We were supposed to meet on the top of a mountain one day when I heard he'd gone heli-skiing with another woman. When I pouted about it to my ski instructor, Grady Burnett, he said, "How about if I take *you* heli-skiing?"

Linda was against it. "It's too dangerous, Donna. You're not experienced enough."

But lack of experience has never stopped me. I was doing great, zipping up and down the hills. But it was early spring, so by our last run, the snow was starting to turn sludgy from the warmth. Of course I fell—and couldn't stand back up. (Naturally, this happened right after Grady said, "Watch out, be careful.") They had to medevac me out, and the last thing I saw was Lynn Kohlman holding on to a tree. She and five other skiers, including Secretary of State John Kerry, were stuck on the mountain for at least another hour until the helicopter went back for them. My right knee was badly broken—I had a tibial plateau fracture—and I had to have surgery in New York a few days later. Seven screws were implanted, and I was in a wheelchair for what felt like forever. I finally understood why we needed ramps in our store, as well as handrails and an elevator—all the required details that I didn't appreciate while building it. I also understood why Stephan so valued his nurses and caregivers. They mean the world to you when you're compromised.

———

Then, in September, something happened that put all my troubles in perspective: Lynn was diagnosed with cancer in her right breast. I immediately called my friend Evelyn Lauder, and she paved the way for Lynn at Memorial Sloan Kettering, where she had a lumpectomy a month later. During the procedure, they discovered that her left breast had suspicious areas, too. My fierce and brave best friend decided to have a double mastectomy, followed by chemo. We were devastated. How could this be? But as you must with cancer, you regroup and resolve to fight it with all your might. Lynn's mother had had breast cancer in her fifties and had gone on to live another thirty years. We told each other Lynn would do the same.

I went to all of her doctor's appointments with her and her husband, Mark. I was right by her side when she had her surgeries. I asked Jill Pettijohn to cook and care for her. And most of all, I tried to keep Lynn laughing with silly stories. I showed her photos from Halloween, when I dressed like a human cyclone (how perfect, right?) and Gabby dressed up as me, with bangs, a Cold Shoulder dress, and too much gold jewelry. I told her how Barbra had me chasing down a particular Prada bag all over Europe, and how I recently wouldn't let my plane land because I was watching the show 24 and it was a really good part. "I swear, Donna," she would say, cracking up at my latest caper. "You really are *Ab Fab*. If people only knew. . . ."

Once again, illness and birth came hand in hand. As we absorbed Lynn's news, Gabby announced that she was pregnant with Gianpaolo's baby and that they wanted to get married. I was ecstatic. I was a grandmother five times over at that point, but now *my* baby was having a baby. This was a whole new level of bliss. I adored Gianpaolo. Handsome, warm, and unpretentious, he reminded me so much of Stephan. He was also a Virgo. And just like Stephan, he was totally unimpressed with my world, which he knew nothing about. I'd met Gianpaolo three years earlier. The first night I took him to a rather edgy birthday party; there were people gyrating on the bar. Then I took him to a restaurant where the waitstaff were transvestites. (I swear, neither was intentional.) The following night was the Met Gala. The only suit he had was his Alitalia pilot uniform, so I took him to our publicity office so we could outfit him in a tux while the car waited outside.

"Gabby, why is your mother's name everywhere in this building?" he wondered. This young pilot from Naples had no idea who I was, and Gabby had kept it that way for as long as she could. Within the hour, we were walking the red carpet surrounded by celebrities. He didn't know what hit him, but he handled it with ease and grace, just as Stephan had.

While planning their wedding, Gabby was clear: "Mommy, we want a small wedding like you and Daddy had on the beach in Parrot Cay. Really intimate. And I want a dress like yours." So I made her a dress like mine: simple, circular, perfect for a pregnant woman. She hated it. "I want one more like Barbra's," she said. "Only for the beach."

That was my first clue this wasn't going to be the bare-bones, barefoot beach ceremony Stephan and I had had. There was nothing simple about Barbra's dress, which I'd designed for her 1998 wedding to Jim. I had been on a silent retreat when Barbra tracked me down and asked me to do it. "Oh, come on, Donna," she said to me on the phone. "I'll do all the talking. You design it in silence." She had such a clear idea about what she wanted that I broke my vow of silence and said, "You design one, and I'll design one. I'll make both, and you choose." She sent me countless sketches, which I studied in silence.

After my retreat, I flew to Barbra's house in Malibu with our master seamstress, Nelly Bidon, for muslin fittings, and went again when the fabric arrived (it was hand-beaded in India). My design was a crystal-on-tulle lace pattern with tiny lock-rose diamonds; Barbra's was Chantilly lace with crystal seed pearls and diamanté. Mine wrapped around the body; hers flowed away from it. But even two dresses weren't enough for Barbra to choose from. I discovered six more in her closet that she'd found online and would later return. In the end, Barbra chose my design, and we finished it with a crown of antique hand-knotted flowers atop a beaded veil. It was one of the most intricate couture pieces I have ever created, and she looked stunning.

We had a month to plan Gabby's December 2002 wedding. You'd be amazed at how ridiculously over the top a wedding you can plan in a month. Because that's what it was—a no-holds-barred beach fantasy under the stars. First I rented a huge plane to fly our one hundred or so guests to Parrot Cay. We took over Como Shambhala, and some guests had to stay on a nearby island. When our boat pulled into the harbor, the most remarkable rainbow encircled it, which I chose to view as an embrace from Stephan. The night before the wedding, we built a bonfire on our property, and everyone wore the brightest, most saturated colors, in contrast to the all-white day ahead.

I'm serious when I say *all white*. The chuppah was made from hundreds of hand-strung orchids that draped to the ground. The silk aisle was strewn with white rose petals. The Sylvia Weinstock cake flown in from New York (studded with white orchids made of sugar) was the perfect finish to the seafood feast flown in from the restaurant Nobu in London, a gift from the Ongs. And, of course, everyone wore white. It was so pretty, so pure and fresh.

But back to Gabby's dress. Five months pregnant, she wanted to look sexy and bare, so we created a micro-mini slip dress with a dramatic train of beaded, sequined tulle. It took forever to hand-embellish, as we didn't have time to have it done in India. (On the other hand, *my* silk stretch Grecian-style wrap dress took a quick evening to make.) I was incredibly hurt when, in her excitement, Gabby got dressed without me. I couldn't stop crying. I know, I know, it sounds so dramatic. But like every mother, I wanted to experience that moment. Gianpaolo was happy to wear the white serape I made for him. Teamed with a white jacket and tailored shirt, he looked so hot, so Parrot Cay.

Speaking of hot, it was *at least* as hot as it had been at my first wedding to Stephan. The humidity was oppressive, not that any of us noticed as we partied into the night. Gabby cut off the train of her dress to dance, and Nelly had to sew it back on by the next morning for photos. And there was Lynn, with a giant smile, snapping pictures. We ended the night with a spectacular fireworks display to a rousing rendition of music from *Madame Butterfly*. It was a bit much, but it was also perfection. I can only imagine what Gianpaolo's family thought of the whole thing, starting with the family their son was marrying into. About thirty of them made the sixteen-hour trek from Italy. My Italian isn't so great, so I was only able to communicate meaningfully with his father. But if their smiles were any indication, they were having a ball.

The whole day was emotional for me. My past and present were there in the faces of all our family and friends, but I felt profoundly alone as I walked down that aisle. Stephan was in my heart, but I longed for his physical presence.

———————

I came back to New York and back to work. Yves Carcelle had reached out to Peter Speliopoulos to replace Louise as our creative director. After four years of living in Paris, Peter wanted to come home, as his lifelong partner lived in New York. Our first collection this go-round was fall 2003. It was iconic and mostly black and ivory (sorry, Pino). It was based on—surprise!—The Body and The Suit. We started the show with The Body: bodysuits and dresses. We fused body-molded, sculpted silver keyholes by Robert Lee Morris onto draped jersey to expose slices of shoulder, back, and hips. For The Suit, we redefined power dressing with stretch tweed, molded tailoring, and fitted circular coats. The show was a hit with retailers and press alike. Style.com wrote, "With her boss (LVMH chairman Bernard Arnault, in a rare U.S. appearance) and a fresh crop of company executives sitting in the front row, Karan sent out a sensuous, assertive collection that included references to her own groundbreaking designs of two decades ago." The actress Cate Blanchett was our model for the campaign, and the perfect woman to convey the clothes' strength and soul.

"I feel like Frida Kahlo," Lynn said one day when she came to see me in the design studio. "I live in constant pain, morning, noon, and night."

Lynn's surgeon had placed expanders under the muscles in her chest after her double mastectomy in preparation for reconstructive surgery. The thinner you are, the more painful that is, and Lynn was as slim as she'd been in her model days. It turned out that she had a terrible infection and needed to be hospitalized. Giving up on the idea of reconstruction, the doctors took out the expanders, and Lynn escaped with me to Parrot Cay for a yoga retreat with Rodney Yee. While at Parrot Cay, Lynn woke up with her head spinning, seeing all sorts of bright colors shooting up out of her body. Rodney and I were excited. "You're experiencing kundalini rising!" we said in unison. Kundalini rising is an explosion of energy coursing through your chakras, usually precipitated by yoga or meditation, which we had been doing in spades. The only problem was that it kept repeating throughout the day. Finally I called my friend Dr. Susan Bressman, a neurologist and the wife of my lawyer David, who said to get Lynn home immediately.

Days later, we learned that Lynn had brain cancer, stage IV. Unrelated to her breast cancer, it was a primary tumor, and she would need aggressive surgery to remove the tumor. Her operation was scheduled for April 11, which happened to be the same day I was supposed to have a facelift. (I was fifty-four years old and single, and thanks to my raw food diet and yoga, my body was looking great. But as my weight dropped, so did my face. I wanted everything to match.) I called my doctor, Dan Baker, to reschedule. "Don't cancel just yet," he said. "Let me talk to your friend." He called Lynn, and the two of them agreed she could photograph my procedure before her brain surgery. He seemed to know that keeping her busy would be the best medicine of all. As planned, Lynn came with me, camera in hand. She only had time to stay for half of my facelift. Somewhere, locked in a vault, I have the photos. We're talking serious blackmail material; may no one ever find them.

Lynn went on to have her brain surgery, which left her with thirty-nine metal staples in a curved line on the side of her head. If anyone could make thirty-nine staples on the head look good, it was Lynn. In fact, a couple of weeks later, some kid came up to her on the street and asked who gave her the cool haircut. Without missing a beat, she replied, "Dr. Hollander at Sloan Kettering."

We recovered together. We went shopping on Madison Avenue, both of us in hats. I wanted to buy her a pair of Ann Demeulemeester boots as a form of retail therapy; they were on her bucket list and seemed like an easy thing to achieve. But they were out of stock. "Please, you have to have them sent to us. We need them for a shoot we have next week with Steven Sebring," I said, referring to the famed fashion photographer. The girl probably thought we were nuts, me with my swollen face and Lynn with her punk hair. But we did have a shoot, just two weeks after our surgeries. Steven, who's a great friend, took a series of photos of the two of us at my East Hampton home. The black-and-white photos are moody, raw, and beautiful. I'm wearing a cashmere blanket, and Lynn is wearing those boots, jeans, and not much else. We imagined doing a glossy book called *Scarred*, a contrasting study of life-affirming and life-saving surgeries. But we had to let the idea go when, just three weeks later, Lynn's tumor returned, requiring chemo and radiation. Still, she survived and, like Stephan before her, began the uneasy path of living with cancer.

My life gave me emotional whiplash: As Lynn was recovering from her second brain surgery, Gabby went into labor. I might not have been with her while she dressed for her wedding day, but I was *not* going to be deprived of this moment. Gabby knew better than to even try. "Gianpaolo, you stay by Gabby's head, and I'll be here at the bottom," I directed him in the delivery room. And sure enough, I witnessed my baby's baby entering this world. On May 28, 2003, baby Stefania Andrea de Felice was born. (Guess who they named her after.) She looked just like me, full head of hair and all. People always said Gabby looked like me, but I never saw it. But now I called the three of us Me, Mini, and Mini Me.

Being a new grandmother didn't slow me down. I was constantly making plans in order to not be alone. That summer I went by sailboat to Corsica with Barbra, Jim, and Richard. Then I headed to the Maldives, where the Ongs had just opened their fabulous Cocoa Island Resort, where the rooms are individual boats positioned on the sand and surrounded by water. I practiced yoga with Rodney Yee and learned to scuba-dive.

Everyone was thinking about who could replace Stephan, or at least someone I could date. Yves Carcelle introduced me to Gregory Colbert, a Canadian filmmaker and photographer best known for his "Ashes and Snow" exhibit, a study of surreally serene interactions between people and animals (picture a child reading to an elephant or kneeling next to a cheetah). He was looking for a place to store his work and asked about Stephan's studio. I couldn't imagine anyone's work there but Stephan's, so I offered my apartment instead. I had just moved into my Central Park West place, and the walls were bare. Gregory came and hung his pieces throughout. I was incredibly flattered—until I got an invoice for them. (They're still hanging in my apartment today.) Clearly, the dating thing was not going to be easy.

In late fall I met Barbra and Jim in Sun Valley. We walked into an art gallery, and I saw a sensational sculpture—soulful and primitive, almost ancient-looking. It was the work of a glassblower named William Morris, whom I had met while Stephan was alive. Bill was my kind of artist and my kind of man: sophisticated but raw, long-haired, built beyond built, and rugged as they come. I called my friend Ingrid Sischy, the editor of *Interview* magazine, and asked if she'd be interested in an article on Bill. "Absolutely," Ingrid said. It turned out that Bill was well known. He'd collaborated with another renowned glassblower, Dale Chihuly, whose work was collected by Elton John, among others. Who knew the glass-art world was so rarefied?

I didn't waste a second. Weeks later, in November, Marni, Ruthie, and I set out for Seattle, where Bill lived, and he took us to the Pilchuck Glass School, where he taught and worked. I was mesmerized. I knew nothing about glassblowing and the physical stamina it took to hoist glass into and out of a 1,700°F furnace. I got burnt twice just trying. My mind raced with design ideas.

"Bill, why don't you make earrings? In fact, why don't you make accessories for me?"

"Sure, why not?" he said. As I quickly found out, Bill was an adventurer, game to try anything, even fashion. He was totally otherworldly. He lived in what looked like a tree house; he was a bow-and-arrow hunter; he spearfished. At one point he put me on his motorcycle, and when we stopped to have coffee, he took off his shirt and did a headstand for me. Turns out he was a yogi, too! I felt like I'd dreamed him up. On the way back to his studio, we passed a sign for Alaska.

"Bill, can you take me to Alaska from here?"

"It's a bit far."

"How about Big Sur, then?" When I was in design school, I had this fantasy about living and designing in Big Sur—wearing a white robe, drawing up designs, and sending them to New York before going for a horseback ride on the beach.

"How would we get there?" he asked.

"I happen to have brought a plane with me," I said. Of course, Marni and Ruth were with us, too, but they promised to hang in the background.

When we arrived, I rented a chocolate Jaguar convertible (just like one I used to own), and away we went. We had a blast. He was fearless, jumping off bluff after bluff into the Pacific. We stayed at the Esalen Institute, the healing arts center and institute. Bill was just as woo-woo as I was. Everything was going swimmingly until we ran of gas—literally—and I let it slip that I didn't know how to pump gas.

"What do you mean, you don't know how to pump gas?" he asked, seriously confused.

"Exactly that."

"Do you cook?"

"I used to."

Catching on, he shook his head. "Let me give you an essential list of what one needs to do in life."

That got my attention. "Give it to me." And he did:

1. Fill your own gas tank.
2. Buy your own groceries.
3. Make your own bed.
4. Do your own laundry.
5. Cook your own meals.

I couldn't pretend I did any of them, at least not anymore. "Look, Bill," I said, as reasonably as I could. "There are certain things in life I had to give up in order to be a designer. It's just how it is."

We weren't a love match, but we continued to collaborate for my fall 2004 collection, one of my all-time favorites. The palette— aubergine, wine, bronze, and black—was borrowed from the earth. We had little fur shrugs over sexy jersey dresses with plunging neck- lines for a vibe that was urban with a savage sensuality. Bill created glass discs and buckle-like pieces that I draped fabric through to give structure to one-shouldered and twist-front looks. He even came to New York for our show and stayed at my apartment, but he wanted to sleep on the terrace. The city was much too much for him.

He was Tarzan, but I was no Jane. Still, my experience with Bill proved that there could be life after Stephan, that I could meet new people and be engaged. Creatively, I was reenergized by discovering a new medium, which I brought into my fashion. I loved the hands- on nature of working with an artisan; it reminded me of collaborat- ing with Robert Lee Morris. I slowly began to think less about what was missing from my life and more about what lay ahead. A world of possibility was starting to open.

24 | ARE YOU COMMITTED?

It was winter 2003, and I was feeling restless. I was living in my new home on Central Park West, the one that Stephan had bought for us and where I still live today. It's a beautiful, sprawling apartment with breathtaking views, a wraparound terrace, limestone floors, and dramatic art everywhere you look. (It's seven thousand square feet, and people are always shocked to see that I knocked out almost every wall and turned it into a one-bedroom apartment with a yoga studio and an enormous closet.) Still, living in such a large place by myself was hard. I have never been good at being alone.

My apartment may have been finished, but creating my dream family home in Parrot Cay was taking forever. At that time, building in the Turks and Caicos was a logistical feat as much as it was a design process. Plans were being drawn up, but we had a long road ahead. Of course, I didn't help the process; I was always changing my mind about what I wanted—what else is new? Stephan used to make decisions for me, as I clearly had commitment issues. Without him, some things were left floating, waiting to land. Kind of like I was.

Early in 2004, I discovered Kabbalah. For a non-practicing Jew, it was the last thing I expected to embrace. Many of my friends, like the jewelry designer Karen Erickson, thought I'd like Kabbalah, but I resisted the idea. Nothing was getting me into a temple. Then, while having dinner with my friend Lisa Fox at Lever House (her husband's restaurant), Lisa called Ruth Rosenberg, her spiritual teacher, and asked her to come join us, which she did. Ruth's husband, Moshe, came with her, and he started reading my face and my hands. Then Ruth talked about astrology. *Now this I can get into*, I thought.

The next night I invited Ruth to join me for dinner with my friends Demi Moore and Ashton Kutcher, then her husband, who were also Kabbalists. I learned that Kabbalah literally means "receiving," and that the practice was about gaining spiritual fulfillment in life by studying the spiritual laws of the universe, including human existence and the journey of the soul. "I've never subscribed to any one ideology," I told Ruth. "Spiritually speaking, I'm a free agent, open to anything and everything."

"I'm not here to change your mind, Donna," Ruth said. She handed me the Zohar, Kabbalah's spiritual text. "Study it and see what you think. Only you know what speaks to you."

It spoke to me soon enough—and right before a fashion show, no less. For my fall 2004 show (the one for which I collaborated with Bill Morris), I had the runway painted a golden color, so all the models would glow in its reflection. Sounds pretty, right? Well, it wasn't. At the rehearsal, the models looked jaundiced. In fact, anyone who came anywhere *near* the runway looked sickly. I was on the phone with Ruth freaking out as this was unfolding. She told me to find a quiet place and hold the Zohar she had given me. I hung up and did exactly that. I'm not exaggerating when I say a powerful bolt of energy flowed through me. I know it sounds crazy, but it's true. It was unlike anything I'd ever experienced. Shunned, I called back Ruth, who identified the energy as light.

"You must come to my show," I said. "I need you here." I just knew that if she came, everything would be okay. And it was. When I returned to the space the next day, the runway was painted black, and the show went smoothly.

Almost immediately afterward, Ruth asked me to join her for Passover in Los Angeles with Rav Philip Berg, the rabbi and dean of Kabbalah Center International, known for his modern, accessible interpretation of ancient Jewish mystical tradition. The first thing the Rav asked me was, "Are you committed?" That threw me. Committing to dinner plans was hard enough. But he was really asking something deeper: Was I a committed person? Could I be? And to what am I committed? We talked and talked throughout that Passover. The clincher for me was learning about Kabbalah's Spirituality for Kids, the part of the religion geared toward children. It was the simple but revolutionary idea of teaching them compassion, caring, and sharing through mind, body, and spirit. I'm such a kid myself— curious, playful—that the philosophy spoke to me. I started speaking to Ruth on a weekly basis and found myself embracing this spirituality born of the light and asking myself how I could become more involved, more committed. Life after Stephan, I was discovering, was full of surprises.

———

Professionally, my biggest surprise at this time was receiving the 2004 CFDA Lifetime Achievement Award. I was only fifty-five—wasn't this an old person's award, a retirement honor of some sort? On the other hand, it felt incredibly validating to be acknowledged by my peers for a career that had spanned thirty years. The actress Susan Sarandon presented the actual award, and we kissed on the lips, which caused a stir. Wonderful as the CFDA honor was, I refused to internalize it. I was far from done; in fact, in so many ways, I felt like I was just beginning. I accepted the award in an atypical Donna Karan dress: a sexy chartreuse green stretch lace wrap-and-drape style.

Work was moving along, but it was frustrating, because we had yet *another* CEO. Fred had moved on to Saks Fifth Avenue and been replaced by Jeffry Aronsson, formerly of Marc Jacobs. I liked Jeffry a lot (I liked *all* the CEOs) but, given the revolving door, found myself leery of getting too invested in any one person. So I stuck to what I knew best: design. Our collections were doing well, critically and commercially. Bonnie was no longer traveling, as she had two children and was starting up her own children's line. So now I got to be Bonnie and travel the world for ideas.

I was trying to stay in the flow, putting myself out there creatively, being there for Gabby and Lynn, and learning to embrace the light through my travels. I won't say I was succeeding, but I was trying.

I met John James (JJ) Biasucci, my first full-fledged romantic partner after Stephan, in Parrot Cay. I was popping over there regularly, usually with a friend or two or three. This time I was there for my birthday, and my friend the producer Sandy Gallin brought JJ, a personal trainer, as a gift for both of us to train with. I had met JJ once, briefly, at a party in Sandy's house in New York. At some point, Sandy took me aside and said, "Donna, I could really see you two together."

"What are you, crazy?" I said, peering at the young, handsome guy with the most ridiculous abs I'd ever seen.

"Give it a chance."

We had nothing in common. Nothing. But in a way, that was the point. We hit it off immediately.

JJ was great-looking, incredibly sweet, and laid back. Nothing bothered him. Yes, he was younger, by almost twenty-five years, but that actually made things simpler. I was completely relaxed in his company and never felt the need to have my hair or makeup done or be "on" around him—a freedom I hadn't known with a new person since high school. It wasn't like I had a lot of experience with men; I had married the only two men I'd been with. So this was new and exciting, and sexy, too. I was slim and feeling fantastic.

In just a short time, JJ came to know me better than anyone. Other than my granddaughter Stefania, I've never known anyone less impressed by what I do. He nicknamed me "Faskowitz," the original name of my father's family, and we loved going to the movies and eating popcorn and drinking Diet Cokes. To the surprise of my friends and family, we started dating seriously and traveling together. I asked him to go to Bali with me, and that trip sealed the deal. After the twenty-four-hour journey and nonstop time together, I could safely say we clicked. He loved Bali as much as I did. JJ became my private life, the person I hung out with when I didn't want to be Donna Karan and all that implied.

———————

The very next month, I set off on a three-week trip to Africa. My dear friend Richard Baskin and new friend Steve Reuther (the one who'd gone heli-skiing with another woman and was now like a brother to me) organized the whole thing, and we included our Sun Valley friend Nettie Frehling and her children. We were going on the ultimate safari: a tour of Kenya, Tanzania, Botswana, and South Africa.

The experience was transformative, transcendent, enlightening. And humbling. Because in Africa, I felt like a tiny grain of sand, a witness to something so much bigger than myself. I was instantly obsessed with the African bush, sleeping in a tent, not caring about my appearance, and being in nature untouched by man. We saw the migration of the wildebeest and more elephants than I thought lived on earth. And don't get me started about the hippos, my personal favorite. Of course, my fashion sense prevailed. The minute I saw the zebras, I thought, *But of course, graphic black and white! They're the best-dressed animals of all.*

The tribes we met were so happy and pure. The Masai had no sense of need or greed. They live in huts and don't care about material possessions. I started thinking maybe I had been a warrior in a past life because of how easily I can wrap and tie a scarf. I fell so in love with Africa and the Africans I was meeting, I wanted to plan a DKNY shoot in Cape Town. I had Danielle Reuther, Steve's daughter, call up all the local modeling agencies and arrange auditions.

"Donna, do we really have time for this?" Richard asked. "Can't you send your people to do this?"

"What's the worst that could happen?" I said. "You meet a cute girl, and I meet a cute guy."

We met the nicest people imaginable at the casting call. The shoot never happened, but I took everyone out to dinner, and Richard was thrilled to be surrounded by models.

———

Steve, Richard, and I were extremely close after our African safari, and we began planning our next adventure: a trip to Australia for a "Date with Destiny" seminar with the famed life coach Tony Robbins. I had already attended a weekend seminar with him in New Jersey, but this would be far more intensive. My assistant, Marni, who came with us, knew Tony and felt he was just the person who could help me find the inner calm I was looking for. As the seminar progressed, however, I just wasn't getting the appeal. People were having exultations left and right, but I was completely unmoved. *Great,* I thought. *I failed typing and draping, and now I'm failing Tony Robbins.*

On the last day, Tony asked the audience something to the effect of, "Who doesn't get it?"

Embarrassed, I raised my pinky. Next thing I knew, I was on the stage alone with Tony. Richard was mortified. *I* was mortified. There were three thousand people in that audience, and here I was, the globally known Donna Karan, up on the stage, pouring my heart out. But Tony makes you forget the audience. He speaks one-on-one with you until he gets you to reveal what's really going on inside. I started with my same-old same-old, "Leave me alone." I explained how I have all these people around me with expectations, and yet I felt very alone and unloved. Just like I had at est, I repeated the line over and over. Tony made me see that it wasn't people who were holding me back, it was the baggage I was holding. The mental stories I told myself (that I wasn't good enough, that I was an outsider, that I lived in fear of being alone) weighed me down. If I let the baggage go, I would have the space and energy to realize my potential. We kid ourselves that everyone else is the problem. But we have to start with ourselves. I could choose to "be here now," as Tony put it. To live in the present—not regret the past and not worry about the future.

———————

This made sense in theory, but it was hard to do. I often felt as if I was spinning my wheels, making the same mistakes again and again. A year and a half after breaking my knee, I broke the other one, also while skiing. Eight screws later, I was back in New York in a wheelchair. Nettie visited me and came bearing gifts: two little dachshunds, whom I named Cash and Mere. I love Nettie with all my heart, but I am not a small-dog person. They yipped and yapped nonstop, and I didn't know what to do with them. Nettie promised to take them back home to Sun Valley with her. But while she was still in New York, my stepdaughter Lisa called to say that she'd seen the most amazing chocolate Labrador retriever in the window of a pet store called American Kennel, across town on Madison Avenue. The problem was, a major snowstorm was under way, and we couldn't get a car. (Every big event in my life seems to happen during a snowstorm.) I called and asked if they could hold the puppy until after the storm. "We don't hold dogs," was the curt reply.

"I appreciate that," I said, "but I'm in a wheelchair and can't get there today."

"Sorry, lady, we don't hold dogs."

And then I did something I'd never done before: I used my name. "I'm the designer Donna Karan, and it's so important you hold this dog for me."

"I don't care who you are. We don't hold dogs."

I hate the word *no*, so I begged. "Look, my husband died, and I'm lonely. I need that dog!"

Begrudgingly, he said, "I'll hold him for an hour. No more."

So there I was, in my wheelchair, two dachshunds on my lap, with Nettie wheeling me across Central Park in a snowstorm. At one point, the chair tipped over, and the dogs scrambled away. Nettie put us all back in place, and we finally arrived at the store. There was my dog, waiting for me. Kismet! I fell crazy in love on the spot. I named my new baby Steph, because he, too, stole my heart in a snowstorm. He loves East Hampton and Parrot Cay as much as his namesake did, and he loves sleeping next to me every night. And he's best friends with Stefania, of course.

Meanwhile, Stefania was about to have a brother. Gabby was pregnant again—with a boy! Sebastian de Felice joined our world on July 26, 2005. From the start, he was as charming and handsome as his father. Our family seems to specialize in this kind of guy. Stephan was gone, but our family was expanding. I wish Stephan could have met these two amazing children. Then again, there's so much I wish Stephan could have lived to experience.

Within a year of Sebastian's birth, Ruth took me to Israel on a spiritual journey along with Moshe, their two children, and my friend Lisa Fox. It was my first trip there, and I had no idea what I was in for. David Bressman, who was now my personal lawyer, was nervous about me going to such a politically turbulent country and made Ruth assure him we would be protected at all times. The first day or so, Ruth pulled over to the side of a road, walked us down a path to water, and started taking off her clothes.

"What are you doing?" I asked, truly alarmed.

"We're about to experience our first *mikvah*," she answered calmly, then explained that a *mikvah* was a ritual to purify and cleanse one's body and soul. "You need to take off your clothes, too."

"But we're right by the road!"

"I only see cows here, Donna," Ruth said, wading into the water. "Besides, you're a designer. You're around naked women all the time." She had a point. In I went.

We repeated this cleansing ritual again and again. Ruth found all sorts of places for us to physically immerse ourselves in Judaism—maybe fifteen in that one week. We visited ancient burial sites, including the graves of those who wrote the Zohar. I became addicted to *mikvahs* and was constantly asking Ruth where our next one was.

I still Skype with Ruth every week, mostly Thursdays, and every week is a lesson on my journey. I spent a lifetime not having a faith, and now I'm just so grateful to have somewhere to turn for guidance. Ruth, like Stephan, calls me out on my nonsense. She never lets me play the victim or blame someone else for my unhappiness. Instead, she reminds me that I possess the gift of life and light—that we all do—and that the more light I give out, the more I receive. It's the simplest and yet the most empowering knowledge I've ever received.

25 | CONNECTING THE DOTS

I've always believed that if there's a problem, there must be a solution. You just have to get creative. That's how I approach designing and just about everything else in my life. When AIDS was literally killing our industry, I came up with a way to marry philanthropy and commerce in the form of Seventh on Sale. In the same spirit, I was thrilled to collaborate on Kids for Kids, for pediatric AIDS, and then again to create Super Saturday, in support of a cure for ovarian cancer. I've also contributed to countless charities, ready to jump in whenever asked. My instinct is to be proactive. I want to *do* something, fix it, get involved in a way that will bring others together and make a difference. I had been on a path of helping others this way for years; I just didn't know where it was leading me.

Then, right after we went public in 1996, I had a vision—a term I rarely use outside of design. It was quite specific. I saw three connecting buildings: one a gallery; one a retail store, spa, and café; and the third a condo building with a restaurant on the street level. The vision was highly detailed and highly personal. I had spent a lifetime searching for calm at retreats and spas, on nature treks, even at self-help seminars. Why not bring that peace and energy to the city and live with it every day? I wanted to create a community of consciousness and change, and this vision was the answer. It would bring together all the tools people like me needed to cope with living in the chaos of the city. Everything would be integrated—the objectives, the activities, the commitment to solving problems. You could live in the condos or just be a member. The name said it all: Urban Zen. I imagined Urban Zens in major cities across the country—and eventually the world. I talked about it with Stephan, and even half joked that his studio would be a perfect space for the first center. He agreed Urban Zen was something I was born to create; he even put a clause into my LVMH contract that allowed me the creative freedom to do it.

When Stephan asked me to take care of the nurses, the desire to create my own health and caring initiative became especially heartfelt. Sickness had hit home. It was no longer something that happened to other people, it happened to me, my husband, my life. No one escapes illness, and no one is prepared for it, either. My Urban Zen concept could be a way to take care of the patient, the caregivers, and the medical community, starting with the nurses.

Having a concept is one thing, but turning it into reality is another. Two experiences drove me to act, each brought to me by a friend.

In 2005, Barbra called. "We must get tickets to President Clinton's Global Initiative," she said. "It's happening in September at the Sheraton in New York." The former president was gathering the most powerful, highest-profile people he knew and holding workshops to discuss crucial global issues and actionable solutions. I was bowled over. What a brilliant way to solve problems! At that first conference, I wanted to clone myself so I wouldn't miss any of the panel discussions. I met and saw extraordinary people: the king and queen of Jordan, Bono, Tony Blair, Bishop Desmond Tutu, Condoleezza Rice, Rupert Murdoch, Richard Branson, and Laura Bush. It was a nonpolitical event, just a call to action for the greater good.

I was so inspired. I thought this should happen more than once a year; it should be a way of life! That was the first dot leading to Urban Zen.

A year later, my friend Sonja Nuttall, whom I'd met the summer after Stephan died, drew the second dot. "Would you be interested in doing a fundraiser at Stephan's studio for His Holiness [the Dalai Lama] and Norbulingka Institute?" she asked. Sonja worked with the institute, which was dedicated to the preservation of Tibetan history and culture.

"Are you kidding?" I shrieked. "Of course I'd be interested! How soon can we do it?"

Sonja and I organized the fundraiser HOPE. The Dalai Lama wasn't available until the day after we'd planned, so Rodney and Colleen offered to teach yoga instead. The minute I walked into the studio and saw all the mats laid out among beautiful Urban Zen banners, I thought, *This is it. My calm in the chaos. Urban Zen was meant to be.*

His Holiness came the next day, and we also hosted a private lunch that included my whole family, the Tibetan scholar Robert Thurman, Rodney and Colleen, and friends like Trudie Styler and Deb Jackman, the wife of Hugh Jackman. Of course, I hardly spoke to His Holiness. I simply couldn't. His energy, his spirit, and his light just took my breath away. We raised over a million dollars, and the studio was blessed in every sense.

The HOPE event ignited something within me. It touched my heart in a visceral way. I could use my gift of creating and communicating to make a real difference in all the things I valued most— culture, health care, and education—and I drew up a business plan to create a center that would connect them. To me, the vision was so clear. Unfortunately, it wasn't to others: everyone tried to talk me into focusing on just one initiative. But yoga was my model, and yoga represents the union of mind, body, and spirit as well as the past, present, and future. I could go on about this for days, but let me break my initiatives down the way I did my Seven Easy Pieces, since they, too, are interchangeable:

1. **The preservation of culture (the past).** The more I travel, especially to Africa and the East, the more I appreciate the wisdom and beauty of vanishing cultures. I love anything artisan: crafts, beading, vegetable dyes, and have worked to incorporate them into my designs whenever possible. When something is made by hand, you feel the soul that went into it, and the generations that passed down their skills. But globalization threatens to turn us into one homogenous people. If we don't raise awareness now, we will lose individual cultures. We need to keep these traditions alive, and integrate them into modern life, as they have so much to teach us.

2. **Integrative health care (the present).** This came out of my experience with Stephan. When he was sick, I couldn't make him better, but I had the tools to make him *feel* better, including Reiki, yoga, acupuncture, meditation, breath work, and massage therapy—all ancient practices, I might add. I saw what a big difference these integrative therapies made, which led me to ask, where is the "care" in health care? There is a void in the system. Everyone treats the disease, but what about the patient? I have two goals for health care: patient care and patient navigation (directing care in the age of specialists). Let's treat the whole patient, mind, body, and spirit, and guide them through the maze of finding the best help in the first place. Even President Clinton, who got healthy through a vegan diet, has created a separate Health Access Initiative to take on this issue.

3. **Empowering children through education (the future).** I was so inspired by Kabbalah's Spirituality for Kids, which was

founded by Madonna. In Israel, the organization is called Kids Creating Peace, and it brings Israeli and Palestinian children together. How smart and strategic. Change starts on the educational level. You can't preserve culture without creating awareness. You can't improve health care without teaching people what steps to take. You can't build for a peaceful future without bringing kids together. It's so simple it's stupid. Let's bring this mind-set into schools and prepare kids to do better by teaching them the mind, body, and spirit connection, starting with yoga and meditation.

These initiatives weren't about me. They were born of a need to reach out, to give back. I achieved so much at a young age and often wondered what my higher purpose was. Every time I'd get a woman into the dressing room, she'd tell me her problems. And all our issues are the same: we love our families, we want to keep them and ourselves healthy, and we want a better future for our children. I may not have the answers, but I have the platform and the profile to connect, communicate, and create change.

In 2007, we hosted our first full-scale Urban Zen event: a Well-Being Forum spread over ten days with a hundred speakers and more than two hundred attendees a day. I hired Rachel Goldstein, a close friend of Gabby's, as program director, and Richard Baskin flew in to help produce it. Our co-chairs included my doctors Woody Merrell and Frank Lipman, Rodney and Colleen, and model/maternal health advocate Christy Turlington Burns. The experience was a true East-meets-West look at health care.

The list of the speakers says it all: doctors like Memorial Sloan Kettering's Larry Norton, Mehmet Oz, Dean Ornish, Christiane Northrup, and Deepak Chopra; advocates such as Michael J. Fox, Karen Duffy, and Kathy Freston; scholars like Robert Thurman and Reverend Eric Schneider; spiritualists like Buddhist master Joan

Halifax, my Kabbalah teacher Ruth Rosenberg, and Zen master Roshi Pat O'Hara; communicators like Arianna Huffington and Ingrid Sischy; and yogis like Richard Freeman, Gary Kraftsow, and James Murphy, as well as Sharon and David. We also had influencers like Tony Robbins, Marianne Williamson, and Eve Ensler and icons like Lou Reed and Diane von Furstenberg. Patients like Kris Carr, the wellness activist and cancer survivor who made the amazing film *Crazy Sexy Cancer*, took part, as did my dear friends Christina Ong and the retailer Joyce Ma.

I was in my glory. Every day started and ended with a yoga practice. We served nutritious lunches. On the last night of the forum, my spiritual sister, the performing artist Gabrielle Roth, who until her death in 2012 practiced healing and awakening through dance, gave a magical performance and led a group celebration. "This is incredible, Donna," Lynn Kohlman told me on that last day. "Look at all these people. We're really making a difference." Lynn had spoken on a panel and attended as much of the Forum as possible. She was physically weak, her speech was slurred, and she often got confused. But she was engaged—and remained so until her death in 2008, a full six years after her diagnosis of brain cancer. She had the essential tools—a great yoga practice and compassionate caretaking.

———

Of course, I couldn't *just* do a forum. I wear layers, and I think and act in layers, too. Though I had done pop-up stores in the Hamptons, I decided to open a permanent Urban Zen store to coincide with the conference. I called on Kevin Salyers, the Madison Avenue store director, to help set it up. I'd bought the townhouse next door to Stephan's studio, which happened to have a small storefront. We sourced from the many cultural objects in our warehouse and ordered in Young Living essential oils, my personal favorites, which were being used extensively throughout the forum. We sold the

Como Shambhala products I knew and loved as well as wellness books, DVDs, and audio recordings.

Naturally, I had to offer clothes, too. I hired the designer Mark Kroeker to work with me to create the kind of pieces I've always wanted: high-end styles that transcended fashion and were all about comfort. We designed a capsule collection of easy tops, palazzo pants, a jumpsuit, a few cashmere pieces, and some scarves. There was no retail strategy behind them, only the desire to make clothes I personally wanted. It was incredibly freeing to design for myself again and not have to cater to an established customer's expectations or the industry's rigid schedule.

The Urban Zen store was a marriage of commerce and philanthropy, not unlike Seventh on Sale and Super Saturday. But in this case, we were selling soulful, global handcrafted products to support the Urban Zen Foundation. For example, everyone loved the Balinese furniture I designed, and now I could sell it here. Ditto for the many artisan pieces I wore and adored. We had done this kind of thing at 819 Madison Avenue, but we had space limitations. Now we had a whole store to play with. (In 2008, we expanded further with a store in Sag Harbor, and eventually we'd open pop-up stores in places like LA and Aspen.)

Our forum was an amazing success, and Rodney came up with a perfect way to keep it going. "Let's train yoga teachers right here in the studio," he said. "They understand the mind-body-spirit connection better than anyone." So we co-founded our Urban Zen Integrative Therapy (UZIT) program, where we train and certify UZIT practitioners in yoga therapy, aromatherapy, Reiki, therapeutic massage, meditation, nutrition, and palliative care. They would treat what we called PANIC: pain, anxiety, nausea, insomnia, and constipation—the very real inconveniences of being sick. So much of this was inspired by my personal healer, Ruth Pontvianne, and all the ways she cared for Stephan when he was ill.

I'm proud to say our UZIT program is thriving. We had a hundred graduates the first year, and to date have certified more than seven hundred at varying levels. As managed by one of our first UZIT practitioners, Gillian Cilibrasi, we train in partnerships with established health institutions across the country. Dr. Woody Merrell collaborated with Beth Israel Medical Center in New York, where we studied the effects of our program for a year and calculated that it resulted in a savings of $900,099 on just one floor. We've gone on to partner with health care facilities ranging from the UCLA Health System to the American Cancer Society Hope Lodge. Our classes at various yoga conferences around the world are always packed.

Our clothing line, which I now design with Bessie Afnaim and Oliver Corral, is thriving, too. Everything we do is as simple and luxurious as a T-shirt. And like a T-shirt, every item is seasonless and ageless—ready to cross climates and time zones. If I can't travel, work, do yoga, and sleep in something, I don't want to know from it. We're known for our jersey and cashmere-and-silk tube dresses, tunics, leggings, luxe knits, and leather and suede jackets. Layer them as you wish. Add a handmade Haitian artisan necklace, a handwoven scarf by Celine Cannon (an artist who worked with Stephan), or maybe a hand-tooled belt by leather artisan Jason Ross. We also make our own jewelry and accessories. Everything is handcrafted and highly individual. And I have finally achieved my lifelong quest to show and sell in the same season! Miraculous, right?

My love affair with Haiti began right around the time Urban Zen was expanding beyond New York City. In early January 2010, I was consumed by a family crisis. Gianpaolo's father Guido was sick, and we were in the hospital with him around the clock. When I returned to work, Michelle Jean, the Haitian manager of the Urban Zen center at the time, was beside herself. "Haven't you heard about Haiti's earthquake?" she asked, obviously distraught.

I truly hadn't, as we hadn't been reading the news. I quickly learned that the earthquake, which occurred on January 12, had measured 7.0 on the Richter scale and killed more than 230,000 people, injuring another 300,000. Just as troubling, 1.5 million people had been displaced. "We have to do something," Michelle kept saying, and I thoroughly agreed.

But what? I wasn't going to write a check—that's not how I help. I prefer to take action. Sonja and I started to call around. We found out that many aid groups were heading down there, and I offered my plane. We also gathered yoga blankets, oils, and other supplies to help the international doctors and nurses who were exhausted from working around the clock. (They especially appreciated the aromatherapy, given all the death and decay.) But it was the displaced population that I was most worried about. Where do you begin to put 1.5 million homeless people?

My friend Lisa Fox went online and found a disaster-relief pop-up tent that could house ten people at a time. It came in a box along with practical supplies such as cots, blankets, and dishes. Each tent cost $1,000, so we set out to raise money to buy a ton of them. We put one up in our Urban Zen store and mobilized to launch an event called Hope, Help & Relief Haiti, partnering with music executive Andre Harrell, the Mary J. Blige & Steve Stoute Foundation for the Advancement of Women Now, and André Balazs and his Standard Hotels. We also organized an initiative called Tent Today, Home Tomorrow specifically to raise money for the shelters.

So many people were reaching out to help that it became a matter of consolidating efforts. Various groups within the music, fashion, and entertainment industries joined us. Mary J. Blige and Wyclef Jean performed, and we raised over $1 million. (I also had a funny karmic moment. That night Wyclef handed me a check for thousands of dollars. "Is this for the tents?" I asked, confused. "No, it's for you. I owe you," he said, and explained that many years ago he had worked in the shipping department in our New Jersey warehouse. One night he'd fallen asleep and there was a robbery. He'd always felt responsible and had sworn he'd pay me back for the missing merchandise. I was happy to buy more tents with the money.)

While I had never been to Haiti, I had an idea for it based on what I had seen my friend John Hardy, the jewelry designer, do in Bali. John had tapped into the miracle of indigenous bamboo— a plant with the strength of concrete—and was building villages. Bali was a perfect model of people relying on natural resources and artisan traditions to create a sustainable economy—a thought that had struck me on my very first trip there. *What do they grow in Haiti?* I wondered. Someone mentioned the aromatic plant vetiver, and I thought, *Aha—perfume!* We could ask designers to each create a fragrance and a bottle. Ideas started percolating in my head.

I soon found out that the Clinton Global Initiative was knee-deep in all things Haiti, and I also met a woman named Joey Adler, whose organization, OneXOne, was working to build a manufacturing factory there. We organized a trip in late 2010 and brought along Sonja Nuttall and my Urban Zen right arm and chief of staff, Marni Lewis. (For my next trip, we brought photographer Russell James, John Hardy, and our Urban Zen jewelry designer Isabel Encinias.)

I was awestruck from the moment I arrived. The island is breathtakingly beautiful, and under the layers and layers of devastation, I saw potential, promise, and possibilities. I also fell hopelessly in love with the people, who were suffering but also pure and spirited. As we traveled the countryside, we saw the crafts of incredible artisans, from the beautiful tobacco leaf work of Jean-Paul Sylvaince and his girlfriend Yvette Celestin to extraordinary crystal and wrought iron chandeliers by a woman named Karine "Cookie" Villard.

Of course, I felt a connection to Stephan, too. We had just left some metalworkers in Croix-des-Bouquets and were now in a Port-au-Prince hotel. I loved the patina of the hotel's iron railings and details. "We need to find the person who did this work, so we can have them help the guys in Croix-des-Bouquets," I said.

"That's me," said a voice behind me. It was Philippe Dodard, a local artist and sculptor. He was tall and charming, and immediately invited me to his home and studio up a steep hill. That's when I saw how much in common he had with Stephan artistically, starting with his abstract line paintings. Philippe had even built a circular metal staircase like the one Stephan did for our Hamptons home. The only thing he was missing was the ponytail. Like me, he was a yogi and a Reiki master, so I felt even more of a bond.

As Philippe introduced me to the artists he knew and supported, I kept wondering, *Why don't we know about all the talent in this little country?* Then inspiration struck: To get the word out, I'd help develop these gorgeous crafts into something marketable and sustainable for the communities that make them. I collaborated with the Clinton Global Initiative to implement plans while working directly with artisans to create objects of desire to appeal to a global market.

My goal was—and still is—to help Haiti help itself. More than that, I want to help create a model on how to help other countries struck by disaster: Nepal, India. . . . It's similar to a family's illness; disaster strikes and none of us know what to do. Thank God for relief organizations. Rebuilding after a catastrophe is a long road, and it's so rewarding to be a part of that. Bringing awareness is key: I've brought *Vogue* to Haiti and have been filmed with Oprah while she was there, too. The more we can keep a spotlight on Haiti, the better. I'm happy to use my profile in any way possible. I can't think of a better use for my platform.

When the Clinton Global Initiative asked me to design its 2012 Global Citizen Award, I worked closely with Cookie, the chandelier artist, and Nadia Swarovski of the famed crystal family. Our hand-crafted design echoed the CGI logo and was a beautiful expression of raw and refined worlds coming together. Two remarkable things happened during the ceremony. First, President Clinton announced that our design would be the permanent CGI award—an incredible honor considering they had previously given out a different one every other year. Second, the president called me onto the stage. "I think we should give an award to Donna Karan," he said. "I believe that it is overwhelmingly because of her that the arts and crafts center of the Haitian economy may be the first sector that is actually doing better today than it was before the earthquake, and I will never be able to thank her enough." I was floored—and truly humbled. Once again, my life had come full circle. He had inspired me to start Urban Zen, and now he was recognizing its efforts. (Just a year earlier, we had honored President Clinton with The Stephan Weiss Apple Award, a tribute we have also given to New York City, as accepted by Michael Bloomberg, Dr. Mehmet Oz, and Courtney Sales Ross.)

———————

Inevitably, Haiti's culture worked its way into my Donna Karan New York designs. Philippe Dodard's bold brushstrokes inspired my spring 2012 collection, which featured sexy printed dresses, pencil skirts, and jackets. Russell James photographed our ad campaign in Jacmel with the gorgeous model Adriana Lima. When the ads first came out, the media criticized me for exploiting Haiti by photo-graphing expensive, glamorous clothes in a poor country. I argued that we had to embrace Haiti into the larger world; otherwise it would be ignored and forgotten. Two years later, we returned to shoot our spring Donna Karan New York 2014 campaign, again with Russell and Adriana, by the iconic Citadel fortress.

These days, I try to go to Haiti at least four times a year to work directly with the artisans. (Conveniently, it's a half-hour flight from Parrot Cay.) I've formed a family there too: after spending the day visiting artisan communities, hospitals, orphanages, and educational centers, I often run into people like Sean Penn, the actress Maria Bello, the director Paul Haggis, and David Belle, founder of Cine Institute (with whom I work closely on my Urban Zen communications). Haiti has become a second home for all of us. And I'm thrilled that Urban Zen now has a presence there in the form of expanding UZIT programs in hospitals and DOT—the Design, Organization, Training Center for Haitian Artisans, a collaboration with my alma mater, Parsons New School of Design and artisan leader Paula Coles (her signature weave bags made out of recycled T-shirts are the only ones I carry year-round).

We've also established an Urban Zen Children's Art Center with the creative visionary Caroline Sada, and we work closely with Maryse Pénette-Kedar, or the "Mother of Haiti," as I call her, who runs the PRODEV educational centers there. Other than playing with my own grandchildren, nothing lifts my heart more than sitting for hours creating crafts with those enchanting kids.

On my very first visit in 2010, we strolled around a small village and ran into dozens of smiling children. They walked us to their school, a little wood shack where a teacher was teaching geography to a class of seven- to thirteen-year-olds. I drew a map of the United States and Haiti on the wall they were using as a blackboard. One of the kids asked, "Why is Haiti so small?" I immediately drew an enormous heart around the tiny island and said, "That's my heart and it belongs to Haiti."

26 | LETTING GO

My life has been a continuous cycle of birth and death, and this book has proven to be another example. Just as I'm releasing my life story to the world, I'm saying goodbye to Donna Karan New York. I had no idea that the end of this book would co-incide with the end of my Donna Karan collection, and I don't have a lot of time to reflect—I've already passed three hard deadlines for this last chapter. So here's the story, unvarnished and unprocessed.

There have been rumors for a while about me stepping down. I had been speculating about it myself. My thirtieth anniversary show for fall 2014 was extraordinary. The photographer Steven Sebring created a film, *Woman in Motion,* to introduce the show, and the model Karlie Kloss wore a new iconic red bodydress designed to bring my bodysuit into the future. The press was abuzz, assuming it was my farewell statement. The timing was logical, but I just couldn't step down. Hard as it was to leave Anne Klein, leaving my own namesake was a whole other matter. *Just one more collection,* I'd tell myself. Then, after that show, I'd swear to Patti, *Okay, I'm done. Next season will be my last.* But I just couldn't let go.

I'm pulled in so many directions—my work in Haiti with Urban

Zen, my travels around the world. And after a lifetime of dressing (and being) the woman who juggles a million roles, I'm here to tell you that it takes a toll. People always ask me "How do you do it all?" The truth is I don't. I can't tell you how much time I spend organizing my schedule, trying to squeeze in this person, that appointment, a fund raiser for this, a quick fabric trip abroad, and, of course, quality time in my design rooms. And then there's my family life and time with friends, as well as my personal time. I've learned that the calendar only holds so many hours, no matter how much you try to pack into it.

Still, I'd been in denial, insisting that I could keep all these balls in the air. Remember when I suggested to Calvin that we combine our "Klein" companies into one so we could both work only half a year? He scoffed at me, saying he loved what he did and didn't need time off. Well, trendsetter that he is, Calvin stepped away more than ten years ago and is happily applying his enormous talent into other amazing creative projects.

The universe was sending me messages to follow his example. While writing this book, my Madison Avenue store closed. Not having a retail home in New York City was the first dot. Then the second dot—my right and left arms left the company: Jane, my co-DKNY designer, and Patti Cohen, my redheaded sister—two people who had been with me from my Anne Klein days. Change was happening all around me. The time had come. I needed to close one chapter to begin the next: nurturing Urban Zen, the Company and the Foundation, as well as my philanthropic pursuits. Long story short, the Collection's been put on hold, at least for a while. It was the right decision at the right time.

I knew I'd be sad, but it was truly heartbreaking. I had to say goodbye to the people who have become my family, who have stood beside me through every professional up and down, every good and bad review, and the many CEOs and management teams. On a personal level, one of my most emotional moments was walking into the design room and seeing all the gorgeous fabrics that had just arrived from Europe for the spring collection that wouldn't be. I immediately started touching the luxe textures, and within minutes, began draping them on a mannequin. I couldn't help myself.

September 2015 (which will have passed by the time you read this) will be only the second season since I was nineteen that I have not presented a spring show. The only other time that happened was on 9/11. How amazing is that?

I've been asking myself, who and what is Donna Karan? Is it a brand? A dress? A person? Where does my story go from here? I wish I could tell you I have it all mapped out, but I don't. I'm nervous and confused, but excited.

For more than thirty years, I signed my fashion show press releases, "To be continued . . ." That was the only way I could let a collection go down the runway. Because my creative process is ongoing. I am never done. There's always something to add: a last-minute thought, an idea I need more time to execute. I feel that way now. There's so much I want to do: hotels, condos, furniture, and yes, fashion. But my biggest focus is on Urban Zen and its three initiatives: healthcare, education, and preserving culture. And I'll never stop designing my Urban Zen fashion collection—after all, I need something to wear.

As I reflect back, I realize that so much of my career has been an adventure, with twists and turns I never could have predicted. Let's start with the fact that I had planned to be a stay-at-home mother. When Anne died, I felt like a spaceship had beamed me up and swooped off into space, taking me on a journey I wasn't prepared for. But I stayed on. Jumping off wasn't an option, because I was committed to continuing Anne's legacy. Ten years later, I did not set out to open the Donna Karan Company. I wanted to have a small collection under the Anne Klein umbrella. I had to be fired—pushed out of the company!—in order to start my own business.

I've never been a woman with a laid-out strategy. I have passion and enthusiasm. The word *no* is not in my vocabulary. Don't tell me something's impossible. In my mind, anything and everything is possible. I just need to stay open and access my gift—the light that flows through me, that flows through all of us—and trust that it will lead me in the right direction.

This is where my spirituality kicks in. I believe we're guided on our journeys. I've had a series of teachers in my life, and the greatest ones have been birth and death. All the unexpected endings and beginnings have happened for a reason. People—like my Kabbalah teacher Ruthie—and events have been placed on my path to steer me forward; sometimes I've listened to them, and other times I've learned the hard way, repeating mistakes over and over until I got things right.

My father's death changed my mother forever. When he died, she disconnected from friends and family and threw herself into work. As much as I swore I'd never be like her, I've gone on to do exactly what she did: fill up the emptiness inside with work. As a child I hated Seventh Avenue, and look where I wound up. Was it destiny or irony? I don't know, but I know Seventh Avenue has been home to some of the greatest moments in my life. It's also where I've felt most connected to my parents.

Years later, when I found my rock on the beach in East Hampton, I was drawn to its stillness, calm, and simplicity. Could I be that rock?, I wondered. I realize now that the answer is no. My personality is to do, do, do. Blame it on my ADD or my fear of stopping and being alone—whatever the reason, chaos is my middle name. I create it better than anything else I do. But it's also brought me an amazing, exciting life. I even named my most favorite fragrance Chaos.

I've been given so much. Mark gave me the gift I wanted more than anything: motherhood. He and I are now grandparents together, and we are a true modern family, getting together for holidays and weekends at the beach. (Mark has been with the same woman, Yvonne, for thirty years, so he has more than recovered from Hurricane Donna.) I still feel guilty about not being a Betty Crocker mom to Gabby, but I gave her the Donna Karan version instead: laughs, high drama, incredible clothes, and most of all, a lifelong best friend. We are inseparable. We look alike, dress alike, vacation together, live next door to each other at the beach, and even have connecting businesses in Sag Harbor: Urban Zen shares a courtyard with Gabby and Gianpaolo's hot restaurant, Tutto il Giorno. Gabby is my life's greatest treasure, bar none.

Then there was Stephan. Where would I have been without his love, strength, belief in me and fierce support, not to mention his remarkable business savvy? He gave me Corey and Lisa as well as my first five grandchildren, Etan, Maya Rose, Mackensie, Mercer, and Miles. When I was young and unsure of myself, I walked away from Stephan. Thank God that the second time around, I had the good sense to glue myself to him and never let go. Our road was long, creative, and soulful. I still feel his presence at Urban Zen (originally his studio), and he continues to guide me.

Gabby and Gianpaolo gave me the gift of Stefania and Sebastian, who bring me pure joy and keep me young. Thanks to Stefania, I'm trying to ride horses again, and Sebastian is trying to teach me how to use the computer. Horses and computers: two lost causes, but I love the bonding they bring.

Just like I can't separate the past from the present, I also can't separate the personal from the professional. My fashion relationships have shaped me into who I am. There would be no Donna Karan it weren't for Anne Klein, period, end of report. But that thought applies to many others, too. You're only as strong as the people you work with. For a woman as creatively liquid as I am, I need a glass to hold me, and I've been blessed with the very best support team in the world. Thanks to countless late nights and quarterly deadlines, we've also become a tight-knit family—hysterical with drama at times, but one that adores and counts on one another. As a kid, I was always looking for a warm, loving family, and fashion has given me that.

———————

I love the process of designing as much as I ever have. I love the conversation with fabric, how it tells me what to do and takes me to places I wasn't planning to go. I love the juxtaposition of combining something fluid, like jersey, with something tailored, like stretch wool. It's a contradiction and a union, just like a man and woman. Relationships fascinate me.

As a designer, the most profound relationship I have is with the body—how to sculpt and release, accent and delete. Black is my muslin, because you're wearing a silhouette that goes from day into night. Your skin, hair, and personality are the focus. I want clothes to be a part of you, a supporting player in your story, never the story itself.

That's why I love stretch. Yes, it's sexy, but it's more about finding comfort. I hate restrictions of any kind (physical or psychological), and stretch gives you mobility. Putting stretch into a man's jacket was pivotal, because they hadn't known such comfort before. To me, comfort is another word for confidence.

My Seven Easy Pieces were born out of wanting to give women

confidence. My customer needed to go to work and feel good, but she didn't have time to figure it out in the morning. So I edited her closet. I told her, "Here, start with a bodysuit, add a handful of pieces, and the outfits will create themselves. You'll look chic, sophisticated, and as authoritative as any man in the room. Only you'll look like a woman." Remember, in 1985 professional women were wearing boxy suits and bowties to emulate men. My feeling was, *You're never going to fool anyone into thinking you're a man, so for God's sake, be a woman!*

One of my greatest pleasures in life is following a woman into the dressing room and taking her left when she thinks she's going right. She wants to conceal, and I want to reveal. My underlying message is, "Don't be afraid of your body. Embrace it. Celebrate it." I'm sure I've improved sex lives.

The artisan hand is integral to my design. I love taking a sculptural piece, whether a Robert Lee Morris gold disc or a Bill Morris glass one, and letting it ground and give shape to the fabric threaded through and around it. Similarly, I'd feel naked without one of my Haitian leather or horn necklaces and my leather arm bracelets. I also love anything that speaks of commitment to a larger cause, whether it's a T-shirt that raises awareness or our leather wrap bracelets: Not One More (for gun safety) and Stand Up for Courage (against bullying).

Inspiration fuels me. Every time I take a trip or spend time in nature, you see it in my clothes. Sometimes the inspiration is practical; Julie Stern jokes that he could always tell when it was a "fat Donna" collection (airy, full silhouettes) or a "skinny Donna" collection (long, lean, and formfitting). Yes, designing is highly personal.

Then there's my never-ending love affair with New York, a city that captures the energy of the world in one place. I've spent more than twenty-five years absorbing that energy and channeling it into the fast-fashion exuberance of DKNY street chic. I've designed clothes with sequins that shimmer like the skyline at night, patterns that echo subway graphics, and palettes that mimic glistening pavement and urban sunsets. DKNY has become a part of New York that touches people in Dubai, England, Russia, Japan—everywhere. I am so proud of what Jane Chung and I created together.

––––––––––

Fashion is evolving. There was a time when you bought an entire new wardrobe every season. Hemlines went up or the pants went narrow, and everything you owned suddenly looked wrong, wrong, wrong. Now women shop for a moment, an item that makes everything feel fresh. Today's way of dressing makes being a fashion designer more challenging than ever. I used to advise aspiring designers to get a job in retail to understand their customer. Now I tell young designers to travel the world, even if it means backpacking and staying in hostels. Working in Haiti showed me how to be creative on a whole new level. As Anne Klein told me, you're a designer whether you're designing a toothbrush, a house, or a bed. I was fortunate to have a mentor, but the world can be your mentor. Go and see it. Everyone is so busy chasing fame, but the real joy and excitement come from the process.

I know that more than ever. I am a child at heart, and I love to play and create. Like a child, I've always felt that I have all the time in the world and so much ahead of me. But I'm older now, and I realize that time is short. The clock is ticking. I have projects to complete with Urban Zen. I have endless plans for Haiti. And then there are the places I need to see, including Cuba, Colombia, and China—yes, all countries that begin with the letter C. It's a big world, and I want to be a part of it.

My career may have turned me into a brand, but I'm a woman first. I'm also a mother, grandmother, friend, sister, philanthropist, yogi, woman on a spiritual quest, caretaker, mentor, teacher, and student—and now I'm a writer, too. I gave birth to one child, and as a designer, I gave birth to a million ideas. I created a brand far larger than I. LVMH plans to take DKNY into the next century and beyond. As the industry and technology shift, so must the creative approach.

Changes like these are exciting—and scary, too. Like Gabby, my brand has grown up and needs to live its own life. I can't wait to see how my legacy unfolds. I can't wait to see how my life unfolds, too. By the time you read this, God knows where I'll be on my personal journey (though I can promise I will finally be attending the Burning Man Festival, something I've never had time to do before). I'm anxious to read the sequel to this book!

———

For my sixtieth birthday, a bunch of friends took me to Lake Powell in Arizona. We rented a houseboat stocked with every water toy under the sun. Lake Powell is beautiful and enormous, and surrounded by rocky canyons, and I wanted to take out the Jet Skis. My friend Richard Baskin agreed to come, but warned me, "No matter what, Donna, we have to stay together. It's dangerous here, and you can get lost."

We were bobbing up and down on the Jet Skis when Richard realized he'd forgotten his sunglasses. "Don't you dare go out on your own," he said. But I fired up and took off anyway. Hours went by, and while I loved the freedom at first, I eventually realized I was lost. *Really* lost. Then I ran out of gas. The sun was setting, and I was in the middle of nowhere, no boats in sight, terrified. Right when I was starting to shiver from fear, Richard and a search party appeared and saved me.

Later that night, Richard said, "Donna, today was the perfect metaphor for how you live your life: You gun it without knowing where the fuck you're going and hope for the best."

He's right. Nothing turns me on like a leap of faith. When I get an idea into my head, I go for it. I put menswear on a runway without a business to support it. I tried crazy designs that were successful and many that flopped, including my now-iconic cold shoulder. If I'd stopped and thought about half the things I wanted to do, they never would have happened. On the one hand, I hate to let go; on the other, I can't wait to jump in. Go figure.

As extraordinary as my career has been, for all the runways and red carpets I've walked and the way my heart still pounds while waiting for a *WWD* review, it's the small, personal moments that stand out most in my memories: Gabby smiling when I picked her up at school. Wrapping my arms around Stephan as we hit the open road on his motorcycle. Laughing with Barbra over a game of gin rummy on a boat surrounded by nothing but blue water. Playfully hitting my sister Gail on the arm when she says I remind her of our mother. Our family embracing me and Stephan on the beach at Parrot Cay when we renewed our vows. Photographing Stefania on her horse while she takes on the next hurdle; Stefania braiding my hair after a long day at work. Sebastian delighting in going with me to Haiti. Taking Polaroids of Ethiopian children who'd never seen their photos before. Going anywhere Gianpaolo steers us, whether by plane, boat, Ferrari or, like Stephan before him, by motorcycle. And of course the excitement experienced every time I step off a plane in an unfamiliar country.

I'll never stop exploring, because it's what I haven't done that excites me most. That's my journey: learning from the past, living in the present, and journeying into the future with the light as my guide. Even more important, though, is who's by my side for the ride. Because at the end of the day, it's not what you wear or even what you've accomplished that matters. It's who you are, who you love, and how you live. *To be continued.*

ACKNOWLEDGMENTS

Writing *My Journey* was a joyful, sad, exhausting, surprising, wonderful, spiritual, and therapeutic experience. It took a world of people and memories to pull it together, and I couldn't be more grateful to those who made it possible.

First, I must thank my co-author and friend Kathleen Boyes, who has been my voice for more than thirty years. Without her brilliance, memory, compassion, diligence, and devotion, this book would not exist. No one else could have done it. And thanks to our talented editor, Jennifer Tung, who patiently kept us on track while pressing for details that enriched the story immensely.

To my soul sister, Barbra Streisand, for her generous words, her great love, and the many lessons we learned together over the years. Barbra connects the dots for me, personally, creatively, and professionally. We're two of a kind.

To President Bill Clinton and Hillary Clinton, who by their example, inspire me to utilize my gift of creating and caring each and every day. And to Anna Wintour, who has made so many dreams come true, from fashion to philanthropy. She inspires me enormously.

To my partner in crime, Patti Cohen, the redheaded Donna Karan in the fashion world, who speaks for me while advising and guiding me with love, loyalty, and humor. I could not have done any of it without her by my side. She will always be my best friend, and we will always be there for each other.

To Jane Chung, my student who became my teacher and dear friend. Jane inspires me day after day with her extraordinary gift of creativity. In every way, she's the yin to my yang.

Behind every great woman is a greater man, and I've had the greatest creative partners of all, each helping me achieve things I had never dreamed were possible: Louis Dell'Olio, Robert Lee Morris, Peter Speliopoulos, Peter Arnell, Trey Laird, Hans Dorsinville, Dominic Kozerski, and Kevin Salyers.

To the many designers and creative hands who have been by my side, inspiring me forward: Cristina Azario, Nelly Bidon, Georgina Bartlett, Istvan Francer, Xiomara Grossett, Chris Hodge, Huguette Hubbard, Jackie Marshall, Rozann Marsi, Kyoko Nagamori, Narciso Rodriguez, Ingrid Solomonson, Tommy Tong, and Edward Wilkerson.

To Tomio Taki, Frank Mori, and Julie Stern, the extraordinary men who started me on this journey at Anne Klein and knew when to fire me. There wouldn't be a Donna Karan New York if not for their vision and support.

To the many executives responsible for our amazing success: Linda Beauchamp, David Bressman, Sonja Caproni, Carole Kerner, Cathy Volker, Steve Ruzow, Denise Seegal, Jane Terker, and Mary Wang.

To LVMH and Bernard Arnault, who had the vision to see the power of what we created.

To my Urban Zen family, who create, collaborate, communicate, and inspire change: Bessie Afnaim and Oliver Corral, Gillian Cilibrasi, Rachel Goldstein, Don Hutchinson, and Yonghee Joe.

To my chief of staff and Haiti cohort, Marni Lewis, who helps me find the calm in the chaos of Urban Zen, and to my yoga teachers and great friends Rodney Yee and Colleen Saidman Yee, who taught me that yoga is a way of life and have made my dreams of a UZIT program a powerful and profound reality.

To the many people at Random House who brought their expertise and enthusiasm to this project: Alina Cho, Gina Centrello, Libby McGuire, Richard Callison, Susan Corcoran, Deborah Aroff, Nina Shield, Robbin Schiff, Liz Cosgrove, Benjamin Dreyer, and Shona McCarthy.

To the Laird + Partners amazing team who created, cleared, and organized the many layouts throughout this book, starting with the talented (and very patient) art director Louis Liu, Ray DiPietro, Jessica Feldman Miranda, Kondwani Banda, and John Rizzo. Thanks to Myles Ashby and Kelli Souder Hill for their help in clearing countless images used in this book. A special thank-you to Glen Hoffman, my first nephew, who visually connected the dots as we went through my dozens of photo albums.

To the photographers who allowed us to reprint their work in these pages: Peter Arnell, Luca Babini, Antoine Bootz, Patrick Demarchelier, Pablo Fisk, Bob Frame, Adam Franzino, Douglas Friedman, Hans Gissinger, Marc Hispard, John Huba, Inez and Vinoodh, Russell James, Mikael Jansson, Krisanne Johnson, Neil Kirk, Steven Klein, Lynn Kohlman, Brigitte Lacombe, Annie Leibovitz, Peter Lindbergh, Spike Mafford, Patrick McMullan, Christine Morden, Denis Piel, Kenneth Probst, Bob Richardson, Durston Saylor, Lothar Schmid, Steven Sebring, Gerardo Somoza, Hugh Stewart, Sølve Sundsbø, Martyn Thompson, and Bonnie Young. And thank you to every other photographer who has helped me document my life's journey.

To many who gave their love, thoughts, and reflections: Beverly Adwar, Maurice Antaya, Enrico Bonetti, Jacki Bouza, Ro Cappola,

Ann Culkin, Jean-Pierre Dupre, Francine LeFrak, Dawn Mello, Sheila Parham, Jill Pettijohn, Andrea Pfister, Pam Serure, and Beth Wohlgelernter.

To Harvey Cohen and Hal Neier, the husbands of Patti and Kathleen, who supported them while they shared this journey with me.

To my many dear friends who travel by my side, loving, learning, and laughing along the way: Richard Baskin, Ross Bleckner, Sandy Gallin, Linda and Steve Horn, Russell James, Calvin Klein, Demi Moore, Sonja Nuttall, BS and Christina Ong, Ingrid Sischy and Sandy Brant, and Bonnie Young and Luca Babini.

To Patti Cappalli, my dear friend and mentor, who took a chance on a neurotic young girl and showed me the world of fashion from Broadway to Paris.

To my Kabbalah teacher Ruth Rosenberg, who has stood by my side through my many doubts, guiding and showing me the light filled with love—a true rarity and a lesson all of us must learn.

To Ruth Pontvianne, Susie Lish, and Evelyn Dalisay for creating a home and for being the mothers I never had. And to my driver, Marco Seck, who protects me first thing in the morning to last thing at night.

To Ilene Wetson, my Five Towns bestie, for introducing me to Stephan, the love of my life.

To Mark Karan, my first love and great friend, who gave me two treasures that will always be a part of me, my daughter and my name.

To Gail—my sister, my memories, my mother who has been protecting me since the day I was born.

And to her husband, Hank Hoffman, and their family: Glen and Barbara, Annabel and Jackson; Darin and Dawn, Alexander, Griffin, and Olivia.

To my beloved family: Corey and Suzanne Weiss, Etan, and

Maya Rose; Lisa Weiss, Mackensie, Miles, and Mercer. Thank you for making me a proud grandma at such a young age.

To Gabby, my identical twin and best friend, who despite my Jewish guilt, tells me every day I'm the best mother in the world.

And to her husband, Gianpaolo de Felice, who with Gabby gave me Stefania and Sebastian, my youngest teachers of all, who are completely unimpressed with the Donna Karan name. They keep me grounded and pure and have taught me the meaning of unconditional love.

To Stephan, who has shown me that love lives on forever.

INDEX

ILLUSTRATIONS CREDITS

Author's collection (pp. vi, xii, 2, 17, 18, 29, 30, 38, 50, 61, 62, 75, 89, 102, 113, 114, 121, 146, 186, 201, 228, 240, 257, 278, 288, 306), *The Business of New York Manhattan, Inc.* from October 1989 "The New Queen of New York" article (p. 122), George Chinsee (endpapers: Patti Cohen's wall), Bob Frame (p. 157), Steven Klein/Art Partner Licensing (p. 211), Annie Leibovitz (p. 212), Peter Lindbergh (pp. 174, 202), Christine Morden (title-page spread), Denis Piel (p. 130: © Denis Piel 2015, "Excerpts from Denis Piel's Film 'Donna Karan, New York' 1986," p. 158: © Denis Piel 2015, "Rosemary's Flight, Donna Karan, 1987"), Kenneth Probst (p. 76), Bob Richardson (p. 90), Steven Sebring (p. 316), Hugh Stewart (p. 258), Sølve Sundsbø/Art + Commerce (p. 330)

First Insert:

Queenie and Gabby (author's collection), Donna as a baby (author's collection), Donna and her sister as children (author's collection), Gabby and his girls as children (author's collection), Queenie in polka dots with young Donna (author's collection), Queenie and Donna before camp (author's collection), young Queenie by her car (author's collection), Donna's school photo (author's collection), Queenie and Harold dancing (author's collection), Donna and Gail at Gail's wedding (author's collection), Donna's prom dress (author's collection), Donna's early modeling (author's collection), Donna in high school (author's collection), Gabby's hanger (author's collection), Anne Klein model in silver top and striped skirt (courtesy of Lothar Schmid), young adult Donna designing (courtesy of Kenneth Probst), in the AK design room with Louis Dell'Olio (Rose Hartman/Getty Images), Donna and Louis black-and-white (author's collection), Donna in a fur coat (author's collection), Donna and baby Gabby (author's collection), Donna with Mark and Gabby at the beach (author's collection), Donna and Gabby doing yoga (author's collection), Donna and Gabby in AK design room (author's collection), Donna and friends at Fire Island (author's collection), Donna with a cigarette (author's collection), Donna and Stephan at their wedding (author's collection), Gabby with Corey and Lisa at Donna's wedding (author's collection), Stephan's proposal telegram (author's collection), Donna and friend kissing Stephan (author's collection), Donna with her uncle Burt Wayne (author's collection), *The New York Times Magazine* "How a Fashion Star is Born" cover (author's collection), Donna swearing in (© Peter Lindbergh), black-and-white of models in bodysuits (author's collection), Donna fitting a dress (courtesy of Peter Arnell), "The Cold Shoulder" article (from *The New York Times,* 2/7/1993 © *The New York Times.* All rights reserved. Used by permission and protected by the Copyright Laws of the United States. The printing, copying, redistribution, or retransmission of this Content without express written permission is prohibited.), all four Seven Easy Pieces modeling shots (courtesy of Mark Hispard), DKNY design team (author's collection), New York City DKNY ad (© Peter Lindbergh), Donna sitting while wearing an orange coat and jeans (© Bridgitte Lacombe), DKNY model "family" (courtesy of Peter Arnell), Donna with Jane Chung (author's collection), taxicabs (© Peter Lindbergh), model in pink dress with surfboard (© Peter Lindbergh), model in black celebrating in the rain (© Peter Lindbergh), male model with newspaper (© Peter Lindbergh), guy and girl kissing in first perfume ad (courtesy of Mikael Jansson), City of Jeans billboard ad (courtesy of Gerardo Somoza), Donna and Stephan black-and-white (courtesy of Lynn Kohlman), Donna and Stephan on balcony with DKNY billboard in background (author's collection), Donna and Stephan in studio (David Turner © Condé Nast), Donna and Stephan hiking (author's collection), Donna and Barbra Streisand with their husbands (author's collection), Donna's friend Susie Lish (author's collection), Stephan on his Ducati (author's collection), Stephan and Barbra Streisand (author's collection), Stephan with long hair (author's collection), Donna and Gabby in white dresses (courtesy of Hugh Stewart), Donna and friend on boat (author's collection), Donna and family at Parrot Cay (author's collection), CFDA uniting after 9/11 (Walter Weissman/Star Max/Newscom), Donna with Anna Wintour and Carolyne Roehm (Ron Galella/Getty Images), Donna at Kids for Kids with Hillary Clinton and others (author's collection), Donna with Gabby and Stefania at Super Saturday (author's collection) black-and-white of Donna and friend at Kids for Kids (author's collection), Donna at Kids for Kids with Johnny Depp and others (author's collection), Kathleen Boyes with Patti Cohen and Marni Lewis (photograph by PatrickMcMullan.com), Donna with Peter Speliopoulos and Nicoletta Santoro (photograph by PatrickMc-Mullan.com), Bonnie Young and Gabby (author's collection), Donna with Denise Seegal and three others (photograph by PatrickMcMullan.com), Tommy Tong with Julie Stern and two others (photograph by PatrickMcMullan.com), Patti Cohen and ten others (photograph by PatrickMcMullan.com), Bessie Afnaim and Oliver Corral (author's collection), Lynn Kohlman with Rodney Yee and Colleen Saidman Yee (author's collection), Donna with Marisa Berenson (Dimitrios Kambouris/FFR/Getty Images), Donna with Christy Turlington Burns (courtesy of Neil Kirk), Donna with Trudie Styler and Sting (Evan Agostini/Getty Images), Barbra wearing Donna Karan (courtesy of Russell James), Donna and Ralph Lauren (Peter Kramer/Getty Images), Donna and Russell Simmons (© Michael Filonow/Corbis Outline), Donna and Giorgio Armani (author's collection), Donna with Deepak Chopra and Arianna Huffington (author's collection), Donna with Bernadette Peters (Evan Agostini/Getty Images), Donna with Oprah and Mary J. Blige (E. Charbonneau/Getty Images), Donna with Natasha Richardson and Gabby (Larry Busacca/Getty Images), Donna with Susan Sarandon (Dimitrios Kambouris/Getty Images), Donna and Angelica Huston (Gregory Pace/Getty Images), Donna and Demi Moore (Evan Agostini/Getty Images), Donna and Richard Baskin (author's collection), Donna and Patti Cohen (author's collection), Donna and Leonard Lauder (Associated Press), Donna and Sandy Gallin (author's collection), Donna with Michelle Obama and Gabby (author's collection), Donna and Calvin Klein (author's collection), Donna and Robert Lee Morris (Evan Agostini/Getty Images), Donna and Hans Dorsinville (author's collection), Donna and Trey Laird (author's collection), Peter Arnell and Patti Cohen (photograph by PatrickMcMullan.com), Donna on cover of *New York* magazine (author's collection), Donna shaking hands with four others (author's collection), Donna yelling with hands on head (Inez Van Lamsweerde and Vinoodh Matadin), "LMVH: A Deal for Donna" article (author's collection), "The Flag Flies High for Wall St. Donna" article (author's collection), Donna and friend near Statue of Liberty (author's collection)

Second Insert:

Gabrielle Roth with Christina Ong and two others (author's collection), Donna and the Dalai Lama (courtesy of Luca Babini), Ruth Rosenberg (author's collection), Karen Berg (author's collection), Donna on a rock (author's collection), Donna and friends in Israel (author's collection), Donna and Sonja Nuttall (author's collection), vow renewals at Parrot Cay (author's collection), family portrait from Gabby's wedding (author's collection), Gabby's bridal party (author's collection), Donna and Gabby at Gabby's wedding (author's collection), Donna with Gail and family (author's collection), Donna and Gail (author's collection), black-and-white image on ski slopes (author's collection), Donna in sunglasses at Sun Valley (author's collection), black-and-white family photo (author's collection), Donna and her adult children on Stephan's Larger than Life Apple sculpture (author's collection), Gabby and Mark Karan (author's collection), Donna and her grandson doing yoga (Previously published in *Harper's Bazaar* magazine, November 2001 issue. Photographer: Patrick Demarchelier.), Stefania at Parrot Cay (author's collection), family photo with Stephan's Dressage Horse (author's collection), Donna with Gabby, her husband and their child (Courtesy of the Artist © Annie Leibovitz), Donna and Stefania on runway (author's collection), Stefania riding a horse (author's collection), Sebastian and his dad (author's collection), Donna and Sebastian on an airplane (author's collection), Francis Bacon painting (author's collection), Donna in a red dress with two upside-down men (courtesy of Douglas Friedman), Donna in a draped white robe while sitting on a wooden lounge (courtesy of Hugh Stewart), inside 819 Madison Avenue store (courtesy of Antoine Bootz), Donna and Dominic Kozerski (Jesse Chehak/Getty Images), Donna in her all-black closet (© John Huba/Art + Commerce), inside Donna's Parrot Cay bedroom (author's collection), Donna and Gabby in Parrot Cay (Saylor H. Durston/Originally published in *Architectural Digest*), the view from Donna's Parrot Cay bedroom (Saylor H. Durston/Originally published in *Architectural Digest*), Urban Warrior campaign ad in Morocco (courtesy of Mikael Jansson), Jeremy Irons and Milla Jovovich (courtesy of Mikael Jansson), dress with a Bill Morris glass buckle (© Peter Lindbergh), Demi Moore (© Peter Lindbergh), Black Cashmere fragrance ad (courtesy of Mikael Jansson), Demi Moore from the back (© Peter Lindbergh), Cate Blanchette from the back (courtesy of Mikael Jansson), Cate Blanchette (courtesy of Mikael Jansson), Signature perfume bottle (courtesy of Hans Gissinger), Donna with Dr. David Feinberg and three others (author's collection), Rodney and Collen Yee at Urban Zen (author's collection), the launch of Urban Zen (author's collection), Ruth Pontivanne giving a massage (author's collection), Donna at ribbon-cutting ceremony (author's collection), Urban Zen model with black bracelets (courtesy of Pablo Fisk), Urban Zen model with brown necklace (courtest of Pablo Fisk), blue sofa (courtesy of

Martyn Thompson), Urban Zen model wearing suede jacket (courtesy of Adam Franzino), vases and candles (author's collection), three runway models in red dresses (courtesy of Gerardo Somoza), children wearing red robes (author's collection), Donna and a cow (author's collection), Donna and a man in India (author's collection), Donna and John James "JJ" Biasucci (author's collection), Donna with Gabby and BS Ong in Nepal (author's collection), Donna and her team arriving in Haiti (author's collection), Donna and an artist in Haiti (author's collection), Donna and a child in a Haitian hospital (author's collection), Donna and Sebastian in Haiti (author's collection), Donna with Marni Lewis and five others in Haiti (author's collection), Donna and Philippe Dodard (author's collection), Donna and Russell James (author's collection), ad campaign with model in leather and male model cutting more (courtesy of Russell James), ad campaign with a model in a black top and black-and-white skirt (courtesy of Russell James), Donna and Kevin Salyers (author's collection), a little girl Donna met in Haiti (author's collection), Donna and Bryn Mooser (author's collection), Sandra Brant and Ingrid Sischy (Mike Coppola/Getty Images), Zainab Salbi (author's collection), Donna and Lisa Evans (courtesy of Russell James), Donna and Uma Thurman (Stephen Lovekin/Getty Images), Anna Wintour (courtesy of Krisanne Johnson), Donna with Deb and Hugh Jackman (photograph by PatrickMcMullan.com), President Bill Clinton (courtesy of Krisanne Johnson), Patti Hansen and Keith Richards (courtesy of Krisanne Johnson), Stephan's Apple sculpture (courtesy of Spike Mafford), Donna pulling a face at the camera (author's collection)

ABOUT THE AUTHOR

DONNA KARAN was born in Queens and raised on Long Island, New York. She attended Parsons School of Design before beginning her career with an internship at Anne Klein, where she rose to head designer in 1974 at age twenty-five. She and her husband, Stephan Weiss, founded Donna Karan International, launching the Donna Karan New York collection in 1985, DKNY in 1989, and a beauty line in 1992. Karan's philanthropic efforts are extensive: A longtime board member of the CFDA (Council of Fashion Designers of America), she conceived its Seventh on Sale benefit to raise funds for AIDS awareness and education, and has co-chaired the New York Kids for Kids event for the Elizabeth Glaser Pediatric AIDS Foundation. Since 1993 she has co-chaired Super Saturday, an annual designer flea market/barbecue to benefit the Ovarian Cancer Research Fund. In 2007, Karan established Urban Zen, a luxury lifestyle brand and foundation that addresses wellness, education, and the preservation of culture through their artisan communities, most notably in Haiti where she is now partnering with Parsons School of Design for vocational education. The CFDA has honored Karan six times; in 2004 she received its Lifetime Achievement Award. Karan has a daughter, Gabby Karan de Felice; two stepchildren, Corey and Lisa Weiss; and a total of seven grandchildren.

Instagram.com/donnakaranthewoman
Facebook.com/urbanzen
@Urban_Zen
Instagram.com/urbanzen
Pinterest.com/urbanzenpins